# COLLINS
# HOME IMPROVEMENTS
# PRICE GUIDE

Bryan Spain is a quantity surveyor who specialises in building and civil engineering costs. He is the editor of the *Spon's Contractors' Handbook* series covering roofing, electrical work, painting and glazing, plumbing and heating, finishings, and minor works. He is the author of *Spon's Budget Estimating Handbook* and contributor to a wide variety of magazines and journals on construction-related matters with a particular emphasis on costs.

In his professional life he worked in local government, private practice and for contracting organisations. Until his recent retirement, he managed his own quantity surveying practice which merged with Tweeds, a national practice of quantity surveyors, three years ago. He now acts as a consultant to Tweeds.

He is married with four grown-up children and his hobby is 'worrying' about Sunderland FC.

# COLLINS
# HOME
# IMPROVEMENTS
# PRICE GUIDE

**Bryan Spain**

HarperCollins*Publishers*

New edition published in 1993 by
HarperCollins Publishers
London

First published in 1987 by
E. & F.N. Spon Ltd
Reprinted 1987, 1988
Second edition 1989

A catalogue record for this book is available from the
British Library

Illustrations: Jessica Stockham
Cover design: Ian Butterworth

ISBN 0 00 412835 7

Typeset by Wearset, Boldon, Tyne and Wear
Printed and bound in Great Britain by
Butler & Tanner Ltd, Frome and London

# PREFACE

It seems that not a week goes by without the newspapers reporting some 'cowboy' horror story concerning a householder being grossly overcharged by some disreputable contractor for carrying out poor quality work. The 'cowboys' rely on creating a feeling that a quick decision is needed to secure a real bargain.

For example, there will be a knock at your door and Jack-the-lad is waiting for you. He won't actually be wearing a cowboy hat and spurs but his patter will soon reveal his Texan antecedents! 'Excuse me, but me and my mates are just finishing a job round the corner and we have some tarmac left over. We could do your drive for you at a knock-down price but I need to know now before your neighbours get in first!' It is advisable not to show any interest as you may be charmed into paying over the odds for a shoddy job. Hopefully this book will help to reduce the number of such cases.

The DIY enthusiast will be able to plan his work more efficiently in both time and financial terms by using the wealth of information contained in the book. Directions on how to use this information are set out in the Introduction on page 12. Most DIY enthusiasts need help on *how* to do the work but this is outside the scope of this book. Reference should be made to the excellent *Collins Complete Do-It-Yourself Manual* which has 500 pages of illustrated advice on the techniques necessary for carrying out DIY work.

Many women work as contractors and where the pronoun 'he' is used it applies to both men and women. While every effort is made to ensure the accuracy of the information given in this publication, neither the author nor the publisher in any way accept liability of any kind resulting from the use made by any person of such information.

I have received help from many firms and organisations in preparing this book and would particularly like to thank Paul Spain, Gil Nicholls, Dorothy Spain, Jason Donald and Hire Service Shops (HSS).

Bryan J.D. Spain

# CONTENTS

# CONTENTS

# INTRODUCTION

The information in this book is intended to help anyone who is responsible for house repairs and improvements. If you have the time, skill and inclination to do the work yourself, you will be able to assess the cost of the materials you will need to buy and how long it should take to do the work.

Alternatively if you have to employ a contractor you should be able to judge whether you are paying the right amount for his services.

Most of the information on cost and time is laid out In tables and the left hand column describes the materials needed and work to be carried out. There are two main types of description:

1. A complete operation usually involving only one skill or trade e.g. replacing a broken roof tile.

2. The unit cost of an item e.g. the cost per square yard or metre for laying a concrete path.

The rest of the information on quantity, time, money and skill is displayed under the following symbols.

 ## Quantity

The number, length, area or volume of the work is described under this symbol. The items are given in both imperial and metric where appropriate and the following abbreviations have been used:

| | | | |
|---|---|---|---|
| no | = number | mm | = millimetre |
| yd | = yard | m | = metre |
| sq yd | = square yard | sq m | = square metre |
| cu yd | = cubic yard | cu m | = cubic metre |

This inclusion of both imperial and metric dimensions is intended to help you if you are unfamiliar with either format. Sometimes a metric (or imperial) equivalent has been given even though it is not possible to buy the material in that size. For example, all timber is sold in metric sizes nowadays but most DIY enthusiasts still think in $4 \times 2$ in terms for a piece of timber which is $102 \times 51$ mm actual size. But this would appear in the book as a $100 \times 50$ mm. Generally, however, the materials are described in the sizes they are sold in.

 # Total DIY hours

The time necessary to carry out each operation is expressed in hours and minutes: 2:15 means 2 hours 15 minutes.

These times represent the number of hours and minutes likely to be taken to carry out the work by an average DIY enthusiast. The word 'average' refers to someone who has a basic knowledge of the use of tools, working in normal conditions and interested in producing an acceptable standard of work. This last point is important because a perfectionist who is looking for a mirror finish on paintwork will obviously take longer than someone who will accept a finish which is not of that standard.

In other words the hours represent the time that should be taken by the average person working in average conditions to produce an average finish. If two people are involved the time should be halved. The time taken to prepare for the work, moving furniture, lifting carpets and clearing away at the end of each work session has not been allowed for. Also, the time quoted assumes reasonable access to the work, but if you had to work in cramped conditions or off ladders add up to 25% to the time stated.

 # Total DIY materials

The cost of the materials is based on prices available to the general public in DIY superstores and shops. These prices are based upon using recognised brand names. Savings can sometimes be made by purchasing 'in house' branded products, but quality does vary – so be careful.

An allowance has been made for waste but nothing has been included for the cost of transporting the materials from the store to home.

Materials which are delivered are assumed to be deposited within a reasonable distance of the place of use and no allowance has been made for their removal beyond that point.

## Skill level

Each operation has been awarded a 'skill factor' ranging from 1 to 10 indicating the degree of difficulty likely to be encountered by the average DIY enthusiast. For example, scraping off wallpaper is given a rating of 1 – the simplest of tasks – but plastering is rated at 8.

Generally speaking, jobs which have rating of 8, 9 or 10 should not be attempted by amateurs unless you are particularly gifted or can ask for experienced and professional help. This applies not only to obvious examples like electrical work but also to breaking out large openings and most work involving structural alterations.

## £ Contractor's price

The total costs of the contractor's charges are included here. There is one important qualification which you must remember. Replacing a tap washer may only take a plumber a matter of minutes but you cannot expect his charges to be based solely on the time taken to do the work if that was the only task he was asked to carry out. He will also charge you for the cost of travelling but these hours and costs are not shown in this book.

The question of emergency call out charges must also be considered. A tradesman who responds to an emergency call will almost certainly be looking for a 'disturbance payment' in addition to the cost of his labour and materials. This should be discussed and agreed before the work is carried out to avoid misunderstandings.

It is a mistake to believe that a call out charge is only applicable outside normal working hours. An emergency call during the day can have a disruptive effect on the contractor's normal work pattern and should be paid for.

Some suggested levels of charges are set out below, but they should be regarded only as indicative:

| | |
|---|---|
| Call out charge during working hours | £15–£20 |
| Call out charge 6pm to midnight | £20–£30 |
| Call out charge after midnight, Sundays and Bank Holidays. | £30–£50 |

You should bear in mind that the true cost of employing a contractor is not what you *thought* you should be charged but what you *are* charged. For example, if there is a glut of work for painting contractors at one particular time, the prices they quote will exceed their normal charges because they have less need to be competitive. The opposite is also true, of course, and these factors will directly affect the costs. There are three main types of builders who carry out domestic repair, improvements and maintenance work:

**(a)** the small firm which has a manned office and is registered for VAT;

**(b)** a one man firm working from home;

**(c)** the tradesman who has full time employment but undertakes small jobs outside his normal working day.

In this book it is assumed that firm (a) above will be carrying out the work and that VAT has been included in the contractor's price column. This means that 17½% for VAT will be included in your bill which, in most cases, you cannot reclaim.

The cost of employing contractors varies all over the country and the following table sets out the approximate variations from a norm of 100 on which this book is based.

| | |
|---|---|
| Scotland | 96 |
| Wales | 98 |
| Northern Ireland | 91 |
| England | |
| South West | 94 |
| South East | 109 |
| Home Counties | 110 |
| Inner London | 130 |
| Outer London | 120 |
| East Anglia | 110 |
| Midlands | 102 |
| North West | 101 |
| North East | 96 |

It is important to remember that buying the services of a builder is not like buying any other product. The prices charged by contractors can vary considerably, much more than the price range available if you were buying a car or an electric cooker for example. The reasons for this are not always overcharging or greed but the differing circumstances facing individual estimators. For example, let us assume you ask three contractors to carry out the simplest of jobs: to dig a 1 cubic metre hole and fill it with 1:2:4 concrete (see page 40 for details of concrete mixes):

*Estimator A* reckons it will take about 4 hours to dig the hole by hand but because he is short of transport he will have to drop his labourer off in the morning and not pick him up until the end of the day, so he must charge 8 hours at £8.50 i.e. £68. He then gets a quote from Foulmix, the ready-mix people, who say that the concrete is £48 per cubic metre but the surcharge for a part load is 25%, so the concrete costs £60. The total cost therefore is £68 plus £60 equals £128 plus 15% overheads and profit, so the quotation is £147.20, say £150.

*Estimator B* thinks his labourer can dig the hole in three hours. Furthermore he has his own transport and is based on a site only 1 mile away so he quotes on 3 hours work plus ½ hour travelling time i.e. 3½ hours at £8, plus £2 for petrol, equals £30. He gets a quote from Slowmix, who are supplying the nearby site and they agree to drop a cubic metre off at your site for their standard price of £46. The total therefore is £30 plus £46 equals £76, plus 12½% profit and overheads, is £85.50, say £90.

*Estimator C* is also working in the area and has a JCB working on the site next door. He reckons the travelling time is ½ hour and the work will take about ½ hour so the total machine time is one hour at £20. He contacts a firm specialising in delivering small loads of concrete who quote him £56. The total therefore is £20 plus £56 equals £76, plus 12½ profit and overheads, is £85.50, say £90.

You can see the last two quotes are identical at £90 but for quite different reasons. *Estimator A* however quotes £150, almost 70% higher than the other two but, if asked, he could easily justify this.

And remember this example covers a very simple construction exercise – digging a hole and filling it with concrete! Imagine the permutations when more complicated building projects are involved. So if you receive different quotes from reputable contractors there are probably sound reasons to account for the difference.

Contractors are generally held in low esteem by the general public but the majority are hardworking and honest, and even large variations in quotations can usually be explained.

# HOME IMPROVEMENTS – ARE THEY WORTH IT?

With certain exceptions, you are wasting your money improving your home if you intend moving within a couple of years! There are many reasons for this which are explained later but the general rule is that you should only carry out the kind of improvements listed in this book if you intend to enjoy the amenity yourself. There is a wealth of evidence to show that the cost of constructing extensions, swimming pools, second bathrooms, through lounges and porches will not be recovered in the subsequent sale of the house.

The exceptions are central heating, garages and to a lesser extent double glazing and if you are lucky you may recover up to 75% of their construction costs. Another exception may lie in the prospective purchaser himself. You may be lucky enough to find a buyer with exactly the same taste, family size and social needs as you but it is extremely unlikely.

A further exception occurs in periods of housing shortages when property values increase because of the demand. The cost of the improvements will be recovered but only because of the general lifting of house prices and not because of the intrinsic value of the improvement.

Most estate agents will tell you (although you could argue that they have a vested interest in promoting this view!) that if you have a need for an extra bedroom it is better to change house and move up the housing ladder rather than build an extension. This theory is based upon the premise that it is more sensible to live in a £80,000 house surrounded by £100,000 houses than in a £80,000 house (say £60,000 plus £20,000 extension costs) in a £60,000 area. It follows on, of course, from this argument that you would be prudent to invest £20,000 in a house extension only if it will bring the value of the house up to that of your neighbours.

It is important to remember that all these comments are related to improvements. Carrying out maintenance and repairs such as rewiring, pointing, damp-coursing, roofing repairs and the like are part of any householder's responsibilities and the selling price will drop in favour of the purchaser if they are neglected.

Another useful tip to remember when considering improving your house is that it is very important to maintain the balance of room uses. In other words, providing a second bathroom in a house with only two bedrooms is extravagant (unless of course, as stated earlier, you intend to enjoy the amenity yourself over a number of years). Similarly, constructing a fourth bedroom in a house with only a small, general purpose sitting room would be unwise.

The following table shows the percentage of construction costs likely to be recovered if the property is sold within two years of the work being carried out.

| | |
|---|---|
| Central heating | 50–75 |
| Garage | 50–75 |
| Double glazing | 40–50 |
| Loft conversion | 20–40 |
| Basement conversion | 20–40 |
| Sun lounge | 10–30 |
| Bedroom extension | 0–20 |
| Kitchen extension | 0–20 |
| Porch | 0–10 |

# USING A CONTRACTOR

## WHY USE A CONTRACTOR?

Apart from buying a house or car, your largest expenditure will probably be having major home improvements carried out so it is important that the finished job is a good standard. There are many projects when do-it-yourself skills will be insufficient for the work involved and a contractor must be used.

If you are not interested in DIY work or perhaps incapable of doing it then you will be totally dependent upon contractors for your repairs and improvements. But even if you have only a moderate level of DIY skills you will have several options on how to carry out any particular job.

Take as an example a kitchen extension with a flat roof. This can be broken down into elements and work content as follows:

| Element | Work done by contractor | Work capable of being done by the average enthusiast |
|---|---|---|
| Foundations | Concrete, brickwork | Excavation |
| Roof | Felt | Joists, decking, fascia board, rainwater installation, painting |

| Element | Work done by contractor | Work capable of being done by the average enthusiast |
|---|---|---|
| Internal and external walls | Brickwork, blockwork | – |
| Windows and doors | Joinery, glazing | Painting |
| Finishes | Screeding and floor tiling, plasterboard and plastering | Wall tiling |
| Fittings | – | Kitchen units and worktops |
| Plumbing | – | Copper pipework, waste, soil and overflow pipework, sink top and taps |
| Electrical work | Wiring, outlets, connection to existing | – |
| Drainage | Pipelaying, modifications to existing | Excavation and backfilling |
| External works | – | New paving |

It can be seen that if you have average skills you could carry out a large portion of the work yourself. You should decide which parts, if any, you will do yourself and which you will give a contractor to do. There are several factors which must be considered here.

## Time available

Generally speaking the DIY enthusiast will take longer to carry out the same work than a professional. You must therefore weigh the money you can save against the disadvantage of having your house disrupted for a longer period. This becomes especially relevant if there are young children to be considered or if the house is likely to be open to the wind and rain, especially in winter.

## Programme of the work

Programming is very important particularly if the work is substantial. You must avoid disrupting the contractor otherwise he may claim extra money. For example, if you carry out the excavation as shown in the previous work plan you must ensure that the work is complete before the contractor arrives on site to carry out the concrete and brickwork. This applies to any aspect of the job which you decide to carry out yourself. You must consider not only whether you are capable of doing the work, but whether you can finish it within a set period of time. Don't forget that your good intentions can be upset by bad weather, illness, work or family problems.

## Specialist work

Certain types of work such as electrical installations should be left to the experts unless you are absolutely confident of your own capabilities. Whilst the actual work involved in putting in a spur on a ring main is relatively simple, there are stringent regulations and safety aspects to be considered which you may not be aware of and because of the danger involved you are strongly advised to employ a specialist.

There are other types of work where it would be better to call in an expert but for reasons of skill rather than safety. For example it may seem a straightforward task to lay a 50 mm cement and sand floor screed, but it is extremely difficult to make the screed level and smooth enough to receive floor tiles. This type of work should therefore generally be left to the expert.

## Cost

For most people the cost of the work will probably be the most important factor when it comes to deciding whether to do part of the work yourself, but you must be careful. It is easy to make a decision that could turn out to be a false economy. You must be absolutely sure of your ability to carry out the work properly first time round because it will prove far more costly to have the work put right if it is done incorrectly.

Think about the cost of your own time. If you are self employed or have a job which involves overtime, you may be financially better off working at your own job and having the construction work done for you. The value which you place on leisure time is also a consideration; DIY is a time-consuming activity and you may often find that once a task has begun there is little spare time for anything else and the effect of this on your spouse and family should be considered very carefully. It may be wise not to make up your mind on the basis of money alone. So remember:

- employ a contractor when the time available for any job is limited;
- only carry out parts of the work yourself if you are sure you will not interfere with the contractor's own programme;
- always use a contractor for specialist work unless you are absolutely sure you are capable of doing the work yourself.

## CHOOSING A CONTRACTOR

Deciding which contractor or contractors to use can be extremely difficult. When you are about to spend a large amount of money you have to be confident that it is going to be spent wisely. Everyone has heard horror stories about jobs that went wrong because the builder was a 'cowboy'. What can be done to prevent this happening to you? There are several important points to bear in mind:

1. Always be wary of people knocking on the door and trying to sell you something, whether it is double glazing or roof repairs. Don't be tempted by discounts offered for ordering the work there and then. You can be sure that even if the salesman has to come back you will still get the discount if you give him the work.

2. Try and find a contractor by recommendation. Ask your friends and neighbours if they can recommend someone and inspect examples of his work if possible.

3. If you decide to use your local Yellow Pages, try and pick a contractor who is affiliated to a national body, i.e. associations like the Federation of Master Builders, the Electrical Contractors Association and the Institute of Plumbing. Some of them will provide guarantees of their members' work in return for a modest premium. In the case of the Federation of Master Builders, their warranty scheme would cost you only 1% of the value of the work up to £50,000, and a reducing percentage beyond that figure (minimum fee £5). For this fee you receive protection against:

   - the cost of employing another contractor to complete the work if the first one stops trading;
   - a two year guarantee of materials and workmanship;

- a five year warranty on structural defects caused by faulty materials or workmanship;

- free conciliation and arbitration service in the case of disputes.

Full details can be obtained from the Federation of Master Builders, Gordon Fisher House, 33 John Street, London WC1N 2BB (Telephone 071-242 7583), or look in Yellow Pages for your local regional office.

4. Make sure that the contractor does all or most of the work himself and check which trades he sublets. Contractors who sublet all of their work are not really contractors but just middle men. Having lots of subcontractors doing the job in these circumstances is not likely to give you good value or good workmanship.

5. Only negotiate with a single contractor if you know him well or if he is highly recommended. Even in these circumstances it may be advisable to obtain alternative quotations to be absolutely sure that you are obtaining value for money. In all other instances approach two or three contractors for quotations. Any more than three may lead to unnecessary confusion when you compare their offers.

## OBTAINING ESTIMATES AND QUOTATIONS

Some contractors will tell you that there is a difference between an estimate and a quotation, although in law they are one and the same (see page 32). An estimate might be only an approximation of the cost of the work whereas a quotation is generally seen as an offer to do the work at the price quoted. However, many contractors see the two as the same, so it is always worth confirming with a contractor who says he will do the work for an 'estimate' that his price is firm and not subject to extra charges once the work is complete.

When obtaining quotations from more than one contractor, you must make sure that they are all based on an equal footing. It is no use telling one contractor that you want one type of floor tile and then telling another something entirely different. The best method of establishing this is to use the system of drawings and specification that the professionals use, but on a simplified basis.

Unless you have a knowledge of the building industry the chances are that the drawings for your kitchen extension will be done by a professional, either an architect, a building surveyor, or an advanced technician. As with obtaining quotations for the actual building of your extension, you should also shop around for these services.

For work valued at less than £20,000 architects would negotiate their fee (it is only subject to percentages above that figure) but it is likely that you will be charged between 10 and 12½% of the value of the work for a full service, i.e. obtaining planning permission, building regulations approval, preparing drawings, appointing a contractor and supervising the work. If you agree to pay on an hourly rate basis for professional services, make sure that you agree an overall ceiling figure and that you are advised at regular intervals how many hours have been spent on your work. The current rates are approximately £20 to £25 per hour for an architect or surveyor and £12 to £15 for a technician.

Most of the actual technical specifications should appear on these drawings; plaster type and thickness, floor screed type and thickness and so on. All that would remain is for you to add your particular details; type of floor covering, type of kitchen fittings etc. Unlike the professionals who do this for a living, however, your knowledge of building workmanship will not be sufficient to enable you to specify everything necessary, and the actual workmanship of the job will generally be left up to the builder. As a general guide however, the following check list will be helpful:

| Building element | Main items to include in specification |
|---|---|
| Substructure | Concrete strength; type of brickwork and mortar; type of damp proof membrane and damp proof course. |
| Upper floor | Size and spacing of joists. Type and thickness of flooring. |
| Roof | Size and spacing of joists and other members such as fascia and soffit boards, type of insulating material; type and thickness of roof covering and number of coats for flat roofs; type of roof tile, underlay and battens for pitched roofs; type and sizes of gutters and downspouts; type and thickness of flashings. |

| Building element | Main items to include in specification |
|---|---|
| Walls | Type of brick and mortar and method of bonding and pointing; type and strength of blockwork; type of wall ties. |
| Windows | Size of members if not a standard window; type of ironmongery; type of glass and method of fixing; type and number of coats of paint; type and size of lintol. |
| Doors | Size of frame and architraves; type and size of door; type of ironmongery; type of glass and method of fixing; type and number of coats of paint; type and size of lintol. |
| Finishes | Thickness of floor screed; type of floor finish; type of skirting and decoration; type of plaster and number and thickness of coats; type of wall tiling; type of wall decoration; thickness of ceiling plasterboard; type and thickness of ceiling plaster; ceiling decoration. |
| Fittings | Details of cupboards, shelving and associated decoration. |
| Sanitary fittings | Type of sanitary fittings and colour; type of taps and traps. |
| Plumbing installation | Types and sizes of pipes for waste, soil and overflow and water installations; state whether to be exposed or concealed, and method of concealment. |
| Electrical installation | Type of fittings and outlets; state whether to be exposed or concealed and method of concealment. |

There are many instances where you will not need to ask for a written quotation, for example; changing a tap washer. Where the work is so simple that there is very little chance of anything going wrong then a verbal quotation should be sufficient. However you should always ask for quotations on complete items of work, never on a time basis. The quotation for renewal of the tap washer should be an all-in price for the actual removal and replacement of that washer not a price per hour for the actual time taken to do it. Beware of any quotations which have conditions attached to them: the price for doing that particular job will be a hundred pounds 'if ... etc., etc.' Always try to have the 'ifs' removed so that the contractor cannot come back when the job is done claiming extra money arguing that the 'ifs' were not fulfilled. When obtaining quotations don't forget to clarify who will remove and replace all the existing carpets, fittings and furniture, and to spell out any restrictions you may want to make about the hours contractors will work and the parts of your house they may not use.

You should also discuss the question of the disposal of any surplus materials. If you want them taken away then tell the contractor. On the other hand, if you want your existing kitchen units carefully removed and left for use elsewhere or to be sold, then you must say so because this may influence the quotation price.

When the quotation arrives, make sure that it covers everything that you want. Written quotations should be detailed enough to enable you to check that you are receiving what you are paying for; they should also make it possible to value any extras or variations that may occur. However you should not expect every single nut and bolt to appear on the quotation, only the principal items.

Quotations may take several different forms because each contractor will have his own particular method of pricing work. At the very least it should list the principal materials, priced separately, and show the labour, plant and VAT. It should also be clear and unambiguous and contain all the points raised in any discussions. You will probably find it helpful to take notes of telephone calls and discussions with the contractor. Details of how long the job will take and when it will start should also be included in the quotation, together with the course of action to be taken if the work takes any longer (see page 33). The other two main items which should be included are details of payments and the valuing of variations and extras, both of which are discussed separately later in this chapter.

Finally, it is most important that you read all of the quotation. Many contractors have standard conditions of sale on the back of quotations or fastened to them. You must study them carefully. If there is anything you are not happy about, you should bring it to the contractor's attention and have it changed or taken out. Under no circumstances accept any conditions that you are not satisfied with. Once you are happy with the quotation the only thing which needs to be done is to accept it. A verbal acceptance is sufficient and would constitute a binding agreement but it is always preferable to make the acceptance in writing. Having signed your acceptance ask for a copy of the quotation and keep it somewhere safe.

# METHODS OF PAYMENT

Most disputes that arise between a client and a contractor are money related but difficulties can be reduced by agreeing the method of payment at the start and including it in the written quotation.

There are several ways of making payments to the contractor depending upon the individual circumstances of the job.

*Payment before the work commences* – this is not recommended except where the amount involved is relatively small, the time to do the job is short, and the contractor involved is of unquestionable character and reputation. In any event there is no point in making payment in advance unless there is some benefit to be gained by doing so, e.g. by obtaining a reduction of the quotation price.

*Payment after the work is complete* – this is obviously the most desirable method for the householder but the contractor would probably resist this arrangement unless the job was of low value and could be done quickly. It is not suitable for high value jobs which may take several weeks or months to complete, and small contractors in particular would not be able to finance a job that did not include stage payments.

*Payment on a stage basis* – there are two main methods of doing this. The first is to pay percentages of the total value at agreed intervals. If the job was scheduled to take three months, one third of the price might be paid each month. This method is not recommended because it does not take progress into account and could result in the payments being in advance of the value of the work completed which would reduce the contractor's motivation to finish the job. The second method is to pay agreed amounts at various completed stages of the work. In the example of a house extension these stages could be agreed as:

15% foundations and ground floor slab complete
55% external walls and roof complete
100% completion

*Payment for materials as they are supplied* – here you pay for the cost of the materials as they are delivered with the balance paid when the work is complete. To do this properly you should ask the contractor for copies of his material invoices, although they may not always be available if he is operating on a credit system with his suppliers. If the contractor is unable to provide invoices then it may be necessary to agree the value of the materials in advance. This method of payment is fraught with potential difficulties and is not recommended.

## VARIATIONS AND EXTRAS

Unforeseen extra costs to the original work are probably the largest single cause of disputes, but the problem can be avoided in most cases. Variations, or extras as they are commonly known, may arise for all sorts of reasons, and who pays for them will depend upon the reasons for the extra occurring. Variations can be put into three categories:

1. Those which the contractor is instructed to make – if you ask for a cast iron bath complete with gold taps instead of the plastic type which you originally requested, then you should expect to pay the difference in price.

2. Items which the contractor should have included in the original quotation – if you had always wanted a cast iron bath with gold fittings and the drawings or specification said so, then it is obviously the contractor's mistake if he only priced for a plastic bath and he should bear the extra cost. Variations or extras of this type can often be avoided by insisting on detailed quotations and examining them carefully.

3. Changes which are due to the contractor having to carry out work different from that foreseen at the time the work was quoted for. In this case the liability for the additional cost may not be so clear cut. For instance, the contractor may have thought he could run his plumbing pipework in the floor space but subsequently found that the floor was solid. Who then would be liable for the extra cost of cutting channels? Remember that if your house has fitted carpets throughout this may have prevented him from making a detailed examination at the quotation stage. In this example it is considered that the responsibility lies with the contractor and he should bear the additional cost. If, however, rotten floorboards are discovered upon removing the old bath, it is only fair that you should pay extra for their renewal because it would have been unreasonable for the contractor to have assumed the defect and included the cost in his quotation. There

are times when the problem is not as black and white as these examples and if there is a genuine doubt over liability, then a fair cost-sharing arrangement should be considered.

The valuation of variations and extras can also cause much disagreement but with a little forethought, arguments can be kept to a minimum. The first step in avoiding disputes is to ensure the original quotation is as detailed as reasonably possible. A quotation which simply says 'Kitchen extension as designed and detailed – £14,000' is of little use when it comes to the valuation of extras. A detailed quotation can form the basis for valuing extras, particularly if the additional work is the same or of a similar character to an item which appears separately in the quotation.

A detailed quotation can also prevent arguments about what was included in the original price if variations occur. Even then it may not be possible to relate the cost of extra work to an item in the original quotation so the work must be valued in another manner. The best method is to ask for a firm quotation for the extra work in advance. In this way you will know the cost beforehand and be able to decide whether you can afford to have the additional work carried out. You should not under any circumstances request additional work without knowing the cost nor should you agree to additional work being done on a time basis (sometimes called 'time and lime'). Remember also that leaving out work is also a variation and the same rules apply. All variations should be recorded in writing and signed by both you and the contractor. This will enable you to keep a record of your overall expenditure and will also save time when the final bill is presented.

From your point of view it is obviously better to leave the payment for extras until the end of the job. However, the contractor may request that they are paid for as and when they are complete and this is perfectly reasonable. As with any transaction however, you should ask for proof of payment and if you have followed the advice on agreeing and recording any variations then the contractor simply stamps or writes 'paid' on the agreement sheet together with his signature.

## MAKING A SIMPLE CONTRACT

The law of contract has evolved from the many cases which have passed through the English court system. Contract law is a varied and complex subject and outside the scope of this book. But when you employ a contractor to do your work, you are creating a contract and it is important that you understand the basic rules that apply.

A simple contract is made when an offer is made by one person and accepted by another. The contract is only enforceable in law however, when there is also consideration involved. Consideration is the reward or gain that the person making the offer receives in return for fulfilling the terms of the offer. In the case of a kitchen extension, the offer would be made by the contractor to construct the extension, the acceptance would be made by you saying 'yes go ahead' and the consideration would be the amount of money to be paid to the contractor in return for completing the job. It is not strictly necessary for the offer and acceptance to be written down. But if it is not, and the job goes wrong and ends up in the courts, there would be obvious problems over the establishment of proof. These problems would not arise if the parties recorded their intentions in writing. It should be noted that the consideration does not have to be a sum, it can just as easily be an intention. For instance it is no defence to say that there was no enforceable contract because you had not agreed on a price, if it could be reasonably inferred that you had accepted the offer with the 'intention' to pay. Nor is it necessary for a contractor to say 'I offer to do the work for £1,000' he could just as easily say 'My estimate to do the work is £1,000.' This would constitute a binding offer.

The offer may be withdrawn at any time by the contractor before acceptance but once the acceptance has been communicated to the contractor it cannot be revoked or withdrawn. Note that the actual posting of an acceptance letter constitutes acceptance, but a posted withdrawal of an offer is not effective until received.

Another important point to note in contract law is that an offer is made invalid if a counter offer is made. For example, if the contractor offers to build you a kitchen extension for £14,000 but you think this is too expensive and make a counter offer of £12,500 which the contractor rejects. After shopping around you find that the cheapest you can get the job done for is £15,500 and go back to the original contractor and agree to accept his original asking price. Even if the contractor has not formally withdrawn his original offer he is not bound now to stand by it, because by making the counter offer you have invalidated his offer. An offer is also invalid if not accepted within a reasonable time. There are no rules defining how long is a 'reasonable' time.

Assuming that a valid contract exists between yourself and the contractor, the question may arise of how much compensation, if any, you are entitled to if the contractor does not carry out his obligations, and so breaks the contract.

Damages are the law's method of compensating the injured party for injury, damage or loss. Thus, if you have suffered damage, injury or loss, and you can prove that it was incurred as a direct result of the broken contract, then you would be entitled to damages. Damages represent compensation; they are only awarded to recompense for the actual loss suffered and are not used in order to penalise or punish the contract breaker. The value of damages may be difficult to ascertain. For example, the contractor may take twice as long to complete your kitchen extension as he originally contracted to do. You may be entitled to damages even though you have not lost any money, because damages may be paid for physical inconvenience. They may also be awarded for the mental anguish you have suffered, although this is more difficult to prove.

If your contractor leaves the job incomplete or badly done, you may be entitled to the cost of having the work rectified or completed. You are, by the way, more likely to succeed in your case if you have first tried to have the work put right by the original contractor.

If you should find yourself in the unfortunate position of having to claim against a contractor, how do you go about it? The first course of action is to try to get the contractor to put the job right himself, if necessary by threatening him with legal action. Make your requests in writing and see that they are delivered via a recorded delivery system. Keep copies of all correspondence. Make notes of the times, dates and contents of any telephone conversations. If there is no reply or your requests are rejected, then your only remedy is through the court. Before you decide to sue however, you should make sure that not only do you have a good case, but that if you win, the contractor has the means to pay the amount of the award.

Your claim will normally be heard in the County Court and the procedure in taking out a court action is well defined. A good reference is the form EX50 'Small Claims in the County Court' which can be obtained from the County Court, a Law Centre or a Citizens Advice Bureau. This outlines the procedure for bringing a small claim to court without going to the expense of hiring a solicitor. You should also bear in mind that you may also be entitled to legal aid depending upon your financial status; you should ask your local Law Centre or Citizens Advice Bureau. If the claim warrants the use of a solicitor then try and find one who is used to dealing with your type of case. Remember again to shop around because charges vary. It is advisable to ask the solicitor if he does an initial consultation at a special fee or even free, which would then give you some idea of the likely success of your claim.

# PROGRAMMING

If you are a DIY enthusiast with a reasonable level of skill, you will probably want to carry out part of the work on your kitchen extension yourself. There are two choices:

**(a)** let a contractor do the other work

**(b)** let individual tradesmen do the other work.

If the extension has to be completed within a fixed period of time then careful co-ordination and planning of the work is required. This is most easily done by preparing a simple bar chart (see chart below). This shows the anticipated programme of the kitchen extension in a form which is easy to follow. The main items of work are on the vertical scale with the horizontal scale representing time. As can be seen certain work items cannot start before others have been completed, e.g. the roof cannot commence until the external walls are built. The chart shows how your work affects that to be done by the contractor and this should help to monitor progress.

If you are going to give the balance of the work to tradesmen then care has to be exercised in making sure the tradesmen arrive at the right time to carry out their particular work. This must be given careful thought. But there are financial benefits in doing the work this way because you are cutting out the profit of the main builder.

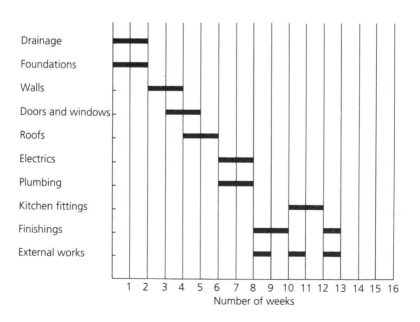

# DESIGN AND BUILD BY A CONTRACTOR

Quite often you may find it easier and cheaper to use a contractor for a complete service rather than having separate drawings done, obtaining planning and building regulation approval and then finding a contractor to do the work. This system, whereby the contractor produces the drawings, obtains the necessary approvals and does the physical work on site is commonly known as 'design and build' and it can have several advantages.

You will only be dealing with one person so there is less likelihood of misunderstandings. If you choose a contractor who is used to doing this sort of scheme you will benefit by his knowledge of the most economic method of carrying out your particular job. He will also be able to advise you on the best choice of materials because he may have special rates of discount with certain suppliers that he can pass on to you. However, it is not guaranteed to be cheaper doing it this way. You will still have to pay for the design and drawings, building regulations and planning fees, although these will not necessarily be shown separately on the quotation.

There are also potential disadvantages. For the very same reasons that a contractor may be able to obtain special discount for certain materials, he may also try and force these upon you, when you may not really want them. He may also try to use up stocks of existing materials lying around his yard. You must therefore be strong-minded about what you want without being unreasonable.

So, on the one hand, with this system an experienced contractor will be able to guide you on what your improvements are going to cost as you develop your thoughts. On the other hand, be aware that you may be more at risk from an unscrupulous contractor because you become totally reliant on him without anyone else to look after your interests. You must be particularly careful in your choice of contractor when adopting this method.

The same can also be said of standard or prefabricated systems such as precast concrete garages or conservatories. Here again personal recommendation is desirable if not essential. You should not overlook the small local specialist in preference to the larger national firm. The larger companies rely heavily upon advertising on a national scale which can be very expensive and must be paid for by the customer. At the same time the products of the national company have usually been tried and tested. Of course the major advantage with these systems lies in the speed of erection compared to traditional methods of construction.

There is no easy method of finding out which contractor is giving you the best value for money with design and build because it is difficult to compare quotations. You will have to rely upon your instinct to some extent but in any case you should always establish whether the contractor will charge you for the cost of design if you do not proceed with the actual construction and if so, how much it will be. If you consider this to be excessive, then you may be able to negotiate a reduction, or if that fails approach someone else.

# DOING IT YOURSELF

## WHEN TO DO IT YOURSELF

There are three main reasons when it makes sense not to employ a contractor and to do the work yourself – if you have the time available, when the nature of the work is within your capabilities, and because you can make substantial savings on the cost of the work. Another reason why you should do the work yourself is the satisfaction and pleasure in planning, carrying out and completing a job. For DIY enthusiasts this is a powerful motivation!

## MEASURING

Before tackling any DIY task it will be necessary to order materials and this will probably involve you in 'measuring up'. A retractable steel measure is the most convenient tool to use and the following simple rules should enable you to calculate the area of most shapes. *Fig. 1* depicts the plan of a room (the strange configuration is intended to make it easier to understand the following examples). The diagram is marked in feet for ease of use.

### Rectangle

For the area, multiply the length by the width. Remember that if the shape you are measuring is irregular, it is usually quicker to calculate the overall area and deduct the voids (see *Fig. 1*) i.e.:

$$28 \times 20 \quad = \quad 560$$

Deduct

$$3 \times 16 \quad = \quad 48$$
$$5 \times 8 \quad = \quad 40$$
$$3 \times 17 \quad = \quad 51 \quad 139$$

$$\overline{421} \text{ sq ft}$$

If *Fig. 1* represented the floor plan of a kitchen, you may also wish to measure the perimeter of the room for a cornice or skirting. This is done quite simply by adding the width and length and multiplying by two. There is no need to work your way round all the indentations:

$$(28 + 20) \times 2 = 96 \text{ ft}$$

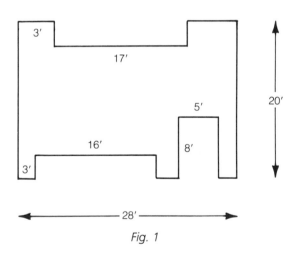

*Fig. 1*

If this calculation was needed for the total length of a skirting you should, of course, deduct any door openings and the like. The assessed perimeter of 96 ft could also be used as a basis for working out the wall area by multiplying it by the storey height (the height from floor to ceiling). If it was 7 ft 6 in, the wall area would be 96 ft × 7 ft 6 in = 720 sq ft divided by 9 = 80 sq yds (less openings).

## Triangle

The triangular area is half the base multiplied by the perpendicular height (see *Fig. 2*) i.e.:

$$\tfrac{1}{2} \times 6 \times 4 = 12 \text{ sq ft}$$

This rule applies to all shapes and sizes of triangles. There is no simple way of calculating the perimeter – you just add the lengths of the three sides together.

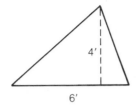 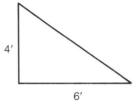

*Fig. 2*

There may be a need sometimes to calculate the area or volume of other shapes and the following tables may prove helpful.

## Circumference or perimeters of planes

| | |
|---|---|
| Circle | Pi (3.1416) × diameter |
| Ellipse | Pi (3.1416) × ½ (major axis + minor axis) |
| Sector | $\dfrac{\text{radius} \times \text{degrees in arc}}{57.3}$ |

## Surface areas of planes and solids

| | |
|---|---|
| Circle | Pi (3.1416) × radius$^2$ or 0.7854 × diameter |
| Cone | ½ circumference × slant height + area of base |
| Frustrum of cone | Pi (3.1416) × slant height × (radius at top + radius at base) + area of top and base |
| Cylinder | (Circumference × length) + area of two ends |
| Ellipse (approx.) | Product of axes × 0.7854 |
| Parallelogram | Base × height |
| Pyramid | ½ (base perimeter × slant height) + area of base |
| Sector of circle | $\dfrac{3.1416 \times \text{degrees in arc} \times \text{radius}^2}{360}$ |
| Sphere | Diameter$^2$ × 3.1416 |

## Volumes

| | |
|---|---|
| Cone | Area of base $\times$ $\frac{1}{2}$ perpendicular height |
| Cylinder | Pi (3.1416) $\times$ radius$^2$ $\times$ height |
| Pyramid | Area of base $\times$ $\frac{1}{4}$ perpendicular height |

# ORDERING MATERIALS

The demand for DIY materials has increased enormously in recent years and a significant change has been the introduction of national DIY superstores which are in most areas. These stores can supply most DIY materials and because they buy in large quantities, they are usually very competitive with builder's merchants. Although some of these outlets have a delivery service, they are usually cash and carry but you would still need to go to a merchant for items like bricks and cement unless you were buying very small quantities.

The ordering of materials is not always straightforward. For instance, you cannot go out and order a cubic yard of concrete (unless it is ready mixed). You must have knowledge of the weight of the cement, sand and aggregate and you must remember the wastage factor. You may find that using only part of a bag of cement is more expensive than buying a premixed bag of concrete of the right quantity. Some thought must go into ordering materials to prevent waste, and the following information will assist you.

Please note that although most of the information in Chapters 4 and 5 is given in both imperial and metric, some of the following materials are only stated in metric terms because that is how they are sold.

## Excavation work

Material bulks when dug out, i.e. it occupies a greater volume after it has been excavated. It would be wrong to order a ten cubic yards skip for ten cubic yards of excavation because the skip would be too small to receive the bulked material. The following are average percentage bulking increases for various types of ground:

| | |
|---|---|
| Sand/gravel | 10–15% |
| Ordinary clay, etc. | 20–30% |
| Hard materials, rock, etc. | 40–50% |

## Concrete work – mixed by hand

The two most common concrete mixes are 1:3:6 and 1:2:4. Usually you would use 1:3:6 in foundations and 1:2:4 in walls, paths and the like. The figures refer to the proportions by volume of the cement:sand:aggregate respectively. In other words there is one part cement, three parts sand and six parts aggregate or gravel in a 1:3:6 mix. But these materials are usually sold by weight or volume and you must know what the proportions are by dry weight for each cubic metre of concrete to be mixed.

|           | 1 cubic yard | | 1 cubic metre | |
|-----------|--------|---------|--------|---------|
|           | 1:2:4  | 1:3:6   | 1:2:4  | 1:3:6   |
| Cement    | 400 lb | 290 lb  | 240 kg | 170 kg  |
| Sand      | 900 lb | 950 lb  | 520 kg | 550 kg  |
| Aggregate | 1600 lb| 1700 lb | 950 kg | 1000 kg |

If you were laying a foundation for a garden wall you should first calculate the volume of the concrete. Say it was 30 ft long × 1 ft wide × 6 in deep (approximately 9 m long × 300 mm wide × 150 mm deep), which produces a volume of 15 cu ft, i.e. 15/27 or 0.55 cu yd (0.41 cu m), and if the foundation was to be laid in 1:3:6 mix, you would need to order the following quantities of materials including the 5% allowance for waste.

| 0.55 cubic yards | 0.41 cubic metres |
|---|---|
| *Cement* | |
| $290 + 5\% \times 0.55 = 170$ lb | $170 + 5\% \times 0.41 = 73$ kg |
| *Sand* | |
| $950 + 5\% \times 0.55 = 550$ lb | $550 + 5\% \times 0.41 = 237$ kg |
| *Aggregate* | |
| $1700 + 5\% \times 0.55 = 980$ lb | $1000 + 5\% \times 0.41 = 430$ kg |

It is unlikely that you will be able to buy the exact quantities you require but you should be able to cut down on waste by being aware of what you actually need.

## Ready mixed concrete

For large jobs it is probably easier to order the concrete ready mixed. Most ready mixed wagons carry 4, 5 or 6 cubic metres of concrete and will deliver part loads but you will have to pay above the full load unit price. Look in your Yellow Pages and you will probably find a firm who specialise in delivering small quantities.

One tip worth remembering is to have somewhere in your garden ready to receive any concrete left over from the job you are carrying out. A little forethought can provide a path extension or a base for a future coal bunker instead of an unsightly heap of unwanted concrete.

## Brickwork

The most common size of bricks is approximately $9 \times 4\frac{1}{2} \times 3$ in ($215 \times 102.5 \times 65$ mm) and the following information is based on the use of bricks of this size:

> **Number of bricks per square metre of wall per half brick thickness = 59**

The number of facing bricks per square metre of one brick thick wall depends upon the bond used. The following table gives the number of facing bricks in walls faced one side only.

| | |
|---|---|
| Stretcher bond | 59 |
| Header bond | 118 |
| English bond | 90 |
| Flemish bond | 80 |
| English garden wall bond | 75 |
| Flemish garden wall bond | 68 |

*Add to the above for wastage – 5%.*

## Mortar

Mortar in brickwork below ground level is usually a 1:3 cement:sand mix and above ground a cement:lime:sand mortar (known as gauged mortar) either 1:1:6 or 1:2:9. Here are the approximate dry weights of materials for each of the above mixes per cubic metre of mixed material:

|  | Cement mortar (1:3) | Gauged mortar (1:1:6) | Gauged mortar (1:2:9) |
|---|---|---|---|
| Cement | 440 kg | 230 kg | 160 kg |
| Lime | – | 120 kg | 160 kg |
| Sand | 1820 kg | 1920 kg | 1980 kg |

*Add to the above for wastage – 7½%.*

The average quantity of mortar per square metre half brick wall is 0.03 cu m. Wall ties should be used at the rate of three per square metre of cavity.

## Woodwork

When buying timber, work out the actual lengths you need for each component and buy slightly longer to allow for sawing.

## Floor and wall tiles

Use this table to work out how many tiles you need:

| Tile size | No. of tiles per sq yard | No. of tiles per sq metre |
|---|---|---|
| 4″ × 4″ (100 × 100 mm) | 84 | 100 |
| 6″ × 3″ (150 × 75 mm) | 75 | 89 |
| 6″ × 6″ (150 × 150 mm) | 37 | 44 |
| 8″ × 4″ (200 × 100 mm) | 28 | 33 |
| 8″ × 8″ (200 × 200 mm) | 21 | 25 |
| 9″ × 9″ (225 × 225 mm) | 17 | 20 |
| 10″ × 2½″ (250 × 62 mm) | 55 | 65 |
| 10″ × 5″ (250 × 125 mm) | 27 | 32 |
| 10″ × 10″ (250 × 250 mm) | 14 | 16 |
| 12″ × 6″ (300 × 150 mm) | 19 | 22 |
| 12″ × 12″ (300 × 300 mm) | 9 | 11 |
| 18″ × 18″ (450 × 450 mm) | 4 | 5 |
| 24″ × 24″ (600 × 600 mm) | 3 | 3 |
| 24″ × 18″ (600 × 450 mm) | 3 | 4 |

The wastage on tiles depends upon several factors; size and shape of room, pattern, size of tile, type of material and hardness.

*Add to the above for wastage – 7½%.*

See if you can obtain refunds if you return unopened packs. If you have to purchase further packs ask whether any discount you may have been given on purchase will still apply.

## Painting

The covering capacity of paints varies enormously depending upon the nature of the surface, type of paint and the skill of the painter; the following figures therefore should only be taken as a guide. Manufacturers often indicate their own coverage capacities on the can and these may be more accurate than the following figures which are issued by the Paint and Painting Industries' Liaison Committee. The figures quoted are coverages regularly achieved in large scale painting work including wastage. They are not optimum figures based upon ideal conditions of surface, nor minimum figures reflecting the reverse of these conditions. The figures are quoted in square metres per litre, except for cement based paint which are in square metres per kilogram.

The texture of roughcast and pebbledash can vary markedly and you could find significant variations in the coverage of paints applied to these surfaces. The figures given are typical but under some conditions much lower coverages could be obtained. In many instances the coverages achieved will be affected by the suction and texture of the backing.

| Paint coverages in square metres per litre | | | | | | | |
|---|---|---|---|---|---|---|---|
| Type of paint | Type of surface | | | | | | |
| | A | B | C | D | E | F | G |
| Water thinned primer/undercoat | | | | | | | |
| as primer | 13–15 | – | – | – | – | 10–14 | – |
| as undercoat | – | – | – | – | – | 12–15 | 12–15 |
| Plaster primer | 9–11 | 8–12 | 7–9 | 5–7 | 2–4 | – | – |
| Alkali resistant primer | 7–11 | 6–8 | 6–8 | 4–6 | 2–4 | – | – |
| External wall primer sealer | 6–8 | 6–7 | 5–7 | 4–6 | 2–4 | – | – |
| Undercoat | 11–14 | 7–9 | 6–8 | 6–8 | 3–4 | 10–12 | 11–14 |
| Gloss finish | 11–14 | 8–10 | 7–9 | 6–8 | – | 10–12 | 11–14 |
| Emulsion paint | | | | | | | |
| standard | 12–15 | 8–12 | 8–12 | 6–10 | 2–4 | 10–12 | 12–15 |
| contract | 10–12 | 7–11 | 7–10 | 5–9 | 2–4 | 10–12 | 10–12 |

**Paint coverages in square metres per litre**

| Type of paint | Type of surface | | | | | | |
|---|---|---|---|---|---|---|---|
| | A | B | C | D | E | F | G |
| Heavy texture coating | 2–4 | 2–4 | 2–4 | 2–4 | 2–4 | 2–4 | 2–4 |
| Masonry paint | 5–7 | 4–6 | 4–6 | 3–5 | 2–4 | – | 6–8 |
| Cement based paint (per kilo) | – | 4–6 | 3–6 | 3–6 | 2–3 | – | – |
| Wood primer (oil based) | – | – | – | – | – | 8–11 | – |

**Key**
A – Finishing plaster
B – Wood floated rendering
C – Fair faced brickwork
D – Blockwork
E – Rough cast/pebbledash
F – Woodwork
G – Smooth primed and
    undercoated surfaces

## Wallpapering

The amount of wallpaper needed to decorate a room will depend on the length of the pattern repeat, the number of doors and windows and the room height. The following table gives the approximate number of rolls required for various size rooms and heights.

| Height of papered wall | Total perimeter of room | | | | |
|---|---|---|---|---|---|
| | 8.5 m | 11 m | 13.5 m | 16 m | 18 m |
| 2.10–2.25 m | 4 | 5 | 6 | 7 | 8 |
| 2.25–2.40 m | 4 | 5 | 6 | 7 | 8 |
| 2.40–2.55 m | 4 | 5 | 6 | 7 | 8 |
| 2.55–2.70 m | 4 | 5 | 7 | 8 | 9 |
| 2.70–2.85 m | 4 | 6 | 7 | 8 | 9 |
| 2.85–3.00 m | 5 | 6 | 7 | 9 | 10 |
| 3.00–3.15 m | 5 | 6 | 8 | 9 | 10 |

| Height of papered wall | Total perimeter of room | | | | |
|---|---|---|---|---|---|
| | 20.5 m | 23 m | 25.5 m | 28 m | 30.5 m |
| 2.10–2.25 m | 9 | 9 | 10 | 11 | 12 |
| 2.25–2.40 m | 9 | 10 | 11 | 12 | 13 |
| 2.40–2.55 m | 9 | 10 | 12 | 13 | 14 |
| 2.55–2.70 m | 10 | 11 | 12 | 13 | 15 |
| 2.70–2.85 m | 10 | 12 | 13 | 14 | 15 |
| 2.85–3.00 m | 11 | 12 | 14 | 15 | 16 |
| 3.00–3.15 m | 12 | 13 | 14 | 16 | 17 |

# BUILDING REGULATIONS

When carrying out home improvements, planning permission and building regulations must be considered. Building regulations deal with the health and safety of people and also with energy conservation.

The latest edition of the Building Regulations was published in 1991 by Her Majesty's Stationery Office (HMSO) and there are copies in most libraries. Building Regulations approval must be obtained whenever a new building or an extension is proposed. However, there are instances when approval is not required. These include:

| | |
|---|---|
| Class 1 | Buildings controlled under other legislation |
| Class 2 | Buildings not frequented by people |
| Class 3 | Greenhouses and agricultural buildings |
| Class 4 | Temporary buildings and mobile homes |
| Class 5 | Ancillary buildings |
| Class 6 | Small detached buildings |
| Class 7 | Extensions to existing buildings |

You should study a copy of the regulations for a definition of the above classes.

You must get approval if the existing building fabric would be materially altered by the proposed work, i.e. where it affects the structure, means of escape, or if the speed at which flame can spread, both internally and externally, necessitates the insertion of insulating materials in a cavity, or underpinning.

If you propose to make certain alterations to building services, approval may also be required. These include the provision, extension or alteration of sanitary equipment, drainage, vented hot water systems, and fixed heating appliances in which fuel is burnt; but not in small buildings not exceeding thirty square metres as previously defined.

Approval may also be required if you propose a change in the use of an existing building or if the building is to be converted to living accommodation or for public use where previously it was not.

There are two ways you can ensure that your improvements comply with the Building Regulations. The first method is to get forms from your local building control officer which will explain precisely what is required. The second method is to appoint a private approved inspector to oversee the work. This person must be independent and the building being improved and the appointment of the inspector is subject to the Building (Approved Inspectors) Regulations 1991.

The plans, drawings and other particulars submitted for approval must be detailed enough for the local authority, or approved inspector, to establish that the work complies with the Building Regulations. Amendments or modifications may be made or requested if the Regulations are being broken and these must be complied with. The amount and level of information which you must submit varies according to the type of work involved and you should read the Regulations for guidance.

You must pay fees in connection with applications for Building Regulations approval. These fees are fixed by the Building (Prescribed Fees, etc.) Regulations 1991. The fees charged cover the inspection of plans and other particulars and the inspection of the work in progress. There are several scales of fees depending upon the nature of the work involved. As an illustration the following are the current fees (including VAT) for work to small garages, carports and certain alterations and extensions.

|  | Plan fee | Inspection fee |
|---|---|---|
| 1. An extension or alteration consisting of the provision of one or more rooms in roof space including means of access | £41.42 | £124.26 |
| 2. Any extension (not falling within paragraph 1 above) which does not have a total floor area exceeding 20 square metres | £20.70 | £62.12 |

| | Plan fee | Inspection fee |
|---|---|---|
| 3. Any extension (not falling within paragraph 1 above) which has a floor area of between 20 square metres and 40 square metres | £41.42 | £124.26 |

The plan fee is payable when you hand in the plans and you will have to pay the inspection fee after the inspection has been made. Details of fees for other types of work should be obtained from your local authority.

## PLANNING PERMISSION

You may also have to obtain planning permission for your home improvement but it depends upon the nature of the work you intend carrying out. All developments are controlled by planning laws in order to protect the interest of the public in development and use of land. Planning permission is quite different from Building Regulation approval and you may need both.

You should check with your local planning authority whether you need planning permission for the work you intend to do. However, you will need planning permission in the cases listed below:

1. If the work will obstruct the view of vehicular traffic using a highway thereby causing danger.

2. If the work will involve a new access to a trunk or classified road, or the widening of an existing one.

3. If the original planning approval for your house has restrictions on the types of work which can be done. These rules do not necessarily mean that you cannot do such work, only that you must apply for planning permission.

4. If you live in a listed building, national park, area of outstanding natural beauty or conservation area, which was designated as such before 1 April 1981, then the rules governing your planning application may be more stringent and permission will often have to be obtained for work which would not otherwise require it. The local planning authority has the right to impose stricter controls. These are generally only in conservation areas or places where the authority wish to preserve the appearance

of character. This is done by what is called an Article 4 direction and the planning authority is obliged to inform you if an Article 4 direction affects your property. If in doubt you should check with your local authority.

5. If the work involves building over a sewer or drain you will have to obtain the consent of the local council under the 1936 Public Health Act.

6. Construction of an access, path or driveway to the road unless the access is to an unclassified road and necessary because of the construction of an extension, porch or hardstanding where planning permission is not required (see later). If the access path or driveway crosses a verge or path in order to meet the road however, the permission of the highway authority must always be given.

7. If you intend to use part of your house as an office to run a business or to let as bedsitters.

8. If you intend to use your house or associated buildings to store goods in connection with your business or sell goods from your house.

9. Conversion of your house or any part of it into flats.

10. Additions of a separate building attached to your house or otherwise to be used as an individual dwelling.

If your property is leasehold or if you are a tenant, then your lease or tenancy agreement may not allow you to carry out certain work even if you have planning permission so before you apply for permission under these circumstances, always check your agreement.

There may be a restrictive covenant which affects your property even if you own the property and if it is freehold. Look closely at your deeds to ensure that no restrictive covenants apply. If they do, check with your planning authority to see if there is anyway round them and if necessary seek legal advice.

The following list shows the type of work where you do not need planning permission but if you are in any doubt, you should talk to your local planning officer.

1. General redecoration, maintenance or improvement work which does not increase the size of your property. Replacement windows providing they do not project beyond the most forward part of any wall of the original house. Changing the

outside appearance of your property (pebbledashing, stone facing, etc.).

2. Internal alterations to the property providing that the internal use of the property is not changed.

3. House extensions provided that:

   **(a)** the volume of the house does not increase by 50 cubic metres, or one tenth of the volume of the original house up to a maximum of 115 cubic metres, whichever is the greater, for a terraced house, or house in a national park, area of outstanding natural beauty or conservation area designated as such before 1 April 1981. For all other houses the limit is the greater size of 70 cubic metres or 15% of the original house volume up to a maximum of 115 cubic metres;

   **(b)** extension is no higher than the original roof;

   **(c)** no part of the extension projects beyond that part of the original house closed to the highway or 20 metres whichever is the nearest;

   **(d)** no part of the extension which is within two metres of the boundary is over four metres high (this does not apply to alterations and extensions to the original roof);

   **(e)** the extension does not cover more than half of the original garden area;

   **(f)** the extension is not intended as a separate or independent dwelling.

   *Note that the original volume is the external volume of the house as originally built or as it stood on 1 July 1984 if built before then.*

4. Conservatories providing they are attached to the house and meet the conditions for house extensions.

5. Small buildings not attached to the house such as greenhouses, sheds, providing:

   **(a)** that the building is for the use of the occupants of the house;

   **(b)** the building does not project beyond that part of the house closest to the highway or 20 metres whichever is the nearest;

**(c)** the height of the building does not exceed three metres (four metres if the roof is ridged).

6. Garages within five metres of the house or garages in national parks, areas of outstanding natural beauty or conservation areas designated before 1 April 1981, providing they meet the criteria for house extensions. Garages over five metres from the house are treated in the same way as small buildings.

7. Loft conversions providing the overall volume of the house does not increase otherwise it is classed as an extension.

8. Porches providing the floor area does not exceed 3 square metres, measured externally, the height does not exceed 3 metres and it is over 2 metres from any boundary between the garden and road or footpath.

9. Television aerials providing they are the normal type attached to the house and used for domestic purposes.

10. Fences providing they do not exceed one metre in height where they run along a boundary which adjoins a vehicular highway or where they do not exceed two metres in height for other locations.

11. Hardstandings for cars providing they are in your garden.

12. Cutting down trees unless they are covered by a tree preservation order or are in a conservation area.

13. Demolition of part of your house or building in the garden unless the building is listed or in a conservation area.

You must of course pay for making a planning application and the current application fee for an alteration/extension is £55.00. If you decide to change the use of an existing building, or convert to flats, then different fees are chargeable and you should consult your local planning officer. There are exceptions however and these are:

**(a)** if the work is for the benefit of a disabled person;

**(b)** if the property is affected by an Article 4 direction;

**(c)** if the application is a variant of a previously unsuccessful application and is made within twelve months of the unsuccessful application, or where an application which has been successful is withdrawn. Only one exemption is allowed for any particular work on your property.

In order to make a planning application you must contact your local planning authority who will send you the relevant forms for completion. In most cases it is better to submit a full and formal application at the beginning. This would mean supplying copies of a plan of the site and sufficient plans, drawings and information to enable the work to be identified clearly and without ambiguity. Your application will be put on the planning register which is open to examination by anyone. Depending on the authority, it may be advertised in the local press, and you may be required to display a notice outside your property or notify your immediate neighbours. Objections to your application may be lodged with the planning authority but no one can insist on a refusal of your application. That decision lies solely with the authority.

Should the authority reject your application they must give you the reasons for doing so. A re-submission may be successful if you can satisfy their objections by making suitable amendments to the work. However if you feel that their decision is unjust or that conditions imposed on an otherwise successful application are too onerous then you have the right to appeal. Appeals are heard by the Secretary of State for the Environment (or the Secretary of State for Scotland or Wales). If you wish to appeal you must do so within six months of the original decision. However it is worth noting that more appeals fail than are successful although there is no fee charged for making an appeal.

## SAFETY

Even though you may have taken out insurance, you owe it to yourself, your family and anyone else on or near to the site, to ensure that there are no unnecessary hazards around. Most accidents on construction sites are caused by slipping, tripping or falling, and from electrical shock. So follow these rules:

1. Plan the job in advance. Make sure you have all the tools and materials to do the job and that the tools are safe and efficient. Inspect all ladders and steps for defects and make sure they are of adequate length. Examine electric plugs, cables and sockets for correct type and ensure that they are in good condition.

2. Clear the site of all unwanted furniture and equipment and let the family know of any 'no-go' areas. Wear overalls or similar clothing including a safety helmet and slip-resistant soles where appropriate. Secure ladders to avoid slipping. Check position of water pipes, electric cables etc.

3. While the work is in progress:

- don't leave tools and materials around where people can fall over them;

- clear up any spillages at once;

- watch where the leads for electrical tools are running and keep them away from heat and sharp edges;

- provide plenty of bags and boxes for small items and loose tools.

4. Always tidy up the site at the end of the day. Don't leave flammable or toxic substances in open containers and sweep up all shavings and sawdust. Ensure that there are no live wires left exposed. Collect and lock away all tools and equipment out of reach of children.

5. One final point: any work which requires the stripping of materials containing asbestos should be done by a contractor licensed under the Asbestos (Licensing) Regulations 1983.

---

**Don't forget, these prices may need adjustment depending on where you live.**
Regional adjustments are provided in the Introduction.

# MONEY MATTERS

It is essential that you give careful consideration to the cost of repairs or improvements *before* you carry them out. There are two questions that must be asked: 'Can I afford it' and 'How should I pay for it'. Unless the work involves urgent repairs (in which case a way must be found to afford it), the decision to proceed can only be taken after the first question has been answered satisfactorily. It is hoped that this book will help you to assess the approximate cost of either, having the work carried out by a contractor, or doing the work yourself, so that you can prepare your budget.

That leaves the question of how to pay for it. The usual options are either use your savings or borrow the money from a bank or building society. There are other sources of finance, such as private borrowing from friends or relations, or using your credit card, but these are unsatisfactory for varying reasons and you are advised to try a bank or building society first. If your present building society or another financial institution turns you down for a mortgage, second mortgage, personal loan or overdraft there must be something radically wrong with your proposal which would make it almost certainly unacceptable to alternative sources of lending unless a very high rate of interest was charged.

Tax relief used to be granted on money borrowed for home improvements but it was withdrawn in April 1988 after widespread abuse. Let us look at the case of three neighbours who each want to borrow £10,000 for a house extension. Mr Brown is retired and pays no tax, Mr Green pays tax at 25% and Mr Jones pays tax at 40%. Each of them has £10,000 savings in a building society at 9% and they have all been offered a loan from a bank at 15%. Let us consider which is the best option for each of them.

|  | Brown | Green | Jones |
|---|---|---|---|
| Income from savings |  |  |  |
| 9% × £10,000 | 900 | 900 | 900 |
| Less income tax | – | 225 | 360 |
| Net income from investment | £900 | 675 | 540 |

So if they used their savings to build the extension they would lose the above net income. If, however, they decided to hold on to their investments and borrow from the bank at 15% the following costs would be incurred:

|  | Brown | Green | Jones |
|---|---|---|---|
| Annual interest on loan |  |  |  |
| 15% × £10,000 | 1500 | 1500 | 1500 |
| Net income from investment | 900 | 675 | 540 |
| Net cost | £600 | 825 | 960 |

This shows that only Mr Brown is better off by borrowing the money from the bank. The paradox is however that being a non-tax paying retired pensioner, he is the one the bank would be least likely to lend the £10,000!

The point is that you should carefully work out your own position to get the best advantage you can for yourself. Consider your income and future prospects, your outgoings and likely future commitments, also the availability of any savings. You might, for instance, decide to take half the cost from savings and borrow the rest, to break the project down and spread it over a longer period, to cut down on contract labour and so on. Remember also all the non-building costs – it greatly reduces the pleasure of a new sun lounge if you have not got enough money left to furnish it!

# GRANTS

In some circumstances grants are available from local authorities for house repairs and improvements. There are four types of grant and some brief notes are set out below to explain them but if you think you qualify you should contact the Citizens Advice Bureau or local authority for a leaflet containing full details. You should note that although the grants are standard some of the rules governing them vary in different local authorities.

## Renovation grant

This grant is available for owner-occupiers, landlords and tenants although there are some restrictions affecting each of these classes. The grant covers six areas of work:

1. To bring a property up to date to the standard of fitness for human habitation (this grant usually applies to very old properties and is mandatory).

2. To repair and/or improve a property beyond the standard of fitness (this grant is discretionary and covers the following types of work: replacement of windows, doors, damp-proof courses, electrical wiring, and defective rainwater pipes and gutters).

3. House insulation (loft insulation, lagging of tanks and pipes, and cavity wall insulation are included in this section and the grant is discretionary. Draught proofing, secondary or double glazing could also be included).

4. Heating (this applies to the provision of heating facilities and although the grant is usually discretionary it could be mandatory if the work is needed to make the building 'fit').

5. Providing satisfactory internal arrangements (in some old properties there may be inconvenient low doorways, steep staircases and the like which could be dangerous. A discretionary grant could be available if the work is part of a wider scheme of development).

6. Conversion (a discretionary grant is available for the conversion of under-used dwellings into flats or the creation of flats above shops or offices).

All the above categories attract discretionary grants except for 1 and part of 3 which are mandatory.

## Common parts grant

The common parts of a building containing flats are the roof, staircase and hall and there are certain restrictions on the types of tenants who are eligible. The grant is discretionary except in the case of a landlord who has been served with a repair notice where it is mandatory.

## HMO grant

Houses in multiple occupation (HMO) where the occupants do not form a single household are eligible for this grant which is usually discretionary and can only be applied for by the landlord. Housing booklets 31 and 32 carry full details.

## Disabled facilities grant

The council must be satisfied that the proposed works are necessary and appropriate to meet the needs of the disabled occupant and that they are reasonable and practicable given the age and condition of the property. If these conditions are fulfilled the grant is mandatory. When completed the work should provide the occupant with one or more of the following benefits:

1. Make it easier to enter and leave the house.
2. Provide kitchen and bathroom facilities that can be used independently.
3. Make heating and lighting controls easier to use.
4. Improve the heating system.
5. Make it easier for a disabled person to look after another person who is dependent on him or her.

There are also discretionary grants for a wide range of other works to make property more suitable for a disabled person and enquiries should be made to the local council.

The amount of the grant, whether mandatory or discretionary depends upon how much the applicant can afford to pay from saving and income. The formula used to assess the grant is complex and application forms explaining how the 'means testing' system works can be obtained from the council offices.

# VAT

Some explanation of VAT ratings is necessary:

*Zero-rating* – Any job which is zero-rated is not liable to VAT and any VAT paid on supplies of goods or labour can be reclaimed from H.M. Customs and Excise.

*Standard-rating* – Any job which is standard-rated is liable to tax at the current rate (at present 17½%) and any tax paid on supplies of goods and labour cannot be reclaimed.

Domestic construction may fall into either category. Broadly, the construction of new private dwellings is zero-rated and all other types of work are standard-rated.

The definition of new private dwellings includes building a new house or bungalow, but if the new building is being erected on the remains of an old one then difficulties arise in deciding whether it is a new building or not. The definition is vital because a new building qualifies for zero-rating but the re-construction of an old one does not.

For example the following would qualify as new buildings:

1. The construction of a building making use of a part or all of the foundations of an existing building, where the whole of the former building has been demolished to foundation level.

2. The construction of a building making use of what remains of an existing building where this is limited to a single wall such as the front facade, or to a single wall plus all or part of the foundations, or to a single continuous facade covering two walls on a corner site.

3. Building-on to an existing house to form two semi-detached houses without internal access to the existing building, and where planning permission etc. does not prevent its separate use, letting or disposal. The new building must stand on its own land.

4. The building of a new house within an existing terrace of houses on the site of a house that has been totally demolished ('infilling').

The following do not qualify as the construction of a new building:

(a) the conversion, reconstruction, alteration or enlargement of an existing building, or an extension or annexe which has internal access to the existing building;

(b) where the outer walls of an existing building remain even without floor or roof; or where internal features are retained in addition to any part of the external wall structure;

(c) the building of an additional flat on top of an existing block.

A new detached garage would qualify for zero-rating if constructed at the same time as the house but not otherwise. Greenhouses, garden sheds are always standard rated.

If you are building a new house for yourself and think your work will qualify for zero-rating, call at the local VAT office (you will find the address under Customs and Excise in the Telephone Directory) and ask for Notice 719 'VAT Refunds for do-it-yourself house builders' and Leaflet 708/2/87 'Construction Industry'. These will tell you what you can and cannot claim for and also how and when to claim.

Zero-rating also applies to certain work, goods and services provided, on or for, protected buildings and disabled persons, details may be found in VAT Leaflets 708/1 and 701/7 respectively.

# INSURANCES

The vast majority of home improvement work is successfully completed without a thought being given to the need for insurance cover, but there could be financial loss if you or a member of the public were injured as a result of your project.

If you intend to engage a contractor to do some of the work you should be certain that he has adequate Public Liability insurance to cover, for example, accidental injury to passers by, or the ruining of their clothes due to paint splashes. Ask your contractor if he has an Inland Revenue '714 certificate'. If he has, he will also have the necessary Public Liability cover for this is a condition for issue of the certificate. If he is not a 714 certificate holder ask to see evidence of current Public Liability insurance before accepting any estimate he has submitted.

For those who are building a house or bungalow for their own occupation with the help of employees and/or labour only subcontractors at least one Insurance Company (Norwich Union) has a 'self build' insurance policy, the cover lasts for 2 years and any extension must be negotiated. This policy covers:

| | |
|---|---|
| Employer's Liability | Injury to an employee or labour-only sub-contractor |
| Public Liability | Injury to members of the public (the limit is £1,000,000 for any one accident) |
| Contract Works | (a) 'All risks' covered – loss or damage to the building and materials on site or in transit. |

| Contract Works (contd) | (b) Plant, tools, and equipment up to £2,000. |
| | (c) Employees personal effects – up to £250 any one employee. |

There is a £250 excess under (a) and (b) and a £50 excess under (c). The insurance is not available for the extension, alteration, repair or renovation of existing buildings.

A general personal accident or sickness policy which provides for weekly payments during temporary disablement as well as lump sums for more serious injuries is a useful safeguard, but do ensure that the type of activity you are proposing to undertake is covered before you pay the premium.

# WHAT'S IT GOING TO COST?

In this chapter information on hours and costs is given under various headings. To find out the total cost or number of hours for a particular job, however, you need to add up the various amounts given for the different elements of the work. For example, if you intend to take out a fireplace consisting of a tiled concrete surround and hearth and then brick up the opening, plaster the new brickwork and fix a length of timber skirting, you would need to collect the hours and costs in the second, third and fourth descriptions set out in 'Fireplaces'. This concept of collecting information from more than one description to build up a composite value or number of hours applies throughout the book.

---

**Don't forget, these prices may need adjustment depending on where you live.**
Regional adjustments are provided in the Introduction.

---

# DISPOSAL OF RUBBISH

Any demolition, excavation and alteration work (pulling down, breaking out) in this book, does not include the cost of removing debris or excavated material. There are two ways of doing this, loading into skips or loading into lorries. It is unlikely that a householder would become involved in the hiring of lorries so only the skip option is considered. Assuming the skips would be loaded to capacity the costs (including VAT) should be:

| Size of skip cu yds | Daily hire rate £ | Cost per cu yd £ |
|---|---|---|
| 2 | 25.85 | 12.43 |
| 3 | 29.38 | 9.79 |
| 4 | 35.23 | 8.81 |
| 5 | 41.13 | 8.23 |
| 6 | 54.05 | 9.00 |
| 8 | 58.75 | 7.34 |

These figures show the advantage of hiring a large skip (providing you can fill it!) and the following figures are based upon using a 5 cu yd skip which holds approximately 5 tons of waste material. Please note that these figures are all based upon imperial units because that is how most skip hire companies serving the domestic market work.

| | | | | | |
|---|---|---|---|---|---|
| Load debris into wheelbarrow, wheel average 25 m, deposit in skip | 1 cu yd (1 cu m) | 1:05 (1:20) | – – | 1 | 7.10 (9.30) |
| Cost of removal of debris in 5 cu yd skip (including tipping charges) | 1 cu yd (1 cu m) | – – | – – | – | 8.23 (10.78) |

You should remember that the above figures apply only to full loads. Hiring a skip and only half filling it would be more expensive per unit.

If for some other reason you wished to hire a lorry it should cost you approximately £25 per hour for lorry and driver, but bear in mind that the minimum hire period would probably be half a day, i.e. £100.

# TREATMENT OF TIMBER

It is estimated that more than 75% of the houses in Britain suffer from insect infestation, the most common being the furniture beetle. Most of the damage they cause is of a minor nature and is confined to unpainted surfaces but if they attack structural timbers, action should be taken immediately. Professional help should be sought but in straightforward cases of minor infestation (or preventative action) the following information should be of use. It is assumed that the insecticidal wood preserver will be applied by brush and that gaining access to the areas requiring treatment is not difficult.

| | 📏 | 🕐 | 🔨 | 🖐 | £ |
|---|---|---|---|---|---|
| Apply one coat insecticidal wood preserver on general surfaces | 1 sq yd (1 sq m) | 0:15 (0.17) | – – | 2 | 3.75 (4.50) |

If you decided to use spraying equipment instead of using a brush, the hire cost of the equipment is £5.50 for the first day, £2.75 for each subsequent day or £11 for a week (all excluding VAT).

> **Don't forget, these prices may need adjustment depending on where you live.**
> Regional adjustments are provided in the Introduction.

# DAMP TREATMENT

There are two main types of dampness in buildings – penetrating and rising damp. Penetrating damp can be observed by patches of dampness on the external walls and is usually caused by one of the following:

- cracked or porous brickwork;
- defective rendering or pointing;
- damaged flashing;
- leaking gutter or rainwater pipe;
- bridged cavity.

Here are some costs and hours associated with this work.

| | 📏 | 🕐 | 🐍 | ✋ | £ |
|---|---|---|---|---|---|
| Cut out single brick and replace with new in external wall and bed and point in cement mortar | 1 no | 1:00 | 0.60 | 4 | 5.50 |
| Hack off defective rendering and renew in one coat cement mortar ¾" (19 mm) thick | 1 sq yd (1 sq m) | 1:25 (1:50) | 1.60 (1.90) | 5 | 10.00 (12.00) |
| Rake out joints of existing mortar and point up in cement mortar | 1 sq yd (1 sq m) | 1:50 (2:10) | 0.40 (0.50) | 5 | 7.50 (9.00) |
| Rake out horizontal joint in wall, refix flashing and point up in cement mortar | 1 yd (1 m) | 0:40 (0:45) | 0.35 (0.40) | 5 | 2.50 (3.00) |
| Rake out horizontal joint in wall, refix stepped flashing and point up in cement mortar | 1 yd (1 m) | 0:50 (0:55) | 0.35 (0.40) | 5 | 3.55 (4.25) |

# DAMP TREATMENT

|  | 🖊 | 🕐 | 🔧 | ✋ | £ |
|---|---|---|---|---|---|
| Remove 6 ft (1.83 m) length of existing rainwater gutter and replace with new gutter | | | | | |
| 4½" (115 mm) half round cast iron | 1 no | 2:20 | 10.50 | 5 | 32.00 |
| 4½" (115 mm) half round plastic | 1 no | 1:30 | 5.20 | 5 | 12.00 |
| Remove 6 ft (1.83 m) length of existing rainwater pipe and replace with new pipe | | | | | |
| 3" (75 mm) diameter cast iron | 1 no | 1:80 | 20.00 | 5 | 40.00 |
| 2½" (63 mm) diameter plastic | 1 no | 1:00 | 5.50 | 5 | 13.00 |
| Remove 6 bricks from external leaf of cavity wall, inspect and remove mortar from wall tie, reset bricks and point up | 1 no | 3:00 | 1.20 | 5 | 30.00 |

Rising damp is usually caused by a defective or non-existent damp-proof course (dpc). There are various methods of inserting a dpc into an existing wall but injecting a chemical waterproofing liquid is probably the most effective one within the range of skills of the DIY enthusiast. The method consists of drilling a series of holes 4½ in (115 mm) apart and pumping in the fluid which permeates the brickwork.

The cost of hiring the equipment is £22.00 for the first day, £11.00 for each subsequent day, £44 for a week or £27.50 for a weekend (the average semi-detached house could be done in a weekend if the holes were pre-drilled). The cost of hiring a drill (¾ in to 1 in chuck) is £12.50, £6.25, £25.00 and £15.50 respectively. All these prices exclude VAT. The following reflect the labour and waterproofing liquid costs for treating *one face* of an external wall.

| | ✏ | 🕐 | ✂ | ✋ | £ |
|---|---|---|---|---|---|
| Drill holes ¾" (18 mm) diameter, 3" (75 mm) deep at 4½" (115 mm) centres, inject chemical dpc and make good holes | 1 yd (1 m) | 2:05 (2:30) | 4.85 (5.30) | 5 | 23.40 (28.00) |

The plaster must be hacked off from the internal face and the skirting removed before work commences and then be replaced.

| | ✏ | 🕐 | ✂ | ✋ | £ |
|---|---|---|---|---|---|
| Hack off existing plaster 3 ft (1 m) high and replaster | 1 yd (1 m) | 2:30 (2:35) | 2.30 (2.50) | 7 | 13.25 (14.50) |
| Take off existing skirting and renew with 4" (100 mm) high painted softwood skirting | 1 yd (1 m) | 0:40 (0:45) | 1.65 (1.80) | 5 | 3.75 (4.50) |

Don't forget, these prices may need adjustment depending on where you live.
Regional adjustments are provided in the Introduction.

# FIREPLACES

The removal and replacement of fireplaces is a task that can be tackled by most DIY enthusiasts – provided they have enough muscle to remove the debris! Unless the old fireplace can be broken up indoors, which is not usually desirable, some help will be required. The DIY hours shown below are for the total man hours necessary to complete the work. The scrap (or antique) value of the fireplace has been ignored. No allowance has been made for removing debris (see page 64).

|  | / | 🕐 | ⚒ | ✋ | £ |
|---|---|---|---|---|---|
| Take out timber fireplace surround size |  |  |  |  |  |
| 3'6" × 3'0" (1050 × 900 mm) | 1 no | 1:00 | – | 3 | 10.00 |
| 4'0" × 3'6" (1200 × 1050 mm) | 1 no | 1:05 | – | 3 | 13.00 |
| 5'0" × 4'0" (1500 × 1200 mm) | 1 no | 1:10 | – | 3 | 16.00 |
| Take out tiled concrete fireplace surround size |  |  |  |  |  |
| 3'6" × 3'0" (1050 × 900 mm) | 1 no | 2:00 | – | 3 | 18.00 |
| 4'0" × 3'6" (1200 × 1050 mm) | 1 no | 2:30 | – | 3 | 24.00 |
| 5'0" × 4'0" (1500 × 1200 mm) | 1 no | 3:00 | – | 3 | 30.00 |
| Take out tiled concrete or stone hearth size |  |  |  |  |  |
| 3'6" × 1'6" (1050 × 450 mm) | 1 no | 1:00 | – | 3 | 10.00 |
| 3'6" × 2'0" (1050 × 600 mm) | 1 no | 1:20 | – | 3 | 12.00 |
| 4'0" × 2'0" (1200 × 600 mm) | 1 no | 1:30 | – | 3 | 14.00 |
| 5'0" × 3'0" (1500 × 900 mm) | 1 no | 2:30 | – | 3 | 20.00 |

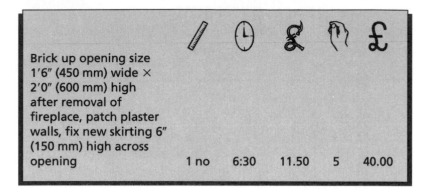

| | / | ① | £ | ♔ | £ |
|---|---|---|---|---|---|
| Brick up opening size 1'6" (450 mm) wide × 2'0" (600 mm) high after removal of fireplace, patch plaster walls, fix new skirting 6" (150 mm) high across opening | 1 no | 6:30 | 11.50 | 5 | 40.00 |

The following prices indicate the time and cost involved in fixing new fireplaces. Due to the wide range of products the information has been based upon the basic price of a selection of fireplaces.

| | / | ① | £ | ♔ | £ |
|---|---|---|---|---|---|
| Fix new fireplace including patch plastering around edges | | | | | |
| Basic price – £100 | 1 no | 6:00 | 105.00 | 3 | 130.00 |
| Basic price – £150 | 1 no | 6:00 | 155.00 | 3 | 190.00 |
| Basic price – £200 | 1 no | 6:00 | 205.00 | 3 | 230.00 |
| Basic price – £300 | 1 no | 6:00 | 305.00 | 3 | 350.00 |

# EXTERNAL WALL TREATMENT
## REPAIRS

The following information relates to the sundry repair and repointing of existing brickwork. It is necessary to re-point old brickwork in order to prevent infiltration of dampness caused by driving rain or leaking pipework penetrating the decayed mortar. Apart from fulfilling this important functional need, re-pointing also improves the appearance of a building. The figures quoted below refer to work carried out at ground level and 20% should be added to the hours and costs for work executed from ladders and 10% from platforms.

| | 📏 | 🕐 | ⚖ | ✋ | £ |
|---|---|---|---|---|---|
| Rake out joints of existing brickwork and point up in cement mortar | 1 sq yd (1 sq m) | 1:50 (2:10) | 0.35 (0.40) | 5 | 11.00 (12.00) |
| Cut out single brick from external wall and replace with new set in cement mortar | 1 no | 1:00 | 0.60 | 4 | 5.50 |
| Cut out terracotta air brick size 9″ × 3″ (220 × 75 mm) and replace with new set in cement mortar | 1 no | 1:00 | 1.40 | 4 | 7.50 |

> **Don't forget, these prices may need adjustment depending on where you live.**
> Regional adjustments are provided in the Introduction.

# CHIMNEY POTS

In the case of the replacement of chimney pots the question of access is critical. The cost of erecting scaffolding and secure walkways to the stack would normally far exceed the cost for the work to be done. It may be possible to gain access to the stack from a rooflight which would reduce the cost considerably. Because of these uncertainties the following costs and hours represent the cost of carrying out the work only and not the cost of the scaffolding or towers.

| | 📏 | 🕐 | ✂ | ✋ | £ |
|---|---|---|---|---|---|
| Remove existing defective chimney pot, hack away flaunching, fix new terracotta pot 8″ (185 mm) diameter × 12″ (300 mm) high and set in cement mortar | 1 no | 4:00 | 14.75 | 4 | 40.00 |
| As above but 18″ (450 mm) high | 1 no | 4:30 | 17.75 | 4 | 50.00 |

**Don't forget, these prices may need adjustment depending on where you live.**
Regional adjustments are provided in the Introduction.

# ROOFING

The skills required to carry out roof repairs can vary enormously. Sometimes the repair work is straightforward but gaining safe and secure access can be difficult and in these circumstances you should use a contractor. This section is divided into three parts – repairs to pitched roofs involving slates and tiles, repairs to flat roofs covered in bituminous roofing felt, and new work. The cost of removing debris is not included in the following costs nor is the cost of hiring any specialist equipment such as roof ladders.

Remember that, as explained in Chapter 1, the contractor's cost only reflects the cost of carrying out the work and not the travelling. Although the cost is given at £9.00 for a contractor to refix one slate, he may charge considerably more when he adds on his travelling time and costs.

## REPAIRS TO PITCHED ROOFS

| | / | ⏱ | ⚒ | ✊ | £ |
|---|---|---|---|---|---|
| Take up covering from pitched roof for disposal | | | | | |
| tiles | 1 sq yd | 0:40 | – | 3 | 5.00 |
| | (1 sq m) | (0:45) | | | (6.00) |
| slates | 1 sq yd | 0:40 | – | 3 | 5.00 |
| | (1 sq m) | (0:45) | | | (6.00) |
| timber boarding | 1 sq yd | 0:42 | – | 3 | 5.40 |
| | (1 sq m) | (0.50) | | | (6.50) |
| battens | 1 sq yd | 0:25 | – | 3 | 2.90 |
| | (1 sq m) | (0:30) | | | (3.50) |
| underfelt | 1 sq yd | 0:08 | – | 3 | 0.85 |
| | (1 sq m) | (0:10) | | | (1.00) |
| flat sheeting | 1 sq yd | 0:25 | – | 3 | 2.90 |
| | (1 sq m) | (0:30) | | | (3.50) |
| corrugated sheeting | 1 sq yd | 0:25 | – | 3 | 2.91 |
| | (1 sq m) | (0:30) | | | (3.50) |

| | 📏 | 🕐 | 🐛 | ✋ | £ |
|---|---|---|---|---|---|
| Carefully take up covering from pitched roof and lay aside for re-use | | | | | |
| tiles | 1 sq yd | 1:15 | – | 3 | 10.00 |
| | (1 sq m) | (1:30) | | | (12.00) |
| slates | 1 sq yd | 1:15 | – | 3 | 10.00 |
| | (1 sq m) | (1:20) | | | (12.00) |
| timber boarding | 1 sq yd | 1:25 | – | 3 | 10.90 |
| | (1 sq m) | (1:40) | | | (13.00) |
| flat sheeting | 1 sq yd | 0:50 | – | 3 | 6.70 |
| | (1 sq m) | (1:00) | | | (8.00) |
| corrugated sheeting | 1 sq yd | 0:50 | – | 3 | 6.70 |
| | (1 sq m) | (1:00) | | | (8.00) |
| Remove single broken slate replace with slate laid aside previously | 1 no | 1:10 | – | 6 | 10.00 |
| Remove single broken slate and replace with new Welsh blue slate size | | | | | |
| 20″ × 10″ (510 × 255 mm) | 1 no | 1:10 | 2.30 | 6 | 14.00 |
| 24″ × 12″ (610 × 305 mm) | 1 no | 1:20 | 4.50 | 6 | 18.00 |
| Remove slates from area approximately 1 sq yd (1 sq m) and replace with new Welsh blue slates size | | | | | |
| 20″ × 10″ | 1 sq yd | 3:00 | 32.60 | 6 | 75.00 |
| (510 × 255 mm) | (1 sq m) | (3:40) | (39.00) | | (90.00) |
| 24″ × 12″ | 1 sq yd | 2:30 | 45.00 | | 80.00 |
| (610 × 305 mm) | (1 sq m) | (3:00) | (54.00) | 6 | (95.00) |
| Remove single broken tile, replace with tile previously laid aside | 1 no | 1:00 | – | 6 | 7.00 |

**Don't forget, these prices may need adjustment depending on where you live.**
Regional adjustments are provided in the Introduction.

| | 📏 | 🕐 | £ | ✋ | £ |
|---|---|---|---|---|---|
| Remove single broken tile replace with new plain tile size 10½″ × 6½″ (265 × 165 mm) | 1 no | 1:00 | 0.30 | 6 | 8.00 |
| interlocking tile size 16″ × 13″ (410 × 330 mm) | 1 no | 1:00 | 0.80 | 6 | 9.00 |
| Take off defective ridge or hip cappings and re-set in cement mortar | 1 yd (1 m) | 1:30 (1:40) | 0.20 (2.00) | 4 | 8.80 (12.00) |
| Take off defective ridge or hip cappings and replace with new bed and point in cement mortar | 1 yd (1 m) | 1:10 (1:20) | 7.50 (9.00) | 4 | 16.80 (20.00) |

## REPAIRS TO FLAT ROOFS

Repairs to built up bituminous felt roofing should only be carried out by an amateur if they are of a minor nature such as small cracks or blisters. If the surface is in poor condition or if there is a profusion of defects it is better to call in a contractor to re-roof the whole area.

| | 📏 | 🕐 | £ | ✋ | £ |
|---|---|---|---|---|---|
| Cut out crack in bituminous felt roofing, apply bituminous compound and apply sealing tape 6″ (150 mm) wide | 1 yd (1 m) | 1:00 (1:10) | 2.50 (3.00) | 5 | 6.30 (7.50) |
| Cut out blister in bituminous felt roofing, apply bituminous compound and apply sealing tape to area approximately 12″ × 12″ (300 × 300 mm) | 1 no | 0:40 | 1.70 | 5 | 5.00 |

# NEW ROOF COVERINGS

The laying of pitched and flat roof coverings is a job for the expert and the following information should give you an indication of what you would expect to pay. Note that the extra items involved in roofing, e.g. extra courses of tiles at verges and eaves, flashings, underfelt, and battens (where applicable), have been allowed for in the overall rate.

| | Quantity | Contractor's Price £ |
|---|---|---|
| Roofing felt | 1 sq yd | 2.00 |
| | (1 sq m) | (2.40) |
| 1" (25 mm) butt jointed softwood boarding | 1 sq yd | 13.00 |
| | (1 sq m) | (15.60) |
| 2" (50 mm) wood wool slabs (unreinforced) | 1 sq yd | 12.50 |
| | (1 sq m) | (15.00) |
| Welsh blue slates size | | |
| 20" × 10" (510 × 255 mm) | 1 sq yd | 58.50 |
| | (1 sq m) | (70.00) |
| 24" × 12" (610 × 305 mm) | 1 sq yd | 71.00 |
| | (1 sq m) | (85.00) |
| Plain concrete tile size 10½" × 6½" (265 × 165 mm) | 1 sq yd | 37.50 |
| | (1 sq m) | (45.00) |
| Interlocking tile size 16" × 13" (410 × 330 mm) | 1 sq yd | 21.00 |
| | (1 sq m) | (25.00) |
| Bituminous fibre-based built up roofing with top layer mineral surface | | |
| two layer | 1 sq yd | 8.40 |
| | (1 sq m) | (10.00) |
| three layer | 1 sq yd | 12.50 |
| | (1 sq m) | (15.00) |
| Bituminous asbestos-based built up roofing with top layer mineral surface | | |
| two layer | 1 sq yd | 12.50 |
| | (1 sq m) | (15.00) |
| three layer | 1 sq yd | 19.20 |
| | (1 sq m) | (23.00) |

# DOORS

Fitting a new door either because of damage or to improve a room's appearance can make a significant improvement for only a few hours work. Although there are a multitude of doors on the market there are only five main types:

| | |
|---|---|
| Panelled | these are traditional doors where panels are set into a surrounding frame; |
| Flush | faced with hardwood or plywood veneer; |
| Glazed | these are normally used where there is a need for light, e.g. in a corridor or an entrance; |
| Ledged and braced | these doors are usually used in situations where appearance is not the main consideration, e.g. a yard entrance or an outhouse (although they are not necessarily the cheapest). |
| Period | these are made from hardwood and usually incorporate panels or fanlights to give a Tudor or Georgian appearance and are mainly used as front entrance doors. |

| Removing doors, frames and ironmongery | 📏 | 🕐 | ⚖️ | ✋ | £ |
|---|---|---|---|---|---|
| Take off existing door | | | | | |
| internal | 1 no | 0:30 | – | 3 | 1.50 |
| external | 1 no | 0:40 | – | 3 | 2.00 |
| Take out existing door frame or lining | 1 no | 0:40 | – | 3 | 2.00 |
| Take off existing ironmongery | | | | | |
| 3″ (75 mm) butt hinges | 1 pr | 0:10 | – | 3 | 1.00 |
| 4″ (100 mm) butt hinges | 1 pr | 0:15 | – | 3 | 1.50 |
| bolt | 1 no | 0:10 | – | 3 | 1.00 |
| deadlock | 1 no | 0:20 | – | 3 | 1.50 |
| mortice lock | 1 no | 0:15 | – | 3 | 1.50 |
| mortice latch | 1 no | 0:15 | – | 3 | 1.50 |
| cylinder lock | 1 no | 0:15 | – | 3 | 1.50 |
| door closer | 1 no | 0:15 | – | 3 | 1.50 |
| casement stay | 1 no | 0:15 | – | 3 | 1.50 |
| casement fastener | 1 no | 0:15 | – | 3 | 1.50 |

There are many doors available and the quality and price can vary significantly. Apart from flush doors most doors are sold by a standard reference code or name and you will find the type of door stated in the item description by referring to *Fig. 3*.

*Garage redwood*

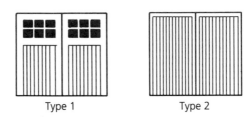

Type 1                    Type 2

*Period*

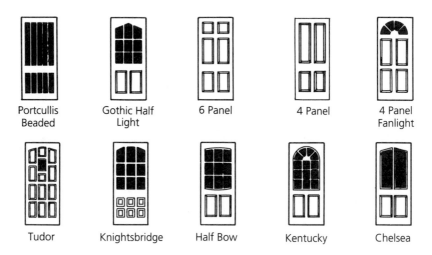

| Portcullis Beaded | Gothic Half Light | 6 Panel | 4 Panel | 4 Panel Fanlight |
| --- | --- | --- | --- | --- |
| Tudor | Knightsbridge | Half Bow | Kentucky | Chelsea |

*Fig. 3*

## Interior flush doors for painting

(These doors are usually unprimed unless you specifically order otherwise)

1⅜" (35 mm) thick
hardboard finish door

| | | | | | |
|---|---|---|---|---|---|
| 1'6" × 6'6" (457 × 1981 mm) | 1 no | 1:30 | 26.00 | 6 | 40.00 |
| 1'9" × 6'6" (533 × 1981 mm) | 1 no | 1:30 | 26.50 | 6 | 40.00 |
| 2'0" × 6'6" (610 × 1981 mm) | 1 no | 1:30 | 26.75 | 6 | 40.00 |
| 2'3" × 6'6" (686 × 1981 mm) | 1 no | 1:30 | 27.00 | 6 | 40.00 |
| 2'6" × 6'6" (762 × 1981 mm) | 1 no | 1:30 | 27.50 | 6 | 40.00 |
| 2'8" × 6'8" (813 × 2032 mm) | 1 no | 1:30 | 28.50 | 6 | 42.00 |
| 2'9" × 6'6" (838 × 1981 mm) | 1 no | 1:30 | 28.50 | 6 | 42.00 |

## Interior flush doors factory finished

(These doors come self finished and only require waxing or polishing to enhance their appearance)

1⅜" (35 mm) thick sapele
veneered door

| | | | | | |
|---|---|---|---|---|---|
| 1'6" × 6'6" (457 × 1981 mm) | 1 no | 1:30 | 31.00 | 6 | 44.00 |
| 1'9" × 6'6" (533 × 1981 mm) | 1 no | 1:30 | 31.00 | 6 | 44.00 |
| 2'0" × 6'6" (610 × 1981 mm) | 1 no | 1:30 | 31.00 | 6 | 44.00 |
| 2'3" × 6'6" (686 × 1981 mm) | 1 no | 1:30 | 31.25 | 6 | 44.00 |
| 2'6" × 6'6" (762 × 1981 mm) | 1 no | 1:30 | 31.50 | 6 | 44.00 |
| 2'8" × 6'8" (813 × 2032 mm) | 1 no | 1:30 | 32.50 | 6 | 46.00 |
| 2'9" × 6'6" (838 × 1981 mm) | 1 no | 1:30 | 32.50 | 6 | 46.00 |

1⅜" (35 mm) thick teak
veneered door

| | | | | | |
|---|---|---|---|---|---|
| 2'0" × 6'6" (610 × 1981 mm) | 1 no | 1:30 | 48.20 | 6 | 60.00 |
| 2'3" × 6'6" (686 × 1981 mm) | 1 no | 1:30 | 48.35 | 6 | 60.00 |
| 2'6" × 6'6" (762 × 1981 mm) | 1 no | 1:30 | 50.00 | 6 | 64.00 |
| 2'9" × 6'6" (838 × 1981 mm) | 1 no | 1:30 | 50.50 | 6 | 65.00 |

| | / | 🕐 | 💷 | 🖐 | £ |
|---|---|---|---|---|---|
| **1⅜" (35 mm) thick maple veneered door** | | | | | |
| 1'6" × 6'6" (457 × 1981 mm) | 1 no | 1:30 | 33.00 | 6 | 46.00 |
| 1'9" × 6'6" (533 × 1981 mm) | 1 no | 1:30 | 33.00 | 6 | 46.00 |
| 2'0" × 6'6" (610 × 1981 mm) | 1 no | 1:30 | 33.25 | 6 | 46.00 |
| 2'3" × 6'6" (686 × 1981 mm) | 1 no | 1:30 | 33.50 | 6 | 46.00 |
| 2'6" × 6'6" (762 × 1981 mm) | 1 no | 1:30 | 33.75 | 6 | 46.00 |
| 2'9" × 6'6" (838 × 1981 mm) | 1 no | 1:30 | 35.00 | 6 | 50.00 |
| **1⅜" (35 mm) thick okoume veneered door** | | | | | |
| 2'0" × 6'6" (610 × 1981 mm) | 1 no | 1:30 | 30.50 | 6 | 44.00 |
| 2'3" × 6'6" (686 × 1981 mm) | 1 no | 1:30 | 30.75 | 6 | 44.00 |
| 2'6" × 6'6" (762 × 1981 mm) | 1 no | 1:30 | 31.00 | 6 | 41.45 |
| 2'8" × 6'8" (813 × 2032 mm) | 1 no | 1:30 | 32.75 | 6 | 46.00 |
| 2'9" × 6'6" (838 × 1981 mm) | 1 no | 1:30 | 32.75 | 6 | 46.00 |
| **1⅝" (40 mm) thick oak veneered door** | | | | | |
| 2'0" × 6'6" (610 × 1981 mm) | 1 no | 1:30 | 64.00 | 6 | 78.00 |
| 2'3" × 6'6" (686 × 1981 mm) | 1 no | 1:30 | 64.00 | 6 | 78.00 |
| 2'6" × 6'6" (762 × 1981 mm) | 1 no | 1:30 | 64.50 | 6 | 78.00 |
| 2'9" × 6'6" (838 × 1981 mm) | 1 no | 1:30 | 67.00 | 6 | 80.00 |
| **1⅝" (40 mm) thick ash veneered door** | | | | | |
| 2'0" × 6'6" (610 × 1981 mm) | 1 no | 1:30 | 64.00 | 6 | 78.00 |
| 2'3" × 6'6" (686 × 1981 mm) | 1 no | 1:30 | 64.00 | 6 | 78.00 |
| 2'6" × 6'6" (762 × 1981 mm) | 1 no | 1:30 | 64.50 | 6 | 78.00 |
| 2'9" × 6'6" (838 × 1981 mm) | 1 no | 1:30 | 67.00 | 6 | 80.00 |
| **1⅜" (35 mm) thick two panel sapele veneered door** | | | | | |
| 2'3" × 6'6" (686 × 1981 mm) | 1 no | 1:30 | 120.00 | 6 | 140.00 |
| 2'6" × 6'6" (762 × 1981 mm) | 1 no | 1:30 | 120.50 | 6 | 141.00 |
| 2'9" × 6'6" (838 × 1981 mm) | 1 no | 1:30 | 128.50 | 6 | 150.00 |
| **1⅜" (35 mm) thick four panel sapele veneered door** | | | | | |
| 2'3" × 6'6" (686 × 1981 mm) | 1 no | 1:30 | 101.00 | 6 | 118.00 |
| 2'6" × 6'6" (762 × 1981 mm) | 1 no | 1:30 | 102.00 | 6 | 120.00 |
| 2'9" × 6'6" (838 × 1981 mm) | 1 no | 1:30 | 109.00 | 6 | 128.00 |
| **1⅜" (35 mm) thick six panel sapele veneered door** | | | | | |
| 2'3" × 6'6" (686 × 1981 mm) | 1 no | 1:30 | 108.50 | 6 | 128.00 |
| 2'6" × 6'6" (762 × 1981 mm) | 1 no | 1:30 | 109.50 | 6 | 130.00 |
| 2'9" × 6'6" (838 × 1981 mm) | 1 no | 1:30 | 116.50 | 6 | 140.00 |

| | / | 🕐 | ✂ | 👆 | £ |
|---|---|---|---|---|---|

**Pine louvred doors**
1" (26 mm) thick doors

| | | | | | |
|---|---|---|---|---|---|
| 1'0" × 1'6" (305 × 457 mm) | 1 no | 1:00 | 5.30 | 6 | 14.00 |
| 1'6" × 1'6" (457 × 457 mm) | 1 no | 1:00 | 7.35 | 6 | 16.00 |
| 1'6" × 2'0" (457 × 610 mm) | 1 no | 1:00 | 9.40 | 6 | 18.00 |
| 2'0" × 1'0" (610 × 305 mm) | 1 no | 1:00 | 6.60 | 6 | 15.00 |
| 2'0" × 2'0" (610 × 610 mm) | 1 no | 1:00 | 11.50 | 6 | 22.00 |
| 1'6" × 2'6" (457 × 762 mm) | 1 no | 1:00 | 10.70 | 6 | 20.00 |
| 1'6" × 3'0" (457 × 914 mm) | 1 no | 1:00 | 12.25 | 6 | 24.00 |
| 2'0" × 3'0" (610 × 914 mm) | 1 no | 1:00 | 15.30 | 6 | 28.00 |
| 1'6" × 4'0" (457 × 1220 mm) | 1 no | 1:10 | 16.40 | 6 | 30.00 |
| 1'6" × 5'0" (457 × 1524 mm) | 1 no | 1:20 | 20.80 | 6 | 35.00 |
| 1'0" × 5'6" (305 × 1676 mm) | 1 no | 1:20 | 17.20 | 6 | 32.00 |
| 1'6" × 5'6" (457 × 1676 mm) | 1 no | 1:20 | 22.70 | 6 | 38.00 |
| 1'0" × 6'0" (305 × 1829 mm) | 1 no | 1:20 | 18.40 | 6 | 33.00 |
| 1'6" × 6'0" (457 × 1829 mm) | 1 no | 1:20 | 25.00 | 6 | 42.00 |
| 2'0" × 6'0" (610 × 1829 mm) | 1 no | 1:20 | 30.00 | 6 | 45.00 |
| 1'6" × 6'6" (457 × 1981 mm) | 1 no | 1:50 | 26.80 | 6 | 42.00 |
| 2'0" × 6'6" (610 × 1981 mm) | 1 no | 1:50 | 32.80 | 6 | 48.00 |
| 2'6" × 6'6" (762 × 1981 mm) | 1 no | 1:50 | 38.70 | 6 | 55.00 |

**Exterior doors for painting**

1¾" (44 mm) thick flush
plywood faced door

| | | | | | |
|---|---|---|---|---|---|
| 2'3" × 6'6" (686 × 1981 mm) | 1 no | 1:45 | 40.50 | 6 | 65.00 |
| 2'6" × 6'6" (762 × 1981 mm) | 1 no | 1:45 | 40.50 | 6 | 65.00 |
| 2'8" × 6'8" (813 × 2032 mm) | 1 no | 1:45 | 41.75 | 6 | 66.00 |
| 2'9" × 6'6" (838 × 1981 mm) | 1 no | 1:45 | 41.75 | 6 | 66.00 |
| 807 × 2000 mm | 1 no | 1:45 | 41.75 | 6 | 66.00 |
| 826 × 2040 mm | 1 no | 1:45 | 41.75 | 6 | 66.00 |

**Exterior casement and
panel doors**

1¾" (44 mm) thick flush
plywood faced door with
glazing opening size
2'10" × 2'8" (864 × 559 mm)
with loose beads

| | | | | | |
|---|---|---|---|---|---|
| 2'3" × 6'6" (686 × 1981 mm) | 1 no | 1:45 | 52.90 | 6 | 75.00 |
| 2'6" × 6'8" (762 × 2032 mm) | 1 no | 1:45 | 54.25 | 6 | 75.00 |
| 2'9" × 6'6" (838 × 1981 mm) | 1 no | 1:45 | 54.25 | 6 | 75.00 |
| 826 × 2040 mm | 1 no | 1:45 | 54.50 | 6 | 75.00 |

1¾" (44 mm) thick flush
plywood faced door with
glazing opening size
1'6" × 1'6" (457 × 457 mm)
with loose beads

| | | | | |
|---|---|---|---|---|
| 2'3" × 6'6" (686 × 1981 mm) | 1 no | 1:45 | 52.90 | 6 | 70.00 |
| 2'6" × 6'8" (762 × 2032 mm) | 1 no | 1:45 | 54.25 | 6 | 72.00 |
| 2'9" × 6'6" (838 × 1981 mm) | 1 no | 1:45 | 54.25 | 6 | 72.00 |

1¾" (44 mm) thick flush
plywood faced door with
glazing opening size
1'8" × 1'8" (508 × 508 mm)
with loose beads

| | | | | |
|---|---|---|---|---|
| 2'3" × 6'6" (686 × 1981 mm) | 1 no | 1:45 | 52.90 | 6 | 75.00 |
| 2'6" × 6'8" (762 × 2032 mm) | 1 no | 1:45 | 54.25 | 6 | 75.00 |
| 2'9" × 6'6" (838 × 1981 mm) | 1 no | 1:45 | 54.25 | 6 | 75.00 |

1¾" (44 mm) thick flush
plywood faced door with
glazing opening size
9" × 3'0" (229 × 914 mm)
with loose beads

| | | | | |
|---|---|---|---|---|
| 2'3" × 6'6" (686 × 1981 mm) | 1 no | 1:45 | 52.90 | 6 | 75.00 |
| 2'6" × 6'8" (762 × 2032 mm) | 1 no | 1:45 | 54.25 | 6 | 75.00 |
| 2'9" × 6'6" (838 × 1981 mm) | 1 no | 1:45 | 54.25 | 6 | 75.00 |

1¾" (44 mm) thick flush
plywood faced door with
glazing opening size
9" × 4'0" (229 × 1219 mm)
with loose beads

| | | | | |
|---|---|---|---|---|
| 2'3" × 6'6" (686 × 1981 mm) | 1 no | 1:45 | 52.90 | 6 | 75.00 |
| 2'6" × 6'8" (762 × 2032 mm) | 1 no | 1:45 | 54.25 | 6 | 75.00 |
| 2'9" × 6'6" (838 × 1981 mm) | 1 no | 1:45 | 54.25 | 6 | 75.00 |

**Matchboarded doors in
redwood**

1⅝" (40 mm) thick ledged
and braced door

| | | | | |
|---|---|---|---|---|
| 2'6" × 6'6" (762 × 1981 mm) | 1 no | 1:45 | 50.70 | 6 | 70.00 |
| 2'8" × 6'8" (813 × 2032 mm) | 1 no | 1:45 | 53.80 | 6 | 75.00 |
| 2'9" × 6'6" (833 × 1981 mm) | 1 no | 1:45 | 53.80 | 6 | 75.00 |
| 726 × 2040 mm | 1 no | 1:45 | 50.70 | 6 | 70.00 |

| | | / | ⏱ | 🔧 | ✋ | £ |
|---|---|---|---|---|---|---|
| **1¾″ (44 mm) thick ledged and braced door** | | | | | | |
| 2′3″ × 6′6″ (686 × 1981 mm) | 1 no | 1:45 | | 65.40 | 6 | 85.00 |
| 2′6″ × 6′6″ (762 × 1981 mm) | 1 no | 1:45 | | 66.50 | 6 | 85.00 |
| 2′8″ × 6′8″ (813 × 2032 mm) | 1 no | 1:45 | | 66.50 | 6 | 85.00 |
| 2′9″ × 6′6″ (838 × 1981 mm) | 1 no | 1:45 | | 66.50 | 6 | 85.00 |
| 726 × 2040 mm | 1 no | 1:45 | | 65.30 | 6 | 85.00 |
| 826 × 2040 mm | 1 no | 1:45 | | 68.00 | 6 | 90.00 |
| **Garage doors in redwood** | | | | | | |
| **1¾″ (44 mm) thick doors** | | | | | | |
| 7′0″ × 6′6″ (2135 × 1981 mm) | 1 pr | 8:00 | | 185.00 | 6 | 300.00 |
| 7′0″ × 7′0″ (2135 × 2135 mm) | 1 pr | 8:00 | | 190.00 | 6 | 305.00 |
| **1¾″ (44 mm) thick doors with 6 openings for glass per leaf** | | | | | | |
| 7′0″ × 6′6″ (2135 × 1981 mm) | 1 pr | 8:00 | | 210.00 | 6 | 325.00 |
| 7′0″ × 7′0″ (2135 × 2135 mm) | 1 pr | 8:00 | | 215.00 | 6 | 330.00 |

## PERIOD DOORS

These doors can provide a very attractive feature to the front entrance of your house. There is a wide variation in the quality of wood used in the construction of hardwood doors as can be seen and this is reflected in the prices. They are bought ready for decoration and glazing. There are four standard sizes all of which cost the same:

2 ft 9 in × 6 ft 6 in (838 × 1981 mm), 2 ft 8 in × 6 ft 8 in (813 × 2032 mm), 2 ft 6 in × 6 ft 6 in (762 × 1981 mm) and 807 × 2000 mm (no imperial size equivalent).

---

**Don't forget, these prices may need adjustment depending on where you live.**
Regional adjustments are provided in the Introduction.

---

|  | ✏ | 🕐 | 🔧 | ✋ | £ |
|---|---|---|---|---|---|
| 1¾" (44 mm) thick door in Far Eastern hardwood | | | | | |
| Portcullis | 1 no | 2:00 | 110.00 | 6 | 140.00 |
| Gothic half light | 1 no | 2:00 | 113.00 | 6 | 145.00 |
| 6 panel | 1 no | 2:00 | 122.00 | 6 | 170.00 |
| Tudor | 1 no | 2:00 | 127.00 | 6 | 180.00 |
| Knightsbridge | 1 no | 2:00 | 113.00 | 6 | 145.00 |
| Half bow | 1 no | 2:00 | 130.00 | 6 | 185.00 |
| Kentucky | 1 no | 2:00 | 113.00 | 6 | 145.00 |
| Chelsea | 1 no | 2:00 | 113.00 | 6 | 145.00 |
| 1¾" (44 mm) thick door in Red Meranti softwood in sizes | | | | | |
| 4 panel fanlight | 1 no | 2:00 | 265.00 | 6 | 310.00 |
| Kentucky | 1 no | 2:00 | 255.00 | 6 | 300.00 |
| Tudor | 1 no | 2:00 | 320.00 | 6 | 370.00 |
| 6 panel | 1 no | 2:00 | 290.00 | 6 | 340.00 |
| Chelsea | 1 no | 2:00 | 210.00 | 6 | 250.00 |
| 1¾" (44 mm) thick door in North American hardwood in sizes | | | | | |
| Carolina | 1 no | 2:00 | 200.00 | 6 | 240.00 |
| Kentucky | 1 no | 2:00 | 195.00 | 6 | 235.00 |
| Elizabethan | 1 no | 2:00 | 245.00 | 6 | 290.00 |
| Chelsea | 1 no | 2:00 | 150.00 | 6 | 185.00 |
| 6 panel | 1 no | 2:00 | 220.00 | 6 | 265.00 |
| Gothic half light | 1 no | 2:00 | 180.00 | 6 | 220.00 |
| Portcullis | 1 no | 2:00 | 165.00 | 6 | 200.00 |

Don't forget, these prices may need adjustment
depending on where you live.
Regional adjustments are provided in the Introduction.

# IRONMONGERY

There is a wide variation in the range and quality of ironmongery that you can buy and the following list is based upon average quality products.

The following hours are based upon fixing the ironmongery to softwood and you should add approximately 15% to the figures quoted for fixing to hardwood.

| | | | | | |
|---|---|---|---|---|---|
| **Hinges** | | | | | |
| Light steel butts | | | | | |
| 2" (50 mm) | 1 pair | 0:30 | 0.70 | 4 | 5.00 |
| 3" (75 mm) | 1 pair | 0:35 | 0.80 | 4 | 5.00 |
| 4" (100 mm) | 1 pair | 0:40 | 1.00 | 4 | 5.50 |
| Medium steel butts | | | | | |
| 3" (75 mm) | 1 pair | 0:35 | 1.30 | 4 | 6.00 |
| 4" (100 mm) | 1 pair | 0:40 | 2.00 | 4 | 7.50 |
| Heavy steel butts | | | | | |
| 4" (100 mm) | 1 pair | 0:40 | 3.00 | 4 | 10.00 |
| Brass butts with brass pins | | | | | |
| 2" (50 mm) | 1 pair | 0:30 | 2.20 | 4 | 7.80 |
| 3" (75 mm) | 1 pair | 0:35 | 3.20 | 4 | 8.50 |
| 4" (100 mm) | 1 pair | 0:40 | 7.00 | 4 | 12.00 |
| Heavy duty hook and band hinges | | | | | |
| 12" (300 mm) | 1 pair | 1:80 | 18.00 | 4 | 30.00 |
| 18" (450 mm) | 1 pair | 2:00 | 19.00 | 4 | 35.00 |
| 24" (600 mm) | 1 pair | 2:20 | 20.00 | 4 | 40.00 |
| **Bolts** | | | | | |
| Steel barrel bolts | | | | | |
| 4" (100 mm) | 1 no | 0:20 | 1.90 | 5 | 3.00 |
| 6" (150 mm) | 1 no | 0:20 | 2.10 | 5 | 3.25 |
| 8" (200 mm) | 1 no | 0:25 | 2.60 | 5 | 4.00 |
| 12" (300 mm) | 1 no | 0:25 | 3.70 | 5 | 5.00 |
| Brass barrel bolts | | | | | |
| 3" (75 mm) | 1 no | 0:20 | 2.10 | 5 | 3.25 |
| 4" (100 mm) | 1 no | 0:20 | 2.25 | 5 | 3.50 |
| 6" (150 mm) | 1 no | 0:20 | 2.50 | 5 | 4.00 |

| | | | | | |
|---|---|---|---|---|---|
| Aluminium barrel bolt | | | | | |
| 3" (75 mm) | 1 no | 0:20 | 1.65 | 5 | 2.50 |
| 4" (100 mm) | 1 no | 0:20 | 1.75 | 5 | 3.00 |
| 6" (150 mm) | 1 no | 0:20 | 2.10 | 5 | 3.25 |
| **Locks** | | | | | |
| Black japanned rim lock | 1 no | 2:00 | 6.80 | 5 | 16.00 |
| Black japanned rim dead lock | 1 no | 2:00 | 5.50 | 5 | 14.00 |
| Mortice lock | 1 no | 2:00 | 7.80 | 5 | 20.00 |
| Mortice dead lock | 1 no | 2:00 | 8.00 | 5 | 22.00 |
| **Latches** | | | | | |
| Cylinder night latch | 1 no | 2:30 | 15.50 | 5 | 30.00 |
| Thumb latch | 1 no | 1:00 | 4.80 | 5 | 10.00 |
| Mortice latch | 1 no | 2:00 | 5.20 | 5 | 15.00 |
| Rebated mortice latch | 1 no | 2:00 | 6.00 | 5 | 15.00 |
| **Door furniture** | | | | | |
| Aluminium pull handle | | | | | |
| 6" (150 mm) | 1 no | 0:15 | 3.20 | 5 | 7.00 |
| 9" (225 mm) | 1 no | 0:35 | 4.00 | 5 | 9.00 |
| Aluminium lever handle | 1 set | 0:30 | 10.00 | 5 | 15.00 |
| Aluminium letter plate (hole in door already cut) | 1 no | 0:30 | 7.50 | 5 | 12.00 |
| Door viewer | 1 no | 1:00 | 12.25 | 5 | 25.00 |
| Door chain | 1 no | 0:30 | 4.20 | 5 | 10.00 |

Don't forget, these prices may need adjustment
depending on where you live.
Regional adjustments are provided in the Introduction.

# WINDOWS

One of the most dramatic changes you can make to the appearance of your house that does not involve structural alterations is the fitting of new windows.

Standard windows are manufactured both in metric and imperial sizes and it is likely that if your house is over ten to fifteen years old you would probably require windows in imperial dimensions. You can buy windows which are already glazed at the factory in single and double glazing or leaded lights. This option is only available for double glazing if you buy six or more windows, but you can buy glass cut to size for all windows in any quantity to fix yourself. The prices quoted include easy clean hinges and glazing beads. The purpose of the illustration in *Fig. 4* is to show the style of the window and it is not drawn to scale. Only the most popular sizes are given and there are many more standard sizes available.

## Types of window          *Fig. 4*

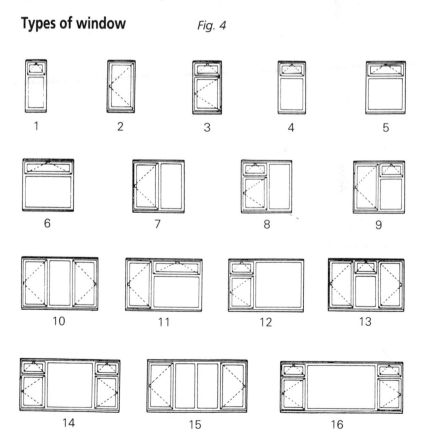

## Types of window

*Fig. 4*

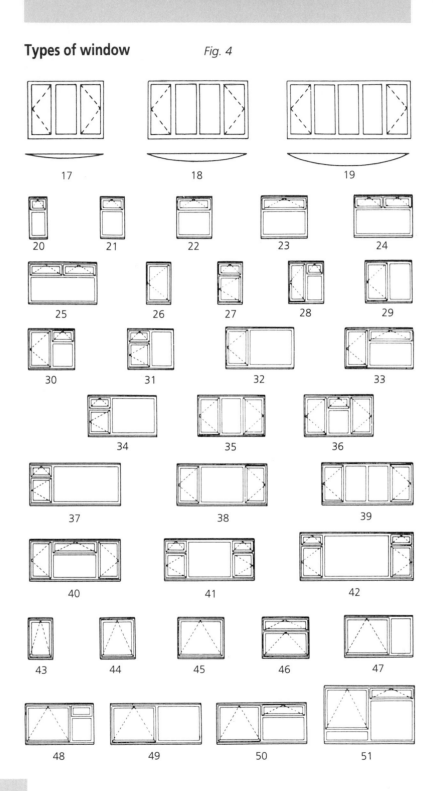

**Hardwood windows in metric sizes (width/height)**

Red mahogany casement windows

| | | | | | |
|---|---|---|---|---|---|
| Type 1 488 × 900 mm | 1 no | 1:10 | 97.00 | 5 | 120.00 |
| Type 2 630 × 1050 mm | 1 no | 1:30 | 115.00 | 5 | 145.00 |
| Type 2 630 × 1200 mm | 1 no | 1:30 | 118.00 | 5 | 150.00 |
| Type 3 630 × 1200 mm | 1 no | 1:30 | 164.00 | 5 | 200.00 |
| Type 4 630 × 900 mm | 1 no | 1:30 | 106.00 | 5 | 135.00 |
| Type 4 630 × 1050 mm | 1 no | 1:30 | 110.00 | 5 | 140.00 |
| Type 4 630 × 1200 mm | 1 no | 1:30 | 112.00 | 5 | 145.00 |
| Type 5 915 × 900 mm | 1 no | 1:45 | 124.00 | 5 | 155.00 |
| Type 5 915 × 1050 mm | 1 no | 1:45 | 126.00 | 5 | 158.00 |
| Type 5 915 × 1200 mm | 1 no | 1:45 | 130.00 | 5 | 160.00 |
| Type 6 1200 × 1050 mm | 1 no | 2:30 | 150.00 | 5 | 195.00 |
| Type 6 1200 × 1050 mm | 1 no | 2:30 | 152.00 | 5 | 200.00 |
| Type 7 1200 × 900 mm | 1 no | 2:30 | 148.00 | 5 | 190.00 |
| Type 7 1200 × 1050 mm | 1 no | 2:30 | 153.00 | 5 | 200.00 |
| Type 7 1200 × 1200 mm | 1 no | 2:30 | 158.00 | 5 | 205.00 |
| Type 7 1200 × 1350 mm | 1 no | 2:30 | 168.00 | 5 | 215.00 |
| Type 8 1200 × 1050 mm | 1 no | 2:30 | 193.00 | 5 | 240.00 |
| Type 9 1200 × 1050 mm | 1 no | 2:30 | 195.00 | 5 | 245.00 |
| Type 9 1200 × 1200 mm | 1 no | 2:30 | 200.00 | 5 | 250.00 |
| Type 10 1200 × 1050 mm | 1 no | 3:00 | 245.00 | 5 | 300.00 |
| Type 10 1700 × 1200 mm | 1 no | 3:00 | 258.00 | 5 | 320.00 |
| Type 10 1700 × 1350 mm | 1 no | 3:00 | 271.00 | 5 | 330.00 |
| Type 11 1700 × 1050 mm | 1 no | 3:00 | 230.00 | 5 | 285.00 |
| Type 11 1770 × 1200 mm | 1 no | 3:00 | 238.00 | 5 | 295.00 |
| Type 12 1770 × 1050 mm | 1 no | 3:00 | 220.00 | 5 | 275.00 |
| Type 12 1700 × 1200 mm | 1 no | 3:00 | 225.00 | 5 | 280.00 |
| Type 13 1700 × 1050 mm | 1 no | 3:00 | 283.00 | 5 | 345.00 |
| Type 13 1770 × 1200 mm | 1 no | 3:00 | 290.00 | 5 | 350.00 |
| Type 13 1700 × 1350 mm | 1 no | 3:00 | 302.00 | 5 | 365.00 |
| Type 14 2339 × 1050 mm | 1 no | 3:30 | 355.00 | 5 | 430.00 |
| Type 14 2339 × 1200 mm | 1 no | 3:30 | 365.00 | 5 | 440.00 |
| Type 14 2339 × 1350 mm | 1 no | 3:30 | 372.00 | 5 | 450.00 |
| Type 15 1200 × 1050 mm | 1 no | 3:30 | 300.00 | 5 | 400.00 |
| Type 15 2339 × 1200 mm | 1 no | 3:30 | 308.00 | 5 | 385.00 |
| Type 15 1200 × 1050 mm | 1 no | 3:30 | 320.00 | 5 | 390.00 |
| Type 16 2908 × 1350 mm | 1 no | 4:00 | 434.00 | 5 | 520.00 |

| | ⌀ | 🕐 | ✂ | ✋ | £ |
|---|---|---|---|---|---|
| **Red mahogany bow windows** | | | | | |
| Type 17 1781 × 1350 mm | 1 no | 3:00 | 480.00 | 5 | 560.00 |
| Type 18 2340 × 1350 mm | 1 no | 3:30 | 585.00 | 5 | 680.00 |
| Type 19 2888 × 1350 mm | 1 no | 4:00 | 695.00 | 5 | 810.00 |

## SOFTWOOD WINDOWS IN IMPERIAL SIZES

The following windows are manufactured in imperial sizes and should be ideal for replacing existing windows if they are more than approximately ten years old. They are manufactured in Scandinavian redwood and stained to give a hardwood appearance and the prices include loose stained glazing beads. Alternatively the windows can be supplied factory-primed for painting at the same price.

| | ⌀ | 🕐 | ✂ | ✋ | £ |
|---|---|---|---|---|---|
| **Softwood windows with butt hinges in imperial sizes (width/height)** | | | | | |
| Type 1 size 1'5¼" × 2'6¼" | 1 no | 1:10 | 39.00 | 5 | 55.00 |
| Type 1 size 1'5¼" × 3'6¼" | 1 no | 1:30 | 42.00 | 5 | 60.00 |
| Type 2 size 2'11¼" × 2'6¼" | 1 no | 1:30 | 45.00 | 5 | 65.00 |
| Type 2 size 2'11¼" × 3'6¼" | 1 no | 1:45 | 48.00 | 5 | 70.00 |
| Type 3 size 2'1¼" × 4'0¼" | 1 no | 1:30 | 68.00 | 5 | 90.00 |
| Type 4 size 2'1¼" × 3'0¼" | 1 no | 1:30 | 45.00 | 5 | 65.00 |
| Type 4 size 2'1¼" × 4'0¼" | 1 no | 1:30 | 48.00 | 5 | 70.00 |
| Type 5 size 3'0¼" × 3'6¼" | 1 no | 1:45 | 55.00 | 5 | 80.00 |
| Type 5 size 3'0¼" × 3'6¼" | 1 no | 1:45 | 57.00 | 5 | 85.00 |
| Type 6 size 4'0¼" × 4'0¼" | 1 no | 2:30 | 69.00 | 5 | 100.00 |
| Type 6 size 4'0¼" × 5'0¼" | 1 no | 2:30 | 70.00 | 5 | 105.00 |
| Type 7 size 4'0¼" × 3'6¼" | 1 no | 2:00 | 64.00 | 5 | 95.00 |
| Type 7 size 4'0¼" × 4'6¼" | 1 no | 2:30 | 71.00 | 5 | 105.00 |
| Type 8 size 4'0¼" × 3'0¼" | 1 no | 2:00 | 76.00 | 5 | 105.00 |
| Type 8 size 4'0¼" × 4'0¼" | 1 no | 2:30 | 82.00 | 5 | 120.00 |
| Type 9 size 3'0¼" × 3'0¼" | 1 no | 1:45 | 77.00 | 5 | 105.00 |
| Type 9 size 4'0¼" × 3'6¼" | 1 no | 2:00 | 80.00 | 5 | 110.00 |
| Type 9 size 4'0¼" × 4'6¼" | 1 no | 2:30 | 86.00 | 5 | 120.00 |
| Type 10 size 5'11¼" × 3'0¼" | 1 no | 3:00 | 96.00 | 5 | 140.00 |
| Type 10 size 5'11¼" × 4'6¼" | 1 no | 3:30 | 112.00 | 5 | 160.00 |
| Type 11 size 5'11¼" × 3'0¼" | 1 no | 3:00 | 97.00 | 5 | 140.00 |

| | | | | | |
|---|---|---|---|---|---|
| Type 11 size 5′11¼″ × 4′6¼″ | 1 no | 3:00 | 106.00 | 5 | 150.00 |
| Type 12 size 5′11¼″ × 4′0¼″ | 1 no | 3:00 | 94.00 | 5 | 135.00 |
| Type 12 size 5′11¼″ × 3′0¼″ | 1 no | 3:00 | 111.00 | 5 | 155.00 |
| Type 12 size 7′10¼″ × 3′6¼″ | 1 no | 3:30 | 103.00 | 5 | 150.00 |
| Type 13 size 7′10¼″ × 4′0¼″ | 1 no | 4:00 | 143.00 | 5 | 200.00 |
| Type 14 size 7′10¼″ × 4′0¼″ | 1 no | 4:00 | 150.00 | 5 | 210.00 |
| Type 14 size 9′9¼″ × 4′6¼″ | 1 no | 5:00 | 171.00 | 5 | 245.00 |
| Type 15 size 7′10¼″ × 4′0¼″ | 1 no | 4:00 | 118.00 | 5 | 175.00 |
| Type 15 size 7′10¼″ × 4′6¼″ | 1 no | 4:30 | 132.00 | 5 | 195.00 |
| Type 20 size 5′0¼″ × 4′0¼″ | 1 no | 2:30 | 84.00 | 5 | 120.00 |
| Type 21 size 5′11½″ × 4′6¼″ | 1 no | 3:00 | 92.00 | 5 | 135.00 |
| Type 22 size 5′11¼″ × 3′6¼″ | 1 no | 3:00 | 75.00 | 5 | 115.00 |
| Type 23 size 2′1¼″ × 2′6¼″ | 1 no | 1:30 | 42.00 | 5 | 60.00 |
| Type 23 size 2′1¼″ × 3′6¼″ | 1 no | 1:30 | 48.00 | 5 | 70.00 |
| Type 23 size 4′0¼″ × 2′0¼″ | 1 no | 1:45 | 53.00 | 5 | 80.00 |
| Type 23 size 3′0¼″ × 3′0¼″ | 1 no | 1:45 | 60.00 | 5 | 85.00 |
| Type 23 size 3′0¼″ × 4′0¼″ | 1 no | 1:45 | 67.00 | 5 | 95.00 |
| Type 23 size 4′0¼″ × 4′0¼″ | 1 no | 2:30 | 71.00 | 5 | 105.00 |
| Type 24 size 4′0¼″ × 3′6¼″ | 1 no | 2:00 | 100.00 | 5 | 130.00 |
| Type 25 size 5′11¼″ × 2′6¼″ | 1 no | 2:30 | 81.00 | 5 | 115.00 |
| Type 25 size 5′11¼″ × 3′6¼″ | 1 no | 2:30 | 85.00 | 5 | 120.00 |
| Type 26 size 5′11¼″ × 4′0¼″ | 1 no | 3:00 | 111.00 | 5 | 155.00 |
| Type 27 size 7′10¼″ × 2′6¼″ | 1 no | 2:30 | 94.00 | 5 | 130.00 |
| Type 27 size 7′10¼″ × 3′6¼″ | 1 no | 3:00 | 99.00 | 5 | 140.00 |
| Type 28 size 7′10¼″ × 4′0¼″ | 1 no | 3:30 | 134.00 | 5 | 185.00 |
| Type 29 size 7′10¼″ × 5′0¼″ | 1 no | 5:00 | 149.00 | 5 | 220.00 |

## GLAZING IN HARDWOOD AND SOFTWOOD WINDOWS

The cost of buying glass cut to size from the window supplier is set out below for some of the above windows. These costs are for the supply of the glass only and not the fixing.

| | Plain double glazing £ | Obscure double glazing £ | Leaded light double glazing £ |
|---|---|---|---|
| **Hardwood windows** | | | |
| Type 2 size 630 × 1050 mm | 24.00 | 28.00 | 60.00 |
| Type 3 size 630 × 1200 mm | 34.00 | 39.00 | 86.00 |

| | Plain double glazing £ | Obscure double glazing £ | Leaded light double glazing £ |
|---|---|---|---|
| **Hardwood windows** | | | |
| Type 4 size 630 × 900 mm | 31.00 | 36.00 | 78.00 |
| Type 5 size 915 × 1050 mm | 39.00 | 45.00 | 98.00 |
| Type 6 size 1200 × 1200 mm | 52.00 | 60.00 | 132.00 |
| Type 7 size 1200 × 1350 mm | 64.00 | 74.00 | 160.00 |
| Type 10 size 1770 × 1050 mm | 76.00 | 88.00 | 190.00 |
| Type 11 size 1770 × 1200 mm | 80.00 | 92.00 | 200.00 |
| Type 13 size 1770 × 1200 mm | 92.00 | 106.00 | 231.00 |
| Type 14 size 2339 × 1200 mm | 120.00 | 138.00 | 300.00 |
| Type 15 size 2339 × 1350 mm | 126.00 | 145.00 | 319.00 |
| Type 16 size 2908 × 1500 mm | 326.00 | 375.00 | 686.00 |
| **Softwood windows** | | | |
| Type 1 size 1'5¼" × 2'6¼" | 28.00 | 32.00 | 70.00 |
| Type 1 size 1'5¼" × 3'6¼" | 32.00 | 37.00 | 81.00 |
| Type 2 size 2'11¼" × 2'6¼" | 20.00 | 23.00 | 50.00 |
| Type 2 size 2'11¼" × 3'6¼" | 26.00 | 30.00 | 64.00 |
| Type 3 size 2'1¼" × 4'0¼" | 37.00 | 43.00 | 93.00 |
| Type 4 size 2'1¼" × 3'0¼" | 33.00 | 38.00 | 84.00 |
| Type 4 size 2'1¼" × 4'0¼" | 40.00 | 46.00 | 101.00 |
| Type 5 size 3'0¼" × 3'6¼" | 42.00 | 48.00 | 106.00 |
| Type 5 size 3'4" × 4'6¼" | 53.00 | 61.00 | 132.00 |
| Type 6 size 4'0¼" × 4'0¼" | 60.00 | 69.00 | 152.00 |
| Type 6 size 4'0¼" × 5'0¼" | 68.00 | 78.00 | 172.00 |
| Type 7 size 4'0¼" × 3'6¼" | 56.00 | 64.00 | 140.00 |
| Type 7 size 4'0¼" × 4'6¼" | 68.00 | 76.00 | 171.00 |
| Type 8 size 4'0¼" × 3'0¼" | 57.00 | 66.00 | 142.00 |
| Type 8 size 4'0¼" × 4'0¼" | 69.00 | 94.00 | 174.00 |
| Type 9 size 3'0¼" × 3'0¼" | 49.00 | 56.00 | 122.00 |
| Type 9 size 4'0¼" × 3'6¼" | 61.00 | 70.00 | 153.00 |
| Type 9 size 4'0¼" × 4'6¼" | 76.00 | 87.00 | 191.00 |
| Type 10 size 5'11¼" × 3'0¼" | 77.00 | 89.00 | 195.00 |
| Type 10 size 5'11¼" × 4'6¼" | 101.00 | 116.00 | 254.00 |
| Type 11 size 5'11¼" × 3'0¼" | 75.00 | 97.00 | 190.00 |
| Type 11 size 5'11¼" × 4'6¼" | 102.00 | 117.00 | 255.00 |
| Type 12 size 5'11¼" × 4'0¼" | 92.00 | 106.00 | 230.00 |
| Type 12 size 7'10¼" × 3'6¼" | 92.00 | 106.00 | 232.00 |
| Type 13 size 5'11¼" × 3'0¼" | 83.00 | 95.00 | 208.00 |
| Type 13 size 7'10¼" × 4'0¼" | 119.00 | 137.00 | 299.00 |
| Type 14 size 7'10¼" × 4'0¼" | 128.00 | 147.00 | 323.00 |

| Softwood windows | Plain double glazing £ | Obscure double glazing £ | Leaded light double glazing £ |
|---|---|---|---|
| Type 14 size 9'9¼" × 4'6¼" | 160.00 | 184.00 | 402.00 |
| Type 15 size 7'10¼" × 4'0¼" | 113.00 | 133.00 | 284.00 |
| Type 15 size 7'10¼" × 4'6¼" | 136.00 | 156.00 | 343.00 |
| Type 20 size 5'0¼" × 4'0¼" | 72.00 | 83.00 | 182.00 |
| Type 21 size 5'11¼" × 4'6¼" | 89.00 | 102.00 | 222.00 |
| Type 22 size 5'11¼" × 3'6¼" | 74.00 | 100.00 | 185.00 |
| Type 23 size 2'1¼" × 2'6¼" | 20.00 | 23.00 | 50.00 |
| Type 23 size 2'1¼" × 3'6¼" | 26.00 | 30.00 | 64.00 |
| Type 23 size 3'0¼" × 2'0¼" | 23.00 | 27.00 | 59.00 |
| Type 23 size 3'0¼" × 3'0¼" | 28.00 | 33.00 | 70.00 |
| Type 23 size 3'0¼" × 4'0¼" | 38.00 | 44.00 | 94.00 |
| Type 23 size 4'0¼" × 4'0¼" | 47.00 | 54.00 | 118.00 |
| Type 24 size 4'0¼" × 3'6¼" | 51.00 | 59.00 | 128.00 |
| Type 25 size 5'11¼" × 2'6¼" | 54.00 | 62.00 | 134.00 |
| Type 25 size 5'11¼" × 3'6¼" | 79.00 | 91.00 | 187.00 |
| Type 26 size 5'11¼" × 4'0¼" | 87.00 | 100.00 | 219.00 |
| Type 27 size 7'10¼" × 2'6¼" | 68.00 | 78.00 | 174.00 |
| Type 27 size 7'10¼" × 3'6¼" | 92.00 | 106.00 | 232.00 |
| Type 28 size 7'10¼" × 4'0¼" | 107.00 | 123.00 | 270.00 |
| Type 29 size 7'10¼" × 5'0¼" | 234.00 | 270.00 | 455.00 |

For information on single glazing see page 121.

## PVC WINDOWS

The replacement of existing windows with PVC (polyvinyl chloride) windows is very popular. PVC is generally marginally dearer than mahogany hardwood windows but the low maintenance costs and longer life must be taken into consideration when making a cost comparison.

The PVC windows listed below *include* plain double glazing and it is assumed that the old window has been removed and the opening prepared to receive the new window.

**PVC windows**

| | | | | | |
|---|---|---|---|---|---|
| Type 1 size 641×921 mm | 1 no | 2:00 | 126.00 | 5 | 160.00 |
| Type 1 size 641×1073 mm | 1 no | 2:00 | 138.00 | 5 | 175.00 |
| Type 4 size 641×921 mm | 1 no | 2:00 | 163.00 | 5 | 200.00 |
| Type 4 size 641×1226 mm | 1 no | 2:00 | 177.00 | 5 | 220.00 |
| Type 5 size 921×921 mm | 1 no | 2:00 | 185.00 | 5 | 225.00 |
| Type 5 size 921×1226 mm | 1 no | 2:00 | 209.00 | 5 | 255.00 |
| Type 6 size 1226×1073 mm | 1 no | 2:30 | 228.00 | 5 | 255.00 |
| Type 6 size 1226×1226 mm | 1 no | 2:30 | 236.00 | 5 | 290.00 |
| Type 7 size 1226×921 mm | 1 no | 2:30 | 207.00 | 5 | 255.00 |
| Type 7 size 1226×1226 mm | 1 no | 2:30 | 250.00 | 5 | 300.00 |
| Type 9 size 1226×921 mm | 1 no | 2:30 | 278.00 | 5 | 335.00 |
| Type 9 size 1226×1266 mm | 1 no | 2:30 | 318.00 | 5 | 375.00 |
| Type 10 size 1810×921 mm | 1 no | 3:00 | 330.00 | 5 | 395.00 |
| Type 10 size 1810×1226 mm | 1 no | 3:00 | 378.00 | 5 | 450.00 |
| Type 11 size 1810×921 mm | 1 no | 3:00 | 315.00 | 5 | 380.00 |
| Type 11 size 1810×1073 mm | 1 no | 3:00 | 343.00 | 5 | 410.00 |
| Type 13 size 1810×1226 mm | 1 no | 3:00 | 460.00 | 5 | 540.00 |
| Type 13 size 2394×1073 mm | 1 no | 3:30 | 478.00 | 5 | 565.00 |
| Type 20 size 1530×1226 mm | 1 no | 2:30 | 321.00 | 5 | 380.00 |
| Type 20 size 1810×1073 mm | 1 no | 2:30 | 377.00 | 5 | 440.00 |
| Type 20 size 1810×1226 mm | 1 no | 3:00 | 392.00 | 5 | 460.00 |
| Type 22 size 1810×921 mm | 1 no | 3:00 | 238.00 | 5 | 295.00 |
| Type 22 size 1810×1226 mm | 1 no | 3:00 | 278.00 | 5 | 340.00 |

As stated before the prices of the PVC windows are for fitted plain double glazed units. If leaded diamond double glazed units are required add approximately 30% on to the material price for the windows.

> **Don't forget, these prices may need adjustment depending on where you live.**
> Regional adjustments are provided in the Introduction.

# KITCHENS

The variation in quality of kitchen fittings varies from adequate to first class with the equivalent difference in cost. In this section the cost of materials and the cost of a contractor carrying out the work is expressed as a range. Although it is unlikely that you could buy any satisfactory products much below the bottom of the range, there is hardly any limit to the amount you could pay above the top figure quoted. For example a hand made imported Italian kitchen could be an extremely expensive item indeed. It is intended that the following figures reflect the range of products you can see in your local DIY supermarket.

Kitchen fittings these days are sold in two ways. First in the traditional product which is assembled and ready to fit in your kitchen. The second are the 'flat pack' or 'self-assembly' units which are sold in kit form for you to make up and fit yourself. The latter is obviously much cheaper to buy but requires more of your time for the assembly and fitting. All the sizes are given in metric and the prices include VAT.

| Ready assembled units | | | | | |
|---|---|---|---|---|---|
| **Base units 870 mm high × 570 mm deep, width** | | | | | |
| 300 mm | 1 no | 1:00 | 60–120 | 5 | 75–140 |
| 500 mm | 1 no | 1:00 | 40–135 | 5 | 55–160 |
| 600 mm | 1 no | 1:00 | 70–145 | 5 | 85–170 |
| 1000 mm corner unit | 1 no | 1:20 | 60–160 | 5 | 75–190 |
| 1000 mm sink/hob unit | 1 no | 1:20 | 40–190 | 5 | 55–220 |
| **Base units with top drawers 870 mm high × 570 mm deep, width** | | | | | |
| 300 mm | 1 no | 1:00 | 90–170 | 5 | 110–200 |
| 500 mm | 1 no | 1:00 | 95–170 | 5 | 115–200 |
| 600 mm | 1 no | 1:00 | 100–180 | 5 | 120–210 |
| 1000 mm | 1 no | 1:20 | 130–270 | 5 | 155–310 |
| 1000 mm corner unit | 1 no | 1:20 | 115–190 | 5 | 150–230 |
| 1000 mm sink unit | 1 no | 1:20 | 120–250 | 5 | 140–290 |
| 1000 mm hob unit | 1 no | 1:20 | 110–240 | 5 | 130–280 |
| **Larder units 570 mm deep × 500 mm wide, height** | | | | | |
| 2060 mm | 1 no | 1:30 | 200–300 | 5 | 230–430 |
| 2351 mm | 1 no | 1:30 | 300–400 | 5 | 340–450 |

| | / | ☉ | ⚖ | ✍ | £ |
|---|---|---|---|---|---|

**Oven housing units**
570 mm deep × 600 mm wide, height

| | | | | | |
|---|---|---|---|---|---|
| 2060 mm | 1 no | 1:30 | 160–340 | 5 | 200–400 |
| 2351 mm | 1 no | 1:30 | 240–470 | 5 | 285–550 |

**Wall units 710 mm high** × 279 mm deep, width

| | | | | | |
|---|---|---|---|---|---|
| 300 mm | 1 no | 1:00 | 60–110 | 5 | 75–130 |
| 500 mm | 1 no | 1:00 | 30–120 | 5 | 45–140 |
| 600 mm | 1 no | 1:00 | 70–140 | 5 | 85–165 |
| 1000 mm | 1 no | 1:20 | 40–180 | 5 | 55–210 |
| 600 mm corner unit | 1 no | 1:20 | 40–130 | 5 | 55–155 |
| 500 mm with glazed door | 1 no | 1:00 | 130–150 | 5 | 155–175 |
| 1000 mm with two glazed doors | 1 no | 1:20 | 200–230 | 5 | 230–265 |

**Wall units 1001 mm high** × 279 mm deep, width

| | | | | | |
|---|---|---|---|---|---|
| 300 mm | 1 no | 1:00 | 110–150 | 5 | 130–175 |
| 500 mm | 1 no | 1:00 | 130–170 | 5 | 155–200 |
| 1000 mm | 1 no | 1:20 | 180–240 | 5 | 285–210 |
| 600 mm corner unit | 1 no | 1:20 | 160–200 | 5 | 200–230 |

**'Flat pack' or 'self-assembly' units**

**Base units 870 mm high** × 570 mm deep, width

| | | | | | |
|---|---|---|---|---|---|
| 300 mm | 1 no | 1:30 | 30–70 | 5 | 45–90 |
| 400 mm | 1 no | 1:30 | 35–75 | 5 | 50–95 |
| 500 mm | 1 no | 1:30 | 30–80 | 5 | 45–100 |
| 600 mm | 1 no | 1:30 | 35–85 | 5 | 45–105 |
| 1000 mm sink/hob unit | 1 no | 1:30 | 35–100 | 5 | 45–130 |
| 900 × 900 mm corner unit | 1 no | 1:30 | 60–110 | 5 | 75–130 |
| 600 mm pan drawer unit | 1 no | 1:30 | 60–150 | 5 | 75–190 |
| Built under oven housing unit | 1 no | 1:30 | 30–65 | 5 | 45–85 |

Don't forget, these prices may need adjustment depending on where you live.
Regional adjustments are provided in the Introduction.

| | | ✎ | 🕐 | ₤ | ✋ | £ |
|---|---|---|---|---|---|---|
| Base units with top drawers 870 mm high × 570 mm deep, width | | | | | | |
| | 300 mm | 1 no | 1:30 | 40–100 | 5 | 55–125 |
| | 400 mm | 1 no | 1:30 | 50–100 | 5 | 65–125 |
| | 500 mm | 1 no | 1:30 | 40–105 | 5 | 55–130 |
| | 600 mm | 1 no | 1:30 | 50–110 | 5 | 65–135 |
| | 600 mm sink/hob unit | 1 no | 1:30 | 50–105 | 5 | 65–130 |
| | 900 × 900 mm corner unit | 1 no | 1:30 | 75–170 | 5 | 90–210 |
| | 1000 mm corner unit | 1 no | 1:30 | 60–110 | 5 | 75–135 |
| | 1000 mm hob unit | 1 no | 1:30 | 60–140 | 5 | 80–180 |
| | 1000 mm sink unit | 1 no | 1:30 | 60–145 | 5 | 75–185 |
| | 1000 mm unit | 1 no | 1:30 | 65–160 | 5 | 80–200 |
| Wall units 710 mm high × 279 mm deep, width | | | | | | |
| | 300 mm | 1 no | 1:30 | 30–70 | 5 | 45–90 |
| | 400 mm | 1 no | 1:30 | 35–60 | 5 | 50–95 |
| | 500 mm | 1 no | 1:30 | 30–80 | 5 | 45–100 |
| | 600 mm | 1 no | 1:30 | 35–85 | 5 | 50–105 |
| | 1000 mm | 1 no | 1:30 | 35–120 | 5 | 50–150 |
| | 600 mm corner unit | 1 no | 1:30 | 35–90 | 5 | 50–110 |
| | 500 mm unit with glazed door | 1 no | 1:30 | 60–100 | 5 | 75–120 |
| | 500 mm peninsula unit | 1 no | 1:30 | 65–100 | 5 | 80–120 |
| | 500 mm dresser unit | 1 no | 1:30 | 75–120 | 5 | 90–140 |
| **Worktops** | | | | | | |
| 30 mm thick × 600 mm wide, length | | | | | | |
| | 1000 mm | 1 no | 0:30 | 15.00 | 5 | 20.00 |
| | 2000 mm | 1 no | 0:40 | 25.00 | 5 | 35.00 |
| | 3000 mm | 1 no | 0:50 | 30.00 | 5 | 40.00 |
| | 1625 × 900 mm breakfast bar | 1 no | 0:50 | 75.00 | 5 | 85.00 |
| 40 mm thick × 600 mm wide, wood effect edging, length | | | | | | |
| | 1500 mm | 1 no | 0:40 | 25–40 | 5 | 35–45 |
| | 3000 mm | 1 no | 0:50 | 40–65 | 5 | 45–80 |
| | 2125 × 900 mm breakfast bar | 1 no | 0:50 | 95–35 | 5 | 100–145 |

## CUPBOARD FRONTS

If the cost of a complete kitchen refit is too expensive for you, it is possible to achieve almost the same effect, without spending so much, by fitting new cupboard doors and drawer fronts to your existing base units.

There are several firms who specialize in supplying these products and the following information gives a brief selection of the choices available. You can also buy a wide selection of new handles and hinges to match the new fronts.

| | | | | | |
|---|---|---|---|---|---|
| **Solid oak fronts** | | | | | |
| Drawer fronts 140 mm high | | | | | |
| 495 mm wide | 1 no | 0:30 | 15.00 | 5 | 20.00 |
| 595 mm wide | 1 no | 0:30 | 17.00 | 5 | 22.00 |
| Doors 570 mm high | | | | | |
| 495 mm wide | 1 no | 1:00 | 48.00 | 5 | 60.00 |
| 595 mm wide | 1 no | 1:00 | 54.00 | 5 | 70.00 |
| Doors 900 mm high | | | | | |
| 495 mm wide | 1 no | 1:20 | 75.00 | 5 | 90.00 |
| 595 mm wide | 1 no | 1:20 | 85.00 | 5 | 105.00 |
| **Solid pine fronts** | | | | | |
| Drawer fronts 140 mm high | | | | | |
| 495 mm wide | 1 no | 0:30 | 16.00 | 6 | 22.00 |
| 595 mm wide | 1 no | 0:30 | 18.00 | 6 | 24.00 |
| Doors 570 mm high | | | | | |
| 495 mm wide | 1 no | 1:00 | 50.00 | 6 | 65.00 |
| 595 mm wide | 1 no | 1:00 | 55.00 | 6 | 70.00 |
| Doors 900 mm high | | | | | |
| 495 mm wide | 1 no | 1:20 | 76.00 | 6 | 95.00 |
| 595 mm wide | 1 no | 1:20 | 90.00 | 6 | 100.00 |
| **Solid maple fronts** | | | | | |
| Drawer fronts 140 mm high | | | | | |
| 495 mm wide | 1 no | 0:30 | 24.00 | 6 | 35.00 |
| 595 mm wide | 1 no | 0:30 | 25.00 | 6 | 35.00 |

| | 📏 | 🕐 | ✂️ | ✋ | £ |
|---|---|---|---|---|---|
| **Doors 570 mm high** | | | | | |
| 495 mm wide | 1 no | 1:00 | 75.00 | 6 | 95.00 |
| 595 mm wide | 1 no | 1:00 | 85.00 | 6 | 105.00 |
| **Doors 900 mm high** | | | | | |
| 495 mm wide | 1 no | 1:20 | 105.00 | 6 | 125.00 |
| 595 mm wide | 1 no | 1:20 | 122.00 | 6 | 140.00 |
| **Melamine fronts with timber edging** | | | | | |
| **Drawer fronts 140 mm high** | | | | | |
| 495 mm wide | 1 no | 0:30 | 15.00 | 6 | 22.00 |
| 595 mm wide | 1 no | 0:30 | 16.00 | 6 | 23.00 |
| **Doors 570 mm high** | | | | | |
| 495 mm wide | 1 no | 1:00 | 24.00 | 6 | 35.00 |
| 595 mm wide | 1 no | 1:00 | 26.00 | 6 | 40.00 |
| **Doors 900 mm high** | | | | | |
| 495 mm wide | 1 no | 1:20 | 34.00 | 6 | 50.00 |
| 595 mm wide | 1 no | 1:20 | 38.00 | 6 | 55.00 |

**Don't forget, these prices may need adjustment depending on where you live.**
Regional adjustments are provided in the Introduction.

# WALL, FLOOR AND CEILING FINISHES

Applying the finishings to a room is probably the most satisfying of all DIY jobs but, because the work will be on permanent view, it also requires the greatest care and skill. Anyone who has not tried plastering before may be surprised to learn that it is one of the hardest skills to master. If you intend to plaster for the first time you would be well advised not to start on the fireplace wall in the lounge which will be facing you every day of your life!

Laying floor and wall tiles can also be more difficult than it seems but patience and care can usually produce an acceptable result.

| | | | | | |
|---|---|---|---|---|---|
| **Alteration work** | | | | | |
| Hack off or take up | | | | | |
| wall plaster | 1 sq yd | 0:55 | – | 3 | 2.90 |
| | (1 sq m) | (1:05) | | | (3.50) |
| lath and plaster | 1 sq yd | 0:55 | – | 3 | 2.90 |
| ceiling | (1 sq m) | (1:05) | | | (3.50) |
| ceramic tiles and | 1 sq yd | 1:10 | – | 3 | 3.20 |
| backing | (1 sq m) | (1:20) | | | (3.80) |
| quarry tiles and | 1 sq yd | 1:15 | – | 3 | 3.35 |
| backing | (1 sq m) | (1:30) | | | (4.00) |
| vinyl tiles and backing | 1 sq yd | 1:10 | – | 3 | 3.35 |
| | (1 sq m) | (1:20) | | | (4.00) |
| woodblock flooring | 1 sq yd | 0:30 | – | 3 | 1.40 |
| | (1 sq m) | (0:35) | | | (1.70) |
| plasterboard and | 1 sq yd | 0:30 | – | 3 | 1.50 |
| skim | (1 sq m) | (0:35) | | | (1.80) |
| suspended ceiling | 1 sq yd | 0:25 | – | 3 | 1.25 |
| | (1 sq m) | (0:30) | | | (1.50) |
| **Floor screeds** | | | | | |
| Cement and sand screed laid on concrete and trowelled smooth | | | | | |
| 1" (25 mm) thick | 1 sq yd | 0:40 | 1.35 | 7 | 4.50 |
| | (1 sq m) | (0:45) | (1.60) | | (5.00) |
| 1½" (38 mm) thick | 1 sq yd | 0:45 | 2.00 | 7 | 5.00 |
| | (1 sq m) | (0:55) | (2.40) | | (6.00) |
| 2" (50 mm) thick | 1 sq yd | 0:55 | 2.70 | 7 | 6.90 |
| | (1 sq m) | (1:05) | (3.20) | | (8.25) |
| 2½" (63 mm) thick | 1 sq yd | 1:05 | 3.40 | 7 | 9.00 |
| | (1 sq m) | (1:20) | (4.10) | | (10.50) |

| | 📏 | 🕐 | £ | 🖐 | £ |
|---|---|---|---|---|---|
| Granolithic (cement and granite chippings) laid on concrete and trowelled smooth | | | | | |
| 1" (25 mm) thick | 1 sq yd | 0:50 | 2.60 | 7 | 7.50 |
| | (1 sq m) | (1:00) | (3.10) | | (9.00) |
| 1½" (38 mm) thick | 1 sq yd | 0:55 | 4.00 | 7 | 9.60 |
| | (1 sq m) | (1:05) | (4.80) | | (11.50) |
| 2" (50 mm) thick | 1 sq yd | 1:05 | 5.30 | 7 | 11.40 |
| | (1 sq m) | (1:20) | (6.40) | | (13.70) |
| 2½" (63 mm) thick | 1 sq yd | 1:15 | 6.60 | 7 | 13.50 |
| | (1 sq m) | (1:30) | (8.00) | | (16.20) |
| **Plastering** | | | | | |
| One coat plaster ¼" (6 mm) thick to plasterboard | | | | | |
| walls | 1 sq yd | 0:45 | 0.84 | 8 | 4.85 |
| | (1 sq m) | (0:55) | (1.00) | | (5.80) |
| ceilings | 1 sq yd | 0:55 | 0.84 | 8 | 5.55 |
| | (1 sq m) | (1:05) | (1.00) | | (6.60) |
| One coat Thistle Universal plaster total thickness ½" (13 mm) on brick walls | 1 sq yd | 0.55 | 1.85 | 8 | 5.39 |
| | (1 sq m) | (1.05) | (2.20) | | (6.40) |
| One coat bonding plaster and one coat finishing plaster total thickness ½" (13 mm) on plasterboard ceilings | 1 sq yd | 1:10 | 2.30 | 8 | 6.90 |
| | (1 sq m) | (1:20) | (2.75) | | (8.25) |
| **Floor tiling** | | | | | |
| Rubber floor tile fixed with adhesive to prepared floor screed | | | | | |
| 2 mm thick, studded, black | 1 sq yd | 0:50 | 5.00 | 6 | 10.00 |
| | (1 sq m) | (1:00) | (6.00) | | (12.00) |
| 2.5 mm thick, studded, coloured | 1 sq yd | 0:50 | 5.70 | 6 | 11.00 |
| | (1 sq m) | (1:00) | (1.85) | | (13.20) |
| 4 mm, studded, black | 1 sq yd | 0:55 | 6.00 | 6 | 11.50 |
| | (1 sq m) | (1:05) | (7.20) | | (13.80) |
| 4 mm thick, studded, coloured | 1 sq yd | 0:35 | 7.00 | 6 | 12.50 |
| | (1 sq m) | (1:05) | (8.40) | | (15.00) |

| | / | ⏱ | 🧵 | ✋ | £ |
|---|---|---|---|---|---|
| **Thermoplastic floor tiles fired with adhesive to prepared floor, screed** | | | | | |
| 2 mm thick | 1 sq yd | 0:40 | 3.00 | 6 | 7.00 |
| | (1 sq m) | (0:50) | (3.60) | | (8.40) |
| 2.5 mm thick | 1 sq yd | 0:40 | 3.30 | 6 | 7.50 |
| | (1 sq m) | (0:50) | (4.00) | | (9.00) |
| 3 mm thick | 1 sq yd | 0:40 | 4.80 | 6 | 9.50 |
| | (1 sq m) | (0:50) | (5.80) | | (11.40) |
| **Vinyl floor tiles fixed with adhesive to prepared floor screed** | | | | | |
| 2 mm thick | 1 sq yd | 0:40 | 4.85 | 6 | 9.20 |
| | (1 sq m) | (0:50) | (5.80) | | (11.00) |
| 3.2 mm thick | 1 sq yd | 0:40 | 6.70 | 6 | 11.30 |
| | (1 sq m) | (0:50) | (8.00) | | (13.50) |
| **Vinyl sheeting fixed with adhesive to prepared floor screed** | | | | | |
| 2 mm thick | 1 sq yd | 0:30 | 5.60 | 7 | 10.50 |
| | (1 sq m) | (0:35) | (6.70) | | (12.60) |
| 2.5 mm thick | 1 sq yd | 0:30 | 6.30 | 7 | 11.50 |
| | (1 sq m) | (0:35) | (7.60) | | (13.80) |
| 3 mm thick | 1 sq yd | 0:30 | 7.50 | 7 | 12.50 |
| | (1 sq m) | (0:35) | (9.50) | | (15.00) |
| **Cork tiling fixed with approved adhesive to prepared screed** | | | | | |
| 3.2 mm thick | 1 sq yd | 0:40 | 7.30 | 7 | 12.00 |
| | (1 sq m) | (0:50) | (8.75) | | (14.40) |
| 4.8 mm thick | 1 sq yd | 0:40 | 9.60 | 7 | 14.50 |
| | (1 sq m) | (0:50) | (11.50) | | (17.40) |
| 6.4 mm thick | 1 sq yd | 0:45 | 11.40 | 7 | 17.00 |
| | (1 sq m) | (0:55) | (13.70) | | (20.40) |
| 8.0 mm thick | 1 sq yd | 0:45 | 13.00 | 7 | 18.50 |
| | (1 sq m) | (0:55) | (15.60) | | (22.20) |

Don't forget, these prices may need adjustment
depending on where you live.
Regional adjustments are provided in the Introduction.

| | | | | | |
|---|---|---|---|---|---|
| Woodblock flooring 1" (25 mm) thick, tongued and grooved, laid to a herringbone pattern, fixing with adhesive and sanding | | | | | |
| Iroko | 1 sq yd | 1:30 | 24.25 | 7 | 42.00 |
| | (1 sq m) | (1:45) | (29.00) | | (50.00) |
| Merbau | 1 sq yd | 1:30 | 24.45 | 7 | 42.50 |
| | (1 sq m) | (1:45) | (29.50) | | (51.00) |
| European oak | 1 sq yd | 1:30 | 28.00 | 7 | 46.00 |
| | (1 sq m) | (1:45) | (33.50) | | (55.00) |
| American oak | 1 sq yd | 1:30 | 32.20 | 7 | 50.00 |
| | (1 sq m) | (1:45) | (38.50) | | (60.00) |
| Sapele | 1 sq yd | 1:30 | 19.70 | 7 | 38.00 |
| | (1 sq m) | (1:45) | (23.50) | | (45.00) |
| Mahogany | 1 sq yd | 1:30 | 24.00 | 7 | 42.00 |
| | (1 sq m) | (1:45) | (28.50) | | (50.00) |
| Maple | 1 sq yd | 1:30 | 20.00 | 7 | 38.50 |
| | (1 sq m) | (1:45) | (24.00) | | (46.00) |
| Terrazzo tile paving 1" (25 mm) thick bedded on screed, joints pointed in white cement | 1 sq yd | 1:35 | 19.25 | 7 | 33.00 |
| | (1 sq m) | (1:55) | (23.00) | | (50.00) |
| Red quarry tiles laid on screed | | | | | |
| ½" (12 mm) thick | 1 sq yd | 1:25 | 16.00 | 7 | 22.00 |
| | (1 sq m) | (1:40) | (19.00) | | (38.00) |
| 1" (25 mm) thick | 1 sq yd | 1:30 | 23.50 | 7 | 28.00 |
| | (1 sq m) | (1:50) | (28.00) | | (48.00) |
| Glazed ceramic tiles size 6" × 6" × ⅜" (150 × 150 × 9 mm) on screed | | | | | |
| grey steel | 1 sq yd | 1:25 | 15.50 | 7 | 25.00 |
| | (1 sq m) | (1:40) | (18.50) | | (40.00) |
| Stone, granite, rockface or russet blend | | | | | |
| black | 1 sq yd | 1:25 | 12.50 | 7 | 23.00 |
| | (1 sq m) | (1:40) | (15.00) | | (36.00) |
| red | 1 sq yd | 1:25 | 10.90 | 7 | 21.00 |
| | (1 sq m) | (1:40) | (13.00) | | (34.00) |

## Wall tiling

Glazed ceramic wall tiles size 8″ × 8″ × ¼″ (200 × 200 × 7 mm) fixed to walls with adhesive and pointed in white cement grout

|  |  |  |  |  |  |
|---|---|---|---|---|---|
| white | 1 sq yd | 1:10 | 12.50 | 6 | 21.80 |
|  | (1 sq m) | (1:20) | (15.00) |  | (26.00) |
| coloured | 1 sq yd | 1:10 | 15.50 | 6 | 25.00 |
|  | (1 sq m) | (1:50) | (18.40) |  | (30.00) |

Glazed ceramic wall tiles size 6″ × 6″ × ¼″ (152 × 152 × 5.5 mm) fixed to walls with adhesive and pointed in white cement grout

|  |  |  |  |  |  |
|---|---|---|---|---|---|
| white | 1 sq yd | 1:25 | 11.70 | 6 | 23.50 |
|  | (1 sq m) | (1:40) | (15.80) |  | (28.00) |
| coloured | 1 sq yd | 1:25 | 15.80 | 6 | 26.75 |
|  | (1 sq m) | (1:40) | (19.00) |  | (32.00) |

## Dry linings

Insulated plasterboard ⅜″ (9.5 mm) thick with taped edges fixed to softwood with galvanised nails, joints taped and filled

|  |  |  |  |  |  |
|---|---|---|---|---|---|
| walls | 1 sq yd | 1:10 | 4.40 | 6 | 11.30 |
|  | (1 sq m) | (1:20) | (5.20) |  | (13.50) |
| ceilings | 1 sq yd | 1:15 | 4.40 | 6 | 11.70 |
|  | (1 sq m) | (1:30) | (5.20) |  | (14.00) |

Paramount dry partition including softwood battens at joints base and head, with all joints taped and filled

|  |  |  |  |  |  |
|---|---|---|---|---|---|
| 2¼″ (57 mm) thick | 1 sq yd | 1:10 | 5.50 | 6 | 18.50 |
|  | (1 sq m) | (1:20) | (6.50) |  | (22.00) |
| 2½″ (63 mm) thick | 1 sq yd | 1:55 | 6.30 | 6 | 20.00 |
|  | (1 sq m) | (1:40) | (7.50) |  | (24.00) |

## RENDERING AND PEBBLE DASHING

Applying render (usually a mixture of cement and sand) is an effective method of completely changing the external appearance of your house. It is quite difficult for a DIY enthusiast to produce an overall uniform effect but it can be achieved. Note that scaffolding or tower hire costs are not included here.

| | 📏 | 🕐 | ⚒ | ✋ | £ |
|---|---|---|---|---|---|
| Render brick wall with cement and sand in one coat ½" (12 mm) thick | 1 sq yd (1 sq m) | 0:50 (1:00) | 1.10 (1.30) | 7 | 9.60 (11.50) |
| Render brick wall with cement and sand in two coats ¾" (18 mm) thick | 1 sq yd (1 sq m) | 1:20 (1:35) | 1.40 (1.70) | 7 | 12.20 (14.50) |
| Add to the above prices for the following | | | | | |
| integral waterproofer | 1 sq yd (1 sq m) | 0:05 (0:06) | 0.30 (0.35) | 3 | 1.21 (1.40) |
| rough cast face | 1 sq yd (1 sq m) | 0:30 (0:35) | – – | 6 | 2.75 (3.30) |
| pebble dash finish | 1 sq yd (1 sq m) | 0:30 (0:35) | 0.25 (0.30) | 6 | 3.15 (3.75) |
| priming and bonding coat | 1 sq yd (1 sq m) | 0:10 (0:12) | 1.25 (1.50) | 3 | 2.10 (2.50) |

**Don't forget, these prices may need adjustment depending on where you live.**
Regional adjustments are provided in the Introduction.

# SHELVING

'Putting up shelves' is one of the most common of all DIY activities. Not only is it a reasonably simple task but it also can be very satisfying to use the shelves within minutes of completing the work!

| | | / | ◔ | ⚷ | ✍ | £ |
|---|---|---|---|---|---|---|
| **Softwood shelving bearers plugged and screwed to brick or blockwork wall** | | | | | | |
| 19 × 50 mm | | 1 yd | 0:13 | 0.73 | 5 | 2.10 |
| | | (1 m) | (0:15) | (0.80) | | (2.30) |
| 25 × 50 mm | | 1 yd | 0:13 | 0.78 | 5 | 2.15 |
| | | (1 m) | (0:15) | (0.85) | | (2.35) |
| **Softwood shelving 19 mm thick fixed to bearers, width** | | | | | | |
| 150 mm | | 1 yd | 0:18 | 1.80 | 5 | 3.65 |
| | | (1 m) | (0:20) | (2.00) | | (4.00) |
| 225 mm | | 1 yd | 0:23 | 2.40 | 5 | 4.65 |
| | | (1 m) | (0:25) | (2.60) | | (5.10) |
| 300 mm | | 1 yd | 0:27 | 2.90 | 5 | 5.65 |
| | | (1 m) | (0:30) | (3.20) | | (6.20) |
| **Birch faced blockboard fixed to bearers, size** | | | | | | |
| 16 × 150 mm | | 1 yd | 0:18 | 2.53 | 5 | 4.40 |
| | | (1 m) | (0:20) | (2.80) | | (4.80) |
| 16 × 225 mm | | 1 yd | 0:23 | 3.40 | 5 | 5.65 |
| | | (1 m) | (0:25) | (3.70) | | (6.20) |
| 25 × 150 mm | | 1 yd | 0:23 | 2.90 | 5 | 4.95 |
| | | (1 m) | (0:25) | (3.20) | | (5.40) |
| 25 × 225 mm | | 1 yd | 0:27 | 4.10 | 5 | 6.85 |
| | | (1 m) | (0:30) | (4.50) | | (7.50) |

**Don't forget, these prices may need adjustment depending on where you live.**
Regional adjustments are provided in the Introduction.

# SHELVING

|  | 📏 | 🕐 | 💷 | 🖐 | £ |
|---|---|---|---|---|---|
| **Birch faced plywood fixed to bearers, size** | | | | | |
| 16 × 150 mm | 1 yd | 0:13 | 1.40 | 5 | 2.75 |
| | (1 m) | (0:15) | (1.50) | | (3.00) |
| 12 × 150 mm | 1 yd | 0:13 | 1.90 | 5 | 3.30 |
| | (1 m) | (0:15) | (2.10) | | (3.60) |
| 19 × 150 mm | 1 yd | 0:18 | 2.20 | 5 | 4.00 |
| | (1 m) | (0:20) | (2.40) | | (4.40) |
| 16 × 225 mm | 1 yd | 0:20 | 1.90 | 5 | 3.75 |
| | (1 m) | (0:22) | (2.10) | | (4.10) |
| 12 × 225 mm | 1 yd | 0:20 | 2.80 | 5 | 4.65 |
| | (1 m) | (0:22) | (3.10) | | (5.10) |
| 19 × 225 mm | 1 yd | 0:23 | 3.30 | 5 | 5.60 |
| | (1 m) | (0:25) | (3.60) | | (6.10) |
| **Chipboard fixed to bearers, size** | | | | | |
| 12 × 150 mm | 1 yd | 0:13 | 0.45 | 5 | 1.80 |
| | (1 m) | (0:15) | (0.50) | | (2.00) |
| 19 × 150 mm | 1 yd | 0:18 | 0.45 | 5 | 1.80 |
| | (1 m) | (0:20) | (0.70) | | (2.70) |
| 25 × 150 mm | 1 yd | 0:23 | 0.90 | 5 | 3.20 |
| | (1 m) | (0:25) | (1.00) | | (3.50) |
| 12 × 225 mm | 1 yd | 0:20 | 0.70 | 5 | 3.00 |
| | (1 m) | (0:22) | (0.75) | | (3.25) |
| 19 × 225 mm | 1 yd | 0:23 | 0.90 | 5 | 3.20 |
| | (1 m) | (0:25) | (1.00) | | (3.50) |
| 25 × 225 mm | 1 yd | 0:27 | 1.40 | 5 | 4.10 |
| | (1 m) | (0:30) | (1.50) | | (4.50) |
| **Plastic faced blockboard fixed to bearers, size** | | | | | |
| 19 × 150 mm | 1 yd | 0:18 | 5.20 | 5 | 7.00 |
| | (1 m) | (0:20) | (5.70) | | (7.70) |
| 25 × 150 mm | 1 yd | 0:23 | 5.65 | 5 | 7.95 |
| | (1 m) | (0:25) | (6.20) | | (8.70) |
| 19 × 225 mm | 1 yd | 0:23 | 7.75 | 5 | 10.05 |
| | (1 m) | (0:25) | (8.50) | | (11.00) |
| 25 × 225 mm | 1 yd | 0:27 | 8.50 | 5 | 11.24 |
| | (1 m) | (0:30) | (9.30) | | (12.30) |

# FLOORING

Floor finishes have been dealt with earlier so this section covers the joists and various types of boarding. If you are laying joists to a new floor (as opposed to replacing a defective joist) you should seek advice on the size of joist necessary to carry the superimposed weight. Don't guess!

| | | 🕐 | £ | 🖐 | £ |
|---|---|---|---|---|---|
| Softwood flooring joists | | | | | |
| 50 × 75 mm | 1 yd | 0:09 | 1.05 | 4 | 2.75 |
| | (1 m) | (0:10) | (1.15) | | (3.00) |
| 50 × 100 mm | 1 yd | 0:11 | 1.30 | 4 | 3.55 |
| | (1 m) | (0:12) | (1.40) | | (3.90) |
| 50 × 125 mm | 1 yd | 0:14 | 1.80 | 4 | 4.20 |
| | (1 m) | (0:15) | (1.95) | | (4.60) |
| 75 × 150 mm | 1 yd | 0:18 | 3.55 | 4 | 6.20 |
| | (1 m) | (0:20) | (3.90) | | (6.80) |
| 75 × 175 mm | 1 yd | 0:23 | 4.10 | 4 | 7.80 |
| | (1 m) | (0:25) | (4.50) | | (8.50) |
| 75 × 200 mm | 1 yd | 0:27 | 4.75 | 4 | 9.30 |
| | (1 m) | (0:30) | (5.20) | | (10.20) |
| Softwood flooring joists impregnated with preservative under pressure | | | | | |
| 50 × 75 mm | 1 yd | 0:09 | 1.40 | 4 | 3.20 |
| | (1 m) | (0:10) | (1.50) | | (3.50) |
| 50 × 100 mm | 1 yd | 0:11 | 1.70 | 4 | 4.10 |
| | (1 m) | (0:12) | (1.85) | | (4.50) |
| 50 × 125 mm | 1 yd | 0:14 | 2.15 | 4 | 4.60 |
| | (1 m) | (0:15) | (2.35) | | (5.00) |
| 75 × 150 mm | 1 yd | 0:18 | 3.95 | 4 | 6.70 |
| | (1 m) | (0:20) | (4.30) | | (7.30) |
| 75 × 175 mm | 1 yd | 0:23 | 4.60 | 4 | 8.80 |
| | (1 m) | (0:25) | (5.00) | | (9.00) |
| 75 × 200 mm | 1 yd | 0:27 | 5.10 | 4 | 9.90 |
| | (1 m) | (0:30) | (5.60) | | (10.75) |
| Softwood butt jointed boarding nailed to joists, size | | | | | |
| 19 × 75 mm | 1 sq yd | 0:53 | 11.90 | 5 | 21.00 |
| | (1 sq m) | (1:00) | (13.00) | | (23.00) |
| 25 × 100 mm | 1 sq yd | 1:05 | 14.15 | 5 | 24.20 |
| | (1 sq m) | (1:10) | (15.50) | | (26.50) |

| | 📏 | 🕐 | 🔧 | ✋ | £ |
|---|---|---|---|---|---|
| **Softwood tongued and grooved boarding nailed to joists, size** | | | | | |
| 19 × 125 mm | 1 sq yd | 1:15 | 14.45 | 5 | 25.40 |
| | (1 sq m) | (1:20) | (15.80) | | (27.80) |
| 25 × 150 mm | 1 sq yd | 1:23 | 15.55 | 5 | 27.40 |
| | (1 sq m) | (1:30) | (17.00) | | (30.00) |
| **Chipboard boarding tongued and grooved joints, nailed to joists, size** | | | | | |
| 18 mm thick | 1 sq yd | 0:30 | 4.65 | 5 | 9.15 |
| | (1 sq m) | (0:35) | (5.10) | | (10.00) |
| 22 mm thick | 1 sq yd | 0:35 | 6.30 | 5 | 11.80 |
| | (1 sq m) | (0:40) | (6.90) | | (12.90) |
| **Plywood boarding, tongued and grooved joists, nailed to joists** | | | | | |
| 15 mm thick | 1 sq yd | 0:30 | 9.30 | 5 | 14.15 |
| | (1 sq m) | (0:35) | (10.20) | | (15.50) |
| 18 mm thick | 1 sq yd | 0:35 | 10.50 | 5 | 16.00 |
| | (1 sq m) | (0:40) | (11.50) | | (17.50) |

**Don't forget, these prices may need adjustment depending on where you live.**
Regional adjustments are provided in the Introduction.

# PLUMBING

The introduction of plastic pipework and 'push-fit' joints in recent years means that you are now able to tackle many plumbing jobs that could previously only be carried out by an expert.

| Repairs and alterations | 📏 | 🕐 | £ | ✋ | £ |
|---|---|---|---|---|---|
| Remove 6 ft (1.83 m) length of existing rainwater gutter and replace with new | | | | | |
|   4″ (100 mm) half round cast iron | 1 no | 1:55 | 13.00 | 4 | 33.00 |
|   4½″ (115 mm) half round plastic | 1 no | 1:30 | 7.00 | 4 | 22.00 |
| Remove 6 ft (1.83 m) length of existing rainwater pipe and replace with new | | | | | |
|   2½″ (63 mm) diameter cast iron | 1 no | 1:50 | 24.00 | 4 | 40.00 |
|   3″ (75 mm) diameter cast iron | 1 no | 1:55 | 24.00 | 4 | 41.00 |
|   2½″ (63 mm) diameter aluminium | 1 no | 1:40 | 23.00 | 4 | 43.00 |
|   3″ (75 mm) diameter aluminium | 1 no | 1:45 | 24.00 | 4 | 40.00 |
|   2½″ (63 mm) diameter plastic | 1 no | 1:00 | 7.00 | 4 | 18.00 |
|   3″ (75 mm) diameter plastic | 1 no | 1:05 | 9.00 | 4 | 20.00 |
| Cut out 2 ft (600 mm) length of copper pipe, insert new length and connect to existing pipe each end with compression fittings, diameter | | | | | |
|   ½″ (15 mm) | 1 no | 1:10 | 4.00 | 5 | 15.00 |
|   ⅞″ (22 mm) | 1 no | 1:20 | 6.00 | 5 | 20.00 |
|   1⅛″ (28 mm) | 1 no | 1:25 | 10.00 | 5 | 23.00 |
|   1⅜″ (35 mm) | 1 no | 1:30 | 18.00 | 5 | 30.00 |

| | | | | |
|---|---|---|---|---|
| Take off defective radiator valve and replace with new including draining down beforehand and bleeding system afterwards | | | | |
| *Single valves* | | | | |
| standard type | 1 no | 1:30 | 7.00 | 5 | 24.00 |
| thermostatic type | 1 no | 1:30 | 18.00 | 5 | 33.00 |
| *Complete system (9 valves)* | | | | |
| standard type | 1 no | 6:00 | 63.00 | 5 | 130.00 |
| thermostatic type | 1 no | 6:00 | 162.00 | 5 | 240.00 |
| Take out existing central heating pump, replace with new, drain down and bleed system | | | | |
| SMC Comet (130-145) | 1 no | 3:30 | 56.00 | 5 | 110.00 |
| SMC Comet (160) bronze | 1 no | 3:30 | 78.00 | 5 | 130.00 |
| Take out defective galvanised steel cold water storage tank and renew complete including connection to existing pipes | | | | |
| 15 gallon | 1 no | 6:00 | 44.00 | 5 | 120.00 |
| 25 gallon | 1 no | 7:00 | 60.00 | 5 | 150.00 |
| 40 gallon | 1 no | 8:00 | 90.00 | 5 | 200.00 |
| Take off existing central heating radiator and refix in new position including re-using all existing materials | 1 no | 4:00 | 12.00 | 5 | 60.00 |
| Take out existing sanitary fittings and renew including all necessary connections and taps | | | | |
| new plastic bath (BP £120) | 1 no | 18:00 | 141.00 | 5 | 230.00 |
| new wash basin (BP £55) | 1 no | 6:00 | 66.00 | 5 | 140.00 |
| new low level WC suite (BP £140) | 1 no | 18:00 | 165.00 | 5 | 280.00 |

111

| New work | | | | | |
|---|---|---|---|---|---|
| Rainwater installation 3″ (75 mm) diameter uPVC rainwater pipe fixed to brickwork | 1 yd (1 m) | 0:27 (0:30) | 5.95 (6.50) | 5 | 9.15 (10.00) |
| Extra for | | | | | |
| bend | 1 no | 0:15 | 5.00 | 5 | 9.00 |
| shoe | 1 no | 0:15 | 2.50 | 5 | 7.50 |
| offset | 1 no | 0:25 | 10.00 | 5 | 14.00 |
| 2½″ (65 mm) diameter aluminium rainwater pipe fixed to brickwork | 1 yd (1 m) | 0:27 (0:30) | 11.90 (13.00) | 5 | 16.00 (17.50) |
| Extra for | | | | | |
| bend | 1 no | 0:15 | 7.00 | 5 | 10.00 |
| shoe | 1 no | 0:15 | 6.00 | 5 | 9.00 |
| offset | 1 no | 0:25 | 11.00 | 5 | 15.00 |
| 2½″ (65 mm) diameter cast iron rainwater pipe fixed to brickwork | 1 yd (1 m) | 0:35 (0:40) | 12.80 (14.00) | 5 | 19.00 (22.80) |
| Extra for | | | | | |
| bend | 1 no | 0:35 | 8.00 | 5 | 11.00 |
| shoe | 1 no | 0:35 | 12.00 | 5 | 15.00 |
| offset | 1 no | 0:40 | 11.00 | 5 | 14.00 |
| 4¼″ (110 mm) half round uPVC gutter fixed to softwood with brackets | 1 yd (1 m) | 0:27 (0:30) | 3.20 (3.50) | 5 | 5.95 (6.50) |
| Extra for | | | | | |
| stop end | 1 no | 0:15 | 2.50 | 5 | 5.00 |
| outlet | 1 no | 0:15 | 3.50 | 5 | 6.50 |
| angle 90 degrees | 1 no | 0:15 | 4.00 | 5 | 7.00 |
| 4½″ (113 mm) half round aluminium gutter fixed to softwood with brackets | 1 yd (1 m) | 0:27 (0:30) | 7.30 (8.00) | 5 | 12.00 (13.10) |
| Extra for | | | | | |
| stop end | 1 no | 0:15 | 2.50 | 5 | 5.00 |
| outlet | 1 no | 0:15 | 5.20 | 5 | 9.00 |
| angle 90 degrees | 1 no | 0:15 | 5.00 | 5 | 9.00 |
| 4½″ (115 mm) half round cast iron gutter fixed to softwood with brackets | 1 yd (1 m) | 0:35 (0:40) | 7.30 (8.00) | 5 | 12.80 (14.00) |

# PLUMBING

| | 📏 | 🕐 | 💰 | ✋ | £ |
|---|---|---|---|---|---|
| Extra for | | | | | |
| stop end | 1 no | 0:30 | 3.00 | 5 | 6.00 |
| outlet | 1 no | 0:30 | 6.00 | 5 | 10.50 |
| angle 90 degrees | 1 no | 0:30 | 6.00 | 5 | 10.50 |
| Rainwater installation complete consisting of 4½″ (112 mm) plastic half round gutters and 3″ (75 mm) diameter plastic down pipes including fittings | | | | | |
| terraced house | 1 no | 15:00 | 80.00 | 5 | 230.00 |
| semi-detached house with gable end | 1 no | 15:00 | 90:00 | 5 | 240.00 |
| semi-detached house with hip end | 1 no | 18:00 | 100.00 | 5 | 280.00 |
| detached house with gable ends | 1 no | 15:00 | 100.00 | 5 | 250.00 |
| detached house with hip ends | 1 no | 21:00 | 210:00 | 5 | 420:00 |
| bungalow with gable ends | 1 no | 18.00 | 150.00 | 5 | 330.00 |
| Rainwater installation complete consisting of 4½″ (115 mm) cast iron round gutters and 3″ (75 mm) diameter cast iron down pipes including fittings | | | | | |
| terraced house | 1 no | 20:00 | 200.00 | 5 | 400.00 |
| semi-detached house with gable end | 1 no | 20:00 | 210.00 | 5 | 410.00 |
| semi-detached house with hip end | 1 no | 24:00 | 260.00 | 5 | 500.00 |
| detached house with gable ends | 1 no | 20:00 | 260.00 | 5 | 460.00 |
| detached house with hip ends | 1 no | 30:00 | 480.00 | 5 | 780.00 |
| bungalow with gable ends | 1 no | 24:00 | 340.00 | 5 | 580.00 |

| | | | | | | | | |
|---|---|---|---|---|---|---|---|---|

Rainwater installation complete consisting of 4½" (113 mm) aluminium gutters and 3" (75 mm) diameter aluminium down pipes including fittings

| | | | | | |
|---|---|---|---|---|---|
| terraced house | 1 no | 15:00 | 330.00 | 5 | 480.00 |
| semi-detached house with gable end | 1 no | 15:00 | 350.00 | 5 | 500.00 |
| semi-detached house with hip end | 1 no | 18:00 | 390.00 | 5 | 570.00 |
| detached house with gable ends | 1 no | 15:00 | 370.00 | 5 | 520.00 |
| detached house with hip ends | 1 no | 21:00 | 570.00 | 5 | 780.00 |

**Pipework**

Copper pipe with pre-soldered capillary joints and fittings

| | | | | | |
|---|---|---|---|---|---|
| 15 mm diameter | 1 yd | 0:27 | 1.55 | 6 | 4.10 |
| | (1 m) | (0:30) | (1.70) | | (4.50) |
| forming bend with spring | 1 no | 0:15 | – | 6 | 1.00 |
| elbow | 1 no | 0:30 | 1.40 | 6 | 4.50 |
| tee | 1 no | 0:35 | 3.00 | 6 | 6.00 |
| tap connector | 1 no | 0:30 | 2.50 | 6 | 5.50 |
| 22 mm diameter | 1 yd | 0:32 | 2.90 | 6 | 7.30 |
| | (1 m) | (0:35) | (3.20) | | (8.00) |
| forming bend with spring | 1 no | 0:20 | – | 6 | 1.25 |
| elbow | 1 no | 0:30 | 2.40 | 6 | 5.50 |
| tee | 1 no | 0:35 | 4.00 | 6 | 7.00 |
| tap connector | 1 no | 0:30 | 5.00 | 6 | 8.00 |
| 28 mm diameter | 1 yd | 0:41 | 3.65 | 6 | 8.50 |
| | (1 m) | (0:45) | (4.00) | | (9.30) |
| forming bend with spring | 1 no | 0:25 | – | 6 | 1.60 |
| elbow | 1 no | 0:35 | 4.00 | 6 | 7.00 |
| tee | 1 no | 0:40 | 4.50 | 6 | 8.50 |

| | / | ⊕ | ₤ | ☝ | £ |
|---|---|---|---|---|---|
| Blue polyethylene pipes and fittings with fusion welded joints laid in trenches (digging trench not included here) | | | | | |
| 25 mm diameter | 1 yd | 0:18 | 0.90 | 6 | 2.75 |
| | (1 m) | (0:20) | (1.00) | | (3.00) |
| tee | 1 no | 0:40 | 4.50 | 6 | 10.00 |
| connection to copper pipe | 1 no | 0:30 | 3.00 | 6 | 8.00 |
| **Stopcock and valves** | | | | | |
| Gunmetal stopcock with brass headwork | | | | | |
| 15 mm diameter | 1 no | 0:30 | 3.30 | 6 | 7.00 |
| 22 mm diameter | 1 no | 0:35 | 6.00 | 6 | 10.00 |
| 28 mm diameter | 1 no | 0:40 | 17.00 | 6 | 25.00 |
| **Cold water storage tanks** | | | | | |
| Plastic tank to BS 4213 complete with lid | | | | | |
| 4 gallons (18 litres) | 1 no | 1:30 | 10.00 | 5 | 25.00 |
| 15 gallons (68 litres) | 1 no | 1:30 | 30.00 | 5 | 45.00 |
| 20 gallons (91 litres) | 1 no | 1:30 | 32.00 | 5 | 48.00 |
| 25 gallons (114 litres) | 1 no | 2:00 | 38.00 | 5 | 60.00 |
| 40 gallons (182 litres) | 1 no | 2:00 | 70.00 | 5 | 90.00 |
| 50 gallons (227 litres) | 1 no | 2:30 | 75.00 | 5 | 100.00 |
| **Cylinders** | | | | | |
| Indirect copper cylinders to BS 699 grade 3 | | | | | |
| ref 1, 21 gallons (96 litres) | 1 no | 2:30 | 110.00 | 5 | 125.00 |
| ref 2, 25 gallons (114 litres) | 1 no | 2:30 | 120.00 | 5 | 135.00 |
| ref 7, 31 gallons (140 litres) | 1 no | 2:30 | 130.00 | 5 | 145.00 |
| Primatic single feed indirect copper cylinder, ready insulated | | | | | |
| 20 gallons (92 litres) | 1 no | 2:30 | 220.00 | 5 | 250.00 |
| 24 gallons (108 litres) | 1 no | 2:30 | 240.00 | 5 | 270.00 |

**Waste pipes and traps**

uPVC pipes and fittings
fixing to walls

| | | | | | |
|---|---|---|---|---|---|
| 32 mm diameter | 1 m | 0:40 | 3.30 | 5 | 6.00 |
| bend | 1 no | 0:35 | 2.00 | 5 | 4.00 |
| tee | 1 no | 0:40 | 3.00 | 5 | 5.20 |
| connection to gully | 1 no | 0:30 | 2.50 | 5 | 3.80 |
| 40 mm diameter | 1 m | 0:45 | 4.00 | 5 | 6.50 |
| bend | 1 no | 0:40 | 2.25 | 5 | 4.50 |
| tee | 1 no | 0:45 | 3.50 | 5 | 6.00 |
| connection to gully | 1 no | 0:35 | 2.50 | 5 | 3.80 |
| 50 mm diameter | 1 m | 0:50 | 5.75 | 5 | 8.50 |
| bend | 1 no | 0:45 | 3.30 | 5 | 5.50 |
| tee | 1 no | 0:50 | 6.20 | 5 | 9.00 |
| connection to gully | 1 no | 0:40 | 2.50 | 5 | 3.80 |

Polypropylene traps with
screwed joints to fittings
outlet and pipe

| | | | | | |
|---|---|---|---|---|---|
| bottle P trap | | | | | |
| 32 mm | 1 no | 0:45 | 5.00 | 4 | 7.50 |
| 40 mm | 1 no | 0:50 | 5.50 | 4 | 9.30 |
| bottle S trap | | | | | |
| 32 mm | 1 no | 0:45 | 5.75 | 4 | 8.20 |
| 40 mm | 1 no | 0:50 | 6.75 | 4 | 9.50 |
| tubular bath trap | | | | | |
| P trap | 1 no | 1:00 | 9.00 | 4 | 12.00 |
| P lowline with overflow | 1 no | 1:00 | 8.00 | 4 | 11.00 |

**Soil and vent pipes**

110 mm diameter uPVC
solvent welded joints
fixed to brickwork with
holderbats at average

| | | | | | |
|---|---|---|---|---|---|
| 1250 mm centres | 1 yd | 0:41 | 8.20 | 5 | 11.45 |
| | (1 m) | (0:45) | (9.00) | | (12.50) |
| access bend | 1 no | 0:45 | 25.00 | 5 | 28.00 |
| single branch | 1 no | 0:45 | 15.00 | 5 | 19.00 |
| single branch with access | 1 no | 0:45 | 28.00 | 5 | 32.00 |
| double branch | 1 no | 0:50 | 35.00 | 5 | 38.00 |
| WC connecting bend | 1 no | 0:35 | 12.00 | 5 | 16.00 |
| WC connector | 1 no | 0:35 | 11.00 | 5 | 15.00 |

**Sanitary fittings**

| | | | | | |
|---|---|---|---|---|---|
| Acrylic bath 5'6" (1700 mm) long complete with 2 chromium plated grips (excluding taps) | | | | | |
| white | 1 no | 4:00 | 110.00 | 6 | 150.00 |
| coloured | 1 no | 4:00 | 120.00 | 6 | 160.00 |
| Acrylic bath panel | | | | | |
| end | 1 no | 0:40 | 9.00 | 4 | 14.00 |
| side | 1 no | 0:50 | 16.00 | 4 | 20.00 |
| Polished aluminium angle strip screwed to corner of bath panels | | | | | |
| 25 × 25 mm | 1 no | 0:30 | 2.00 | 4 | 5.00 |
| Vitreous china wash basin complete (excluding taps) size 570 × 445 mm | | | | | |
| fixed to wall brackets | 1 no | 2:30 | 60.00 | 6 | 85.00 |
| pedestal mounted | 1 no | 2:30 | 90.00 | 6 | 120.00 |
| Coloured close coupled WC suite with plastic seat, 9 litre cistern, ball valve, flush pipe and connect to drain outlet | | | | | |
| washdown type | 1 no | 3:30 | 170.00 | 6 | 210.00 |
| syphonic type | 1 no | 3:30 | 310.00 | 6 | 350.00 |
| Vitreous china freestanding bidet (excluding fittings) | | | | | |
| white | 1 no | 3:30 | 125.00 | 6 | 160.00 |
| coloured | 1 no | 3:30 | 160.00 | 6 | 200.00 |
| Stainless steel sink tops complete (excluding taps) single bowl and single drainer size | | | | | |
| 1000 × 600 mm | 1 no | 2:00 | 60.00 | 5 | 80.00 |
| single bowl and double drainer size | | | | | |
| 1500 × 600 mm | 1 no | 2:30 | 100.00 | 5 | 130.00 |

**Taps**

| | | | | | |
|---|---|---|---|---|---|
| Chromium plated wash basin, sinks and bath pillar taps | | | | | |
| 13 mm diameter | 1 pr | 1:00 | 13.00 | 6 | 25.00 |
| 19 mm diameter | 1 pr | 1:00 | 14.50 | 6 | 28.00 |
| Chromium plated bath mixer taps complete with handspray | 1 no | 1:30 | 140.00 | 6 | 160.00 |
| Chromium plated sink mixer taps with swivel spout | 1 no | 1:30 | 80.00 | 6 | 95.00 |

**Showers**

| | | | | | |
|---|---|---|---|---|---|
| Thermostatic mixing valve fixing to wall | 1 no | 1:30 | 220.00 | 6 | 240.00 |
| Mechanical mixing valve fixing to wall | 1 no | 1:30 | 105.00 | 6 | 125.00 |
| Flexible tube and handspray with sliding bar attachment | 1 no | 1:00 | 38.00 | 6 | 50.00 |
| Glazed fireclay shower tray fixed to floor | | | | | |
| white | 1 no | 2:00 | 165.00 | 5 | 190.00 |
| coloured | 1 no | 2:00 | 190.00 | 5 | 210.00 |
| Acrylic shower tray fixed to floor | | | | | |
| white | 1 no | 1:50 | 65.00 | 5 | 80.00 |
| coloured | 1 no | 1:50 | 70.00 | 5 | 90.00 |

Don't forget, these prices may need adjustment depending on where you live.
Regional adjustments are provided in the Introduction.

# CENTRAL HEATING

| | | / | ① | £ | ⏚ | £ |
|---|---|---|---|---|---|---|
| **Radiators** | | | | | | |
| Steel single panel radiator fixed to brackets plugged to wall | | | | | | |
| 500 × 420 mm high | 1 no | 1:30 | 18.00 | 6 | 35.00 | |
| 1200 × 420 mm high | 1 no | 2:00 | 45.00 | 6 | 65.00 | |
| 1850 × 420 mm high | 1 no | 2:30 | 65.00 | 6 | 90.00 | |
| 500 × 520 mm high | 1 no | 1:45 | 22.00 | 6 | 40.00 | |
| 1200 × 520 mm high | 1 no | 2:15 | 48.00 | 6 | 70.00 | |
| 1850 × 520 mm high | 1 no | 2:40 | 72.00 | 6 | 100.00 | |
| 500 × 620 mm high | 1 no | 1:45 | 25.00 | 6 | 45.00 | |
| 1200 × 620 mm high | 1 no | 2:15 | 55.00 | 6 | 80.00 | |
| 1850 × 620 mm high | 1 no | 2:40 | 90.00 | 6 | 120.00 | |
| 500 × 720 mm high | 1 no | 2:30 | 35.00 | 6 | 65.00 | |
| 1200 × 720 mm high | 1 no | 2:30 | 75.00 | 6 | 110.00 | |
| 1850 × 720 mm high | 1 no | 2:45 | 80.00 | 6 | 115.00 | |
| Steel double panel radiator fixed to brackets plugged to wall | | | | | | |
| 750 × 520 mm high | 1 no | 2:00 | 95.00 | 6 | 120.00 | |
| 1200 × 520 mm high | 1 no | 2:40 | 140.00 | 6 | 170.00 | |
| 1850 × 520 mm high | 1 no | 3:00 | 220.00 | 6 | 260.00 | |
| 500 × 620 mm high | 1 no | 2:20 | 70.00 | 6 | 100.00 | |
| 1200 × 620 mm high | 1 no | 2:50 | 165.00 | 6 | 190.00 | |
| 1850 × 620 mm high | 1 no | 3:00 | 250.00 | 6 | 290.00 | |
| 750 × 720 mm high | 1 no | 2:40 | 125.00 | 6 | 160.00 | |
| 1200 × 720 mm high | 1 no | 3:00 | 190.00 | 6 | 230.00 | |
| 1700 × 720 mm high | 1 no | 3:30 | 260.00 | 6 | 300.00 | |
| **Valves** | | | | | | |
| Thermostatic radiator valves 15 mm diameter | 1 no | 0:45 | 15.00 | 6 | 25.00 | |

**Boilers (for central heating and indirect hot water)**

| | | | | | |
|---|---|---|---|---|---|
| Solid fuel boiler, gravity feed, white stove enamelled casing, thermostat, 125 mm flue socket | | | | | |
| 45,000 BTU | 1 no | 14:00 | 1050.00 | 7 | 1250.00 |
| 60,000 BTU | 1 no | 14:00 | 1250.00 | 7 | 1500.00 |
| 80,000 BTU | 1 no | 15:00 | 1600.00 | 7 | 1950.00 |
| 100,000 BTU | 1 no | 16.00 | 1850.00 | 7 | 2200.00 |
| Oil fired boiler, fully automatic, white stove enamelled casing, for Kerosene or gas oil, conventional flue | | | | | |
| 50,000 BTU | 1 no | 9:00 | 1000.00 | 7 | 1250.00 |
| 60,000 BTU | 1 no | 9:00 | 1050.00 | 7 | 1350.00 |
| 80,000 BTU | 1 no | 10:00 | 1200.00 | 7 | 1500.00 |
| 100,000 BTU | 1 no | 10:00 | 1400.00 | 7 | 1750.00 |
| Gas fired wall hung boiler, for domestic central heating and hot water, balanced flue | | | | | |
| 30,000 BTU | 1 no | 8:00 | 550.00 | 7 | 650.00 |
| 40,000 BTU | 1 no | 8:00 | 650.00 | 7 | 750.00 |
| 50,000 BTU | 1 no | 8:00 | 700.00 | 7 | 800.00 |
| 60,000 BTU | 1 no | 8:00 | 850.00 | 7 | 950.00 |
| 80,000 BTU | 1 no | 8:00 | 1400.00 | 7 | 1500.00 |
| Gas fired boiler, free standing, balanced flue | | | | | |
| 40,000 BTU | 1 no | 8:00 | 700.00 | 7 | 800.00 |
| 50,000 BTU | 1 no | 8:00 | 750.00 | 7 | 850.00 |
| 60,000 BTU | 1 no | 8:00 | 800.00 | 7 | 900.00 |
| 80,000 BTU | 1 no | 8:00 | 1100.00 | 7 | 1200.00 |
| 100,000 BTU | 1 no | 8:00 | 1400.00 | 7 | 1500.00 |

Don't forget, these prices may need adjustment depending on where you live.
Regional adjustments are provided in the Introduction.

# GLAZING

The first part of this section deals with glazing repairs and covers the replacement of broken windows that most households suffer from occasionally. Although the glazing industry normally works in square metres, sample pane sizes have been given to make the figures quoted more helpful.

**Clear float glass 4 mm thick**

Cut out broken glass from wood or metal windows and reglaze in putty, size

| | | | | |
|---|---|---|---|---|
| 6″ × 12″ (150 × 300 mm) | 1 no | 0:30 | 1.80 | 4 | 6.00 |
| 9″ × 18″ (225 × 450 mm) | 1 no | 0:35 | 4.00 | 4 | 8.20 |
| 18″ × 18″ (450 × 450 mm) | 1 no | 0:40 | 8.00 | 4 | 12.30 |
| 30″ × 24″ (750 × 600 mm) | 1 no | 0:45 | 18.00 | 4 | 22.50 |
| 36″ × 30″ (900 × 750 mm) | 1 no | 0:50 | 27.00 | 4 | 31.50 |

Hack out broken glass from wood or metal windows and reglaze in pinned beads previously laid aside

| | | | | |
|---|---|---|---|---|
| 6″ × 12″ (150 × 300 mm) | 1 no | 0:25 | 1.70 | 4 | 5.40 |
| 9″ × 18″ (225 × 450 mm) | 1 no | 0:30 | 3.80 | 4 | 7.80 |
| 18″ × 18″ (450 × 450 mm) | 1 no | 0:35 | 7.70 | 4 | 11.80 |
| 30″ × 24″ (750 × 600 mm) | 1 no | 0:40 | 17.60 | 4 | 22.00 |
| 36″ × 30″ (900 × 750 mm) | 1 no | 0:45 | 26.50 | 4 | 31.00 |

**Obscure glass 6 mm thick**

Hack out broken glass from wood or metal windows and reglaze in putty, size

| | | | | |
|---|---|---|---|---|
| 6″ × 12″ (150 × 300 mm) | 1 no | 0:30 | 2.15 | 4 | 6.50 |
| 9″ × 18″ (225 × 450 mm) | 1 no | 0:35 | 4.85 | 4 | 9.00 |
| 18″ × 18″ (450 × 450 mm) | 1 no | 0:40 | 9.75 | 4 | 15.00 |
| 30″ × 24″ (750 × 600 mm) | 1 no | 0:45 | 21.60 | 4 | 26.00 |
| 36″ × 30″ (900 × 750 mm) | 1 no | 0:50 | 32.50 | 4 | 37.00 |

| | | ✏ | 🕐 | ✂ | ✋ | £ |
|---|---|---|---|---|---|---|
| Hack out broken glass from wood or metal windows and reglaze in pinned beads previously laid aside | | | | | | |
| 6″ × 12″ (150 × 300 mm) | 1 no | | 0:25 | 2.00 | 4 | 6.00 |
| 9″ × 18″ (225 × 450 mm) | 1 no | | 0:30 | 4.70 | 4 | 8.50 |
| 18″ × 18″ (450 × 450 mm) | 1 no | | 0:35 | 9.50 | 4 | 14.00 |
| 30″ × 24″ (750 × 600 mm) | 1 no | | 0:40 | 21.00 | 4 | 25.00 |
| 36″ × 30″ (900 × 750 mm) | 1 no | | 0:45 | 31.80 | 4 | 35.50 |

## DOUBLE GLAZING

The cost of having double glazing fitted at the factory is given in the 'Windows' section but the prices are only applicable when you are also buying a new window. The following prices refer to double glazing fitted in your existing wood windows and include the cost of removing the existing glass and cleaning the rebates.

Note that the price per square metre varies considerably depending upon the size of pane and these have been grouped into 3 categories:

| | |
|---|---|
| **Small** | not exceeding 5 square feet (approximately ½ square metre) |
| **Medium** | between 5 and 10 square feet (approximately ½ to 1 square metre) |
| **Large** | over 10 square feet (approximately 1 square metre) |

Don't forget, these prices may need adjustment depending on where you live.
Regional adjustments are provided in the Introduction.

| | Quantity | Contractor's Price £ |
|---|---|---|
| Hermetically sealed double glazing units consisting of two panes of 4 mm thick clear sheet glass fixed to wood in putty and sprigs in panes | | |
| small | 1 sq yd | 58.00 |
| | (1 sq m) | (70.00) |
| medium | 1 sq yd | 44.00 |
| | (1 sq m) | (53.00) |
| large | 1 sq yd | 40.00 |
| | (1 sq m) | (48.00) |
| Hermetically sealed double glazing units consisting of two panes of 4 mm thick clear sheet glass fixed to wood with screwed beads in panes size | | |
| small | 1 sq yd | 61.00 |
| | (1 sq m) | (73.00) |
| medium | 1 sq yd | 47.00 |
| | (1 sq m) | (56.00) |
| large | 1 sq yd | 42.00 |
| | (1 sq m) | (50.00) |
| Hermetically sealed double glazing units consisting of two panes of 6 mm thick clear sheet glass fixed to wood in putty and sprigs in panes | | |
| small | 1 sq yd | 67.00 |
| | (1 sq m) | (80.00) |
| medium | 1 sq yd | 50.00 |
| | (1 sq m) | (60.00) |
| large | 1 sq yd | 46.00 |
| | (1 sq m) | (55.00) |
| Hermetically sealed double glazing units consisting of two panes of 6 mm thick clear sheet glass fixed to wood with screwed beads in panes size | | |
| small | 1 sq yd | 70.00 |
| | (1 sq m) | (84.00) |
| medium | 1 sq yd | 53.00 |
| | (1 sq m) | (63.00) |
| large | 1 sq yd | 48.00 |
| | (1 sq m) | (58.00) |

# ELECTRIC INSTALLATION

Carrying out electrical work is a mixture of basic DIY skills (lifting floorboards, drilling holes in walls and ceilings) and highly technical tasks which are better left to the professional. Because of this combination of different levels of skills, the prices quoted below are for having the work done by a contractor and are based upon working in situations where there are no major obstructions to the most economical use of cable runs.

| | Quantity | Contractor's Price £ |
|---|---|---|
| Form spur from existing point not exceeding 10 feet (3.3 m) distance to provide | | |
| single 13 amp power point | 1 no | 50.00 |
| twin 13 amp power point | 1 no | 55.00 |
| lighting point with flex and lamp holder | 1 no | 40.00 |
| shaver point | 1 no | 75.00 |
| cooker point control unit | 1 no | 100.00 |
| TV socket outlet | 1 no | 50.00 |
| telephone outlet | 1 no | 45.00 |
| dimmer switch | 1 no | 90.00 |
| bell push | 1 no | 45.00 |
| 4 kW infra red heater | 1 no | 200.00 |
| Window extractor fan | 1 no | 250.00 |
| Floor mounted storage heater | | |
| 0.86 kW | 1 no | 200.00 |
| 1.70 kW | 1 no | 235.00 |
| 2.57 kW | 1 no | 290.00 |
| 3.40 kW | 1 no | 350.00 |
| Panel convector heaters | | |
| 0.75 kW | 1 no | 110.00 |
| 1.25 kW | 1 no | 120.00 |
| 1.50 kW | 1 no | 130.00 |
| 2.00 kW | 1 no | 135.00 |
| 3.00 kW | 1 no | 155.00 |
| Oil filled electric radiators | | |
| 0.50 kW | 1 no | 140.00 |
| 0.75 kW | 1 no | 160.00 |
| 1.00 kW | 1 no | 170.00 |
| 1.50 kW | 1 no | 225.00 |
| 2.00 kW | 1 no | 285.00 |

# ELECTRIC INSTALLATION

| | Quantity | Contractor's Price £ |
|---|---|---|
| Form spur from existing point not exceeding 20 ft (6.6 m) distance to provide | | |
| single 13 amp power point | 1 no | 60.00 |
| twin 13 amp power point | 1 no | 65.00 |
| lighting point with flex and lamp holder | 1 no | 50.00 |
| shaver point | 1 no | 85.00 |
| cooker point control unit | 1 no | 110.00 |
| TV socket outlet | 1 no | 60.00 |
| telephone outlet | 1 no | 55.00 |
| dimmer switch | 1 no | 100.00 |
| bell push | 1 no | 55.00 |
| 4 kW infra red heater | 1 no | 210.00 |
| window extractor fan | 1 no | 260.00 |
| Floor mounted storage heater | | |
| 0.86 kW | 1 no | 210.00 |
| 1.70 kW | 1 no | 245.00 |
| 2.57 kW | 1 no | 300.00 |
| 3.40 kW | 1 no | 360.00 |
| Panel convector heaters | | |
| 0.75 kW | 1 no | 120.00 |
| 1.25 kW | 1 no | 130.00 |
| 1.50 kW | 1 no | 140.00 |
| 2.00 kW | 1 no | 145.00 |
| 3.00 kW | 1 no | 165.00 |
| Oil filled electric radiators | | |
| 0.50 kW | 1 no | 150.00 |
| 0.75 kW | 1 no | 170.00 |
| 1.00 kW | 1 no | 180.00 |
| 1.50 kW | 1 no | 235.00 |
| 2.00 kW | 1 no | 295.00 |
| Supply and fix single tube fluorescent light fittings to adjacent ceiling lighting point | | |
| 600 mm long | 1 no | 28.00 |
| 1200 mm long | 1 no | 35.00 |
| 1500 mm long | 1 no | 45.00 |
| 1800 mm long | 1 no | 50.00 |
| 2400 mm long | 1 no | 65.00 |

| | Quantity | Contractor's Price £ |
|---|---|---|
| Supply and fix twin tube fluorescent light fittings to adjacent ceiling lighting point | | |
| 600 mm long | 1 no | 40.00 |
| 1200 mm long | 1 no | 60.00 |
| 1500 mm long | 1 no | 70.00 |
| 1800 mm long | 1 no | 80.00 |
| 2400 mm long | 1 no | 100.00 |

**Don't forget, these prices may need adjustment depending on where you live.**
Regional adjustments are provided in the Introduction.

# PAINTING AND WALLPAPERING

Painting and wallpapering are probably the most popular of all DIY activities. Everybody sees themselves as capable of painting although the standards achieved vary widely. This section is divided into two parts. The first gives square yard and square metre prices and other information, and the second shows the areas of surfaces to be painted in standard size rooms, together with illustrations of the cost of carrying out the work and the hours involved.

The basic price (BP) of wallpaper shown is an average retail price. All the information given in this section is based upon the use of brushes. If you decide to use spraying equipment you could probably achieve a 30% to 50% saving on labour but would use an extra 10% to 20% materials. If you used a roller you would probably save 15% on labour and use an extra 10% materials. These figures on the use of spraying and rolling are understandably approximate because different people 'load' the equipment with varying levels of paint.

## INTERNAL PAINTING

### TABLE 1

| Existing work | | | | | |
|---|---|---|---|---|---|
| Scrape off one layer of woodchip wallpaper from | | | | | |
| plastered walls | 1 sq yd | 0:25 | – | 2 | 1.40 |
| | (1 sq m) | (0:30) | | | (1.70) |
| plastered ceilings | 1 sq yd | 0:35 | – | 2 | 1.70 |
| | (1 sq m) | (0:40) | | | (2.00) |
| Scrape off two layers of woodchip wallpaper from | | | | | |
| plastered walls | 1 sq yd | 0:35 | – | 2 | 1.90 |
| | (1 sq m) | (0:40) | | | (2.30) |
| plastered ceilings | 1 sq yd | 0:28 | – | 2 | 2.50 |
| | (1 sq m) | (0:34) | | | (3.00) |

|  | / | 🕐 | 💰 | ✋ | £ |
|---|---|---|---|---|---|
| **Scrape off one layer of vinyl wallpaper from** | | | | | |
| plastered walls | 1 sq yd | 0:30 | – | 2 | 1.75 |
| | (1 sq m) | (0:35) | | | (2.10) |
| plastered ceilings | 1 sq yd | 0:33 | – | 2 | 2.10 |
| | (1 sq m) | (0:34) | | | (2.50) |
| **Scrape off two layers of vinyl wallpaper from** | | | | | |
| plastered walls | 1 sq yd | 0:33 | – | 2 | 2.60 |
| | (1 sq m) | (0:40) | | | (3.10) |
| plastered ceilings | 1 sq yd | 0:40 | – | 2 | 3.20 |
| | (1 sq m) | (0:50) | | | (3.80) |
| **Wash down previously painted surfaces and rub down, width** | | | | | |
| over 12" (300 mm) | 1 sq yd | 0:20 | – | 2 | 2.10 |
| | (1 sq m) | (0:22) | | | (2.50) |
| 6"–12" (150–300 mm) | 1 sq yd | 0:08 | – | 2 | 0.85 |
| | (1 sq m) | (0:09) | | | (0.90) |
| not exceeding 6" (150 mm) | 1 sq yd | 0:03 | – | 2 | 0.37 |
| | (1 sq m) | (0:04) | | | (0.40) |
| **Burn off existing paint from general surfaces, width** | | | | | |
| over 12" (300 mm) | 1 sq yd | 1:15 | – | 3 | 7.95 |
| | (1 sq m) | (1:20) | | | (9.50) |
| 6"–12" (150–300 mm) | 1 yd | 0:30 | – | 3 | 2.50 |
| | (1 m) | (0:35) | | | (2.70) |
| not exceeding 6" (150 mm) | 1 yd | 0:20 | – | 3 | 1.20 |
| | (1 m) | (0:22) | | | (1.30) |

Don't forget, these prices may need adjustment
depending on where you live.
Regional adjustments are provided in the Introduction.

**New work**

Note that the material cost varies for each surface because of the different absorption rates.

One coat alkali resisting primer on

| | | | | | |
|---|---|---|---|---|---|
| brickwork | 1 sq yd | 0:17 | 0.50 | 5 | 2.35 |
| | (1 sq m) | (0:19) | (0.60) | | (2.80) |
| blockwork | 1 sq yd | 0:22 | 0.65 | 5 | 2.60 |
| | (1 sq m) | (0:25) | (0.80) | | (3.10) |
| concrete walls | 1 sq yd | 0:14 | 0.38 | 5 | 2.00 |
| | (1 sq m) | (0:16) | (0.45) | | (2.35) |
| concrete ceilings | 1 sq yd | 0:18 | 0.38 | 5 | 2.10 |
| | (1 sq m) | (0:21) | (0.45) | | (2.50) |
| plastered walls | 1 sq yd | 0:12 | 0.38 | 5 | 1.90 |
| | (1 sq m) | (0:14) | (0.45) | | (2.30) |
| plastered ceilings | 1 sq yd | 0:14 | 0.38 | 5 | 2.00 |
| | (1 sq m) | (0:16) | (0.45) | | (2.35) |

One coat matt brilliant white emulsion paint on

| | | | | | |
|---|---|---|---|---|---|
| brickwork | 1 sq yd | 0:15 | 0.38 | 5 | 2.00 |
| | (1 sq m) | (0:18) | (0.45) | | (2.40) |
| blockwork | 1 sq yd | 0:20 | 0.55 | 5 | 2.50 |
| | (1 sq m) | (0:23) | (0.65) | | (3.00) |
| concrete walls | 1 sq yd | 0:12 | 0.35 | 5 | 1.90 |
| | (1 sq m) | (0:14) | (0.40) | | (2.25) |
| concrete ceilings | 1 sq yd | 0:15 | 0.35 | 5 | 2.00 |
| | (1 sq m) | (0:18) | (0.40) | | (2.35) |
| plastered walls | 1 sq yd | 0:10 | 0.35 | 5 | 1.75 |
| | (1 sq m) | (0:12) | (0.40) | | (2.10) |
| plastered ceilings | 1 sq yd | 0:12 | 0.35 | 5 | 1.85 |
| | (1 sq m) | (0:14) | (0.40) | | (2.20) |

| | / | ⏱ | 🧵 | ✋ | £ |
|---|---|---|---|---|---|
| **One coat matt coloured emulsion paint on** | | | | | |
| brickwork | 1 sq yd | 0:15 | 0.45 | 5 | 2.10 |
| | (1 sq m) | (0:18) | (0.55) | | (2.50) |
| blockwork | 1 sq yd | 0:20 | 0.65 | 5 | 2.60 |
| | (1 sq m) | (0:23) | (0.75) | | (3.10) |
| concrete walls | 1 sq yd | 0:12 | 0.38 | 5 | 1.90 |
| | (1 sq m) | (0:14) | (0.45) | | (2.30) |
| concrete ceilings | 1 sq yd | 0:15 | 0.38 | 5 | 2.00 |
| | (1 sq m) | (0:18) | (0.45) | | (2.40) |
| plastered walls | 1 sq yd | 0:10 | 0.38 | 5 | 1.90 |
| | (1 sq m) | (0:12) | (0.45) | | (2.30) |
| plastered ceilings | 1 sq yd | 0:12 | 0.38 | 5 | 1.90 |
| | (1 sq m) | (0:14) | (0.45) | | (2.25) |
| **One coat silk brilliant white emulsion on** | | | | | |
| brickwork | 1 sq yd | 0:13 | 0.32 | 5 | 1.70 |
| | (1 sq m) | (0:15) | (0.38) | | (2.00) |
| blockwork | 1 sq yd | 0:16 | 0.42 | 5 | 2.25 |
| | (1 sq m) | (0:19) | (0.50) | | (2.70) |
| concrete walls | 1 sq yd | 0:10 | 0.28 | 5 | 1.50 |
| | (1 sq m) | (0:12) | (0.32) | | (1.80) |
| concrete ceilings | 1 sq yd | 0:14 | 0.28 | 5 | 1.85 |
| | (1 sq m) | (0:16) | (0.32) | | (2.20) |
| plastered walls | 1 sq yd | 0:09 | 0.28 | 5 | 1.40 |
| | (1 sq m) | (0:11) | (0.32) | | (1.70) |
| plastered ceilings | 1 sq yd | 0:13 | 0.28 | 5 | 1.60 |
| | (1 sq m) | (0:15) | (0.32) | | (1.90) |
| **One coat silk coloured emulsion on** | | | | | |
| brickwork | 1 sq yd | 0:13 | 0.35 | 5 | 1.75 |
| | (1 sq m) | (0:15) | (0.42) | | (2.05) |
| blockwork | 1 sq yd | 0:16 | 0.45 | 5 | 2.30 |
| | (1 sq m) | (0:19) | (0.55) | | (2.75) |
| concrete walls | 1 sq yd | 0:10 | 0.30 | 5 | 1.55 |
| | (1 sq m) | (0:12) | (0.35) | | (1.85) |
| concrete ceilings | 1 sq yd | 0:14 | 0.30 | 5 | 1.90 |
| | (1 sq m) | (0:16) | (0.35) | | (2.25) |
| plastered walls | 1 sq yd | 0:09 | 0.30 | 5 | 1.45 |
| | (1 sq m) | (0:11) | (0.35) | | (1.75) |
| plastered ceilings | 1 sq yd | 0:13 | 0.30 | 5 | 1.65 |
| | (1 sq m) | (0:15) | (0.35) | | (1.95) |

# PAINTING AND WALLPAPERING

|  | | | | | |
|---|---|---|---|---|---|
| One coat brilliant white eggshell on | | | | | |
| brickwork | 1 sq yd | 0:13 | 0.33 | 5 | 1.68 |
|  | (1 sq m) | (0:15) | (0.40) | | (2.02) |
| blockwork | 1 sq yd | 0:16 | 0.44 | 5 | 2.28 |
|  | (1 sq m) | (0:19) | (0.53) | | (2.72) |
| concrete walls | 1 sq yd | 0:10 | 0.27 | 5 | 1.56 |
|  | (1 sq m) | (0:12) | (0.32) | | (1.87) |
| concrete ceilings | 1 sq yd | 0:14 | 0.27 | 5 | 1.85 |
|  | (1 sq m) | (0:16) | (0.32) | | (2.22) |
| plastered walls | 1 sq yd | 0:09 | 0.27 | 5 | 1.44 |
|  | (1 sq m) | (0:11) | (0.32) | | (1.72) |
| plastered ceilings | 1 sq yd | 0:13 | 0.27 | 5 | 1.60 |
|  | (1 sq m) | (0:15) | (0.32) | | (1.92) |
| One coat coloured eggshell on | | | | | |
| brickwork | 1 sq yd | 0:13 | 0.38 | 5 | 1.75 |
|  | (1 sq m) | (0:15) | (0.45) | | (2.10) |
| blockwork | 1 sq yd | 0:16 | 0.45 | 5 | 2.30 |
|  | (1 sq m) | (0:19) | (0.55) | | (2.75) |
| concrete walls | 1 sq yd | 0:10 | 0.34 | 5 | 1.60 |
|  | (1 sq m) | (0:12) | (0.40) | | (1.90) |
| concrete ceilings | 1 sq yd | 0:14 | 0.34 | 5 | 1.90 |
|  | (1 sq m) | (0:16) | (0.40) | | (2.30) |
| plastered walls | 1 sq yd | 0:09 | 0.34 | 5 | 1.50 |
|  | (1 sq m) | (0:11) | (0.40) | | (1.80) |
| plastered ceilings | 1 sq yd | 0:13 | 0.34 | 5 | 1.70 |
|  | (1 sq m) | (0:15) | (0.40) | | (2.00) |
| One coat wood primer on general surfaces, width | | | | | |
| over 12″ (300 mm) | 1 sq yd | 0:20 | 0.42 | 5 | 2.60 |
|  | (1 sq m) | (0:22) | (0.50) | | (3.10) |
| 6″–12″ (150–300 mm) | 1 yd | 0:05 | 0.16 | 5 | 0.92 |
|  | (1 m) | (0:06) | (0.17) | | (1.00) |
| not exceeding 6″ (150 mm) | 1 yd | 0:02 | 0.07 | 5 | 0.80 |
|  | (1 m) | (0:03) | (0.08) | | (0.90) |

Don't forget, these prices may need adjustment
depending on where you live.
Regional adjustments are provided in the Introduction.

| | | | | | |
|---|---|---|---|---|---|
| One coat oil based white undercoat on general surfaces, width | | | | | |
| over 12" (300 mm) | 1 sq yd | 0:20 | 0.32 | 5 | 2.10 |
| | (1 sq m) | (0:22) | (0.38) | | (2.50) |
| 6"–12" (150–300 mm) | 1 yd | 0:05 | 0.11 | 5 | 1.00 |
| | (1 m) | (0:06) | (0.12) | | (1.10) |
| not exceeding 6" (150 mm) | 1 yd | 0:02 | 0.06 | 5 | 0.55 |
| | (1 m) | (0:03) | (0.07) | | (0.60) |
| One coat oil based white gloss on general surfaces, width | | | | | |
| over 12" (300 mm) | 1 sq yd | 0:20 | 0.32 | 5 | 2.10 |
| | (1 sq m) | (0:22) | (0.38) | | (2.50) |
| 6"–12" (150–300 mm) | 1 yd | 0:05 | 0.11 | 5 | 1.00 |
| | (1 m) | (0:06) | (0.12) | | (1.10) |
| not exceeding 6" (150 mm) | 1 sq yd | 0:02 | 0.06 | 5 | 0.55 |
| | (1 sq m) | (0:03) | (0.07) | | (0.60) |
| One coat oil based coloured gloss on general surfaces, width | | | | | |
| over 12" (300 mm) | 1 sq yd | 0:20 | 0.38 | 5 | 2.20 |
| | (1 sq m) | (0:22) | (0.45) | | (2.60) |
| 6"–12" (150–300 mm) | 1 sq yd | 0:05 | 0.14 | 5 | 1.10 |
| | (1 sq m) | (0:06) | (0.15) | | (1.20) |
| not exceeding 6" (150 mm) | 1 sq yd | 0:02 | 0.06 | 5 | 0.65 |
| | (1 sq m) | (0:03) | (0.07) | | (0.70) |

**Stains and varnishes**

| | | | | | |
|---|---|---|---|---|---|
| Prepare and apply one coat oak preserver on general surfaces, width | | | | | |
| over 12" (300 mm) | 1 sq yd | 0:14 | 0.42 | 5 | 1.92 |
| | (1 sq m) | (0:16) | (0.50) | | (2.30) |
| 6"–12" (150–300 mm) | 1 yd | 0:09 | 0.15 | 5 | 1.10 |
| | (1 m) | (0:10) | (0.17) | | (1.20) |
| not exceeding 6" (150 mm) | 1 yd | 0:05 | 0.09 | 5 | 0.73 |
| | (1 m) | (0:06) | (0.10) | | (0.80) |

| | / | ⏲ | £ | ✋ | £ |
|---|---|---|---|---|---|
| Prepare and apply two coats oak preserver on general surfaces, width | | | | | |
| over 12″ (300 mm) | 1 sq yd | 0:25 | 0.85 | 5 | 3.75 |
| | (1 sq m) | (0:28) | (1.00) | | (4.50) |
| 6″–12″ (150–300 mm) | 1 yd | 0:16 | 0.32 | 5 | 2.10 |
| | (1 m) | (0:18) | (0.35) | | (2.30) |
| not exceeding 6″ (150 mm) | 1 yd | 0:10 | 0.18 | 5 | 1.30 |
| | (1 m) | (0:11) | (0.20) | | (1.40) |
| Prepare and apply one coat clear polyurethane on general surfaces, width | | | | | |
| over 12″ (300 mm) | 1 sq yd | 0:14 | 0.25 | 5 | 1.75 |
| | (1 sq m) | (0:16) | (0.30) | | (2.10) |
| 6″–12″ (150–300 mm) | 1 yd | 0:10 | 0.09 | 5 | 0.90 |
| | (1 m) | (0:11) | (0.10) | | (1.00) |
| not exceeding 6″ (150 mm) | 1 yd | 0:07 | 0.05 | 5 | 0.50 |
| | (1 m) | (0:08) | (0.06) | | (0.55) |
| Prepare and apply two coats clear polyurethane on general surfaces, width | | | | | |
| over 12″ (300 mm) | 1 sq yd | 0:27 | 0.50 | 5 | 3.35 |
| | (1 sq m) | (0:30) | (0.60) | | (4.00) |
| 6″–12″ (150–300 mm) | 1 yd | 0:18 | 0.18 | 5 | 1.65 |
| | (1 m) | (0:20) | (0.20) | | (1.80) |
| not exceeding 6″ (150 mm) | 1 yd | 0:12 | 0.11 | 5 | 0.92 |
| | (1 m) | (0:14) | (0.12) | | (1.00) |
| Prepare and apply two coats linseed oil on wood general surfaces, width | | | | | |
| over 12″ (300 mm) | 1 sq yd | 0:30 | 0.50 | 5 | 3.75 |
| | (1 sq m) | (0:35) | (1.20) | | (4.50) |
| 6″–12″ (150–300 mm) | 1 yd | 0:16 | 0.36 | 5 | 2.55 |
| | (1 m) | (0:18) | (0.40) | | (2.80) |
| not exceeding 6″ (150 mm) | 1 yd | 0:09 | 0.23 | 5 | 1.28 |
| | (1 m) | (0:10) | (0.25) | | (1.40) |

| | 📏 | 🕐 | ✂ | ✋ | £ |
|---|---|---|---|---|---|
| **Prepare and apply one coat wax polish on wood** | | | | | |
| over 12" (300 mm) | 1 sq yd | 0:20 | 1.15 | 5 | 3.35 |
| | (1 sq m) | (0:25) | (1.40) | | (4.00) |
| 6"–12" (150–300 mm) | 1 yd | 0:13 | 0.45 | 5 | 1.10 |
| | (1 m) | (0:14) | (0.50) | | (2.20) |
| not exceeding 6" | 1 yd | 0:07 | 0.25 | 5 | 1.10 |
| (150 mm) | (1 m) | (0:08) | (0.30) | | (1.20) |
| **One coat Artex preparation, one coat Artex sealer, one coat Artex AX finish, stippled finish** | | | | | |
| brickwork | 1 sq yd | 0:38 | 1.68 | 5 | 5.40 |
| | (1 sq m) | (0:45) | (2.00) | | (6.50) |
| blockwork | 1 sq yd | 0:38 | 1.85 | 5 | 5.70 |
| | (1 sq m) | (0:45) | (2.20) | | (6.80) |
| concrete walls | 1 sq yd | 0:38 | 1.42 | 5 | 5.25 |
| | (1 sq m) | (0:45) | (1.70) | | (6.30) |
| concrete ceilings | 1 sq yd | 0:42 | 1.35 | 5 | 5.85 |
| | (1 sq m) | (0:50) | (1.60) | | (7.00) |
| plastered walls | 1 sq yd | 0:42 | 1.25 | 5 | 5.00 |
| | (1 sq m) | (0:40) | (1.50) | | (6.00) |
| plastered ceilings | 1 sq yd | 0:38 | 1.25 | 5 | 5.35 |
| | (1 sq m) | (0:45) | (1.50) | | (6.40) |

## WALLPAPERING

The basic price referred to (BP) is the purchase cost of the paper per roll. The net materials column contains an allowance for paste and filling materials for cracks and also for waste. For every 50p variation in the basic price per roll, the material column should be increased or decreased by 12p per square yard (14p per square metre).

> **Don't forget, these prices may need adjustment depending on where you live.**
> Regional adjustments are provided in the Introduction.

| | 📏 | 🕐 | ✂️ | ✋ | £ |
|---|---|---|---|---|---|
| **Hang wallpaper to walls** | | | | | |
| lining paper | 1 sq yd | 0:17 | 0.15 | 6 | 1.50 |
| (BP £0.70) | (1 sq m) | (0:20) | (0.17) | | (1.80) |
| woodchip paper | 1 sq yd | 0:17 | 0.16 | 6 | 1.60 |
| (BP £0.80) | (1 sq m) | (0:20) | (0.19) | | (1.90) |
| flock paper (BP £6.00) | 1 sq yd | 0:20 | 1.15 | 6 | 2.60 |
| | (1 sq m) | (0:25) | (1.40) | | (3.10) |
| Anaglypta paper | 1 sq yd | 0:20 | 0.20 | 6 | 1.65 |
| (BP £1.50) | (1 sq m) | (0:25) | (0.35) | | (2.00) |
| standard patterned | 1 sq yd | 0:20 | 0.90 | 6 | 2.30 |
| paper (BP £4.50) | (1 sq m) | (0:25) | (1.06) | | (2.80) |
| vinyl surface paper | 1 sq yd | 0:20 | 1.10 | 6 | 2.50 |
| (BP £5.50) | (1 sq m) | (0:25) | (1.30) | | (3.00) |
| **Hang wallpaper to ceilings** | | | | | |
| lining paper | 1 sq yd | 0:20 | 0.15 | 6 | 2.30 |
| (BP £0.70) | (1 sq m) | (0:25) | (0.17) | | (2.00) |
| woodchip paper | 1 sq yd | 0:20 | 0.16 | 6 | 1.75 |
| (BP £0.80) | (1 sq m) | (0:25) | (0.19) | | (2.10) |
| flock paper (BP £6.00) | 1 sq yd | 0:20 | 1.15 | 6 | 2.75 |
| | (1 sq m) | (0:25) | (1.40) | | (3.30) |
| Anaglypta paper | 1 sq yd | 0:20 | 0.30 | 6 | 1.90 |
| (BP £1.50) | (1 sq m) | (0:25) | (0.35) | | (2.30) |
| standard patterned | 1 sq yd | 0:20 | 0.90 | 6 | 2.50 |
| paper (BP £4.50) | (1 sq m) | (0:25) | (1.06) | | (3.00) |
| vinyl surface paper | 1 sq yd | 0:20 | 1.10 | 6 | 2.65 |
| (BP £5.50) | (1 sq m) | (0:25) | (1.30) | | (3.20) |

Table 2 shows the net areas and lengths of surfaces to be painted or papered in the average house. The following assumptions have been made:

| | |
|---|---|
| Living room | 1 door, 1 fireplace, 1 large window; |
| Dining room | 2 doors, 1 large window; |
| Bedroom | 1 door, 1 average window; |
| Kitchen | 2 doors, fittings below dado height, 1 large window; |
| WC | 1 door, 1 small window; |
| Bathroom | 1 door, 1 cupboard, 1 average window; |
| Ceiling heights | Ground floor 7'9" (2.4 m); First floor 7'6" (2.2 m). |

## TABLE 2

| | Ceiling sq yd (sq m) | Walls sq yd (sq m) | Window sq yd (sq m) | Door sq yd (sq m) | Skirting yd (m) | Frame yd (m) |
|---|---|---|---|---|---|---|
| **Living room** | | | | | | |
| 12' × 10' (3.6 × 3.0 m) | 13 (11) | 29 (24) | 3 (3) | 2 (2) | 11 (10) | 10 (8) |
| 12' × 12' (3.6 × 3.6 m) | 16 (13) | 31 (26) | 3 (3) | 2 (2) | 12 (11) | 10 (8) |
| 14' × 10' (4.2 × 3.0 m) | 16 (13) | 31 (26) | 3 (3) | 2 (2) | 12 (11) | 10 (8) |
| 14' × 12' (4.2 × 3.6 m) | 19 (15) | 35 (29) | 3 (3) | 2 (2) | 14 (13) | 10 (8) |
| 14' × 14' (4.2 × 4.2 m) | 22 (18) | 38 (32) | 3 (3) | 2 (2) | 15 (14) | 10 (8) |
| 16' × 10' (4.8 × 3.0 m) | 18 (15) | 35 (29) | 3 (3) | 2 (2) | 14 (13) | 10 (8) |
| 16' × 12' (4.8 × 3.6 m) | 21 (17) | 38 (32) | 3 (3) | 2 (2) | 15 (14) | 10 (8) |
| 16' × 14' (4.8 × 4.2 m) | 25 (20) | 41 (34) | 3 (3) | 2 (2) | 17 (15) | 10 (8) |
| 16' × 16' (4.8 × 4.8 m) | 28 (23) | 44 (37) | 3 (3) | 2 (2) | 18 (16) | 10 (8) |
| **Dining room** | | | | | | |
| 10' × 10' (3.0 × 3.0 m) | 11 (9) | 24 (20) | 3 (3) | 4 (4) | 11 (10) | 16 (13) |
| 12' × 10' (3.6 × 3.0 m) | 13 (11) | 29 (24) | 3 (3) | 4 (4) | 12 (11) | 16 (13) |
| 12' × 12' (3.6 × 3.6 m) | 16 (13) | 31 (26) | 3 (3) | 4 (4) | 14 (13) | 16 (13) |
| 14' × 10' (4.2 × 3.0 m) | 16 (13) | 31 (26) | 3 (3) | 4 (4) | 14 (13) | 16 (13) |
| 14' × 12' (4.2 × 3.6 m) | 19 (15) | 35 (29) | 3 (3) | 4 (4) | 17 (15) | 16 (13) |
| 14' × 14' (4.2 × 4.2 m) | 22 (18) | 38 (32) | 3 (3) | 4 (4) | 18 (16) | 16 (13) |

| | Ceiling sq yd (sq m) | Walls sq yd (sq m) | Window sq yd (sq m) | Door sq yd (sq m) | Skirting yd (m) | Frame yd (m) |
|---|---|---|---|---|---|---|
| 16' × 10' (4.8 × 3.0 m) | 18 (15) | 35 (29) | 3 (3) | 4 (4) | 17 (15) | 16 (13) |
| 16' × 12' (4.8 × 3.6 m) | 21 (17) | 38 (32) | 3 (3) | 4 (4) | 18 (16) | 16 (13) |
| 16' × 14' (4.8 × 4.2 m) | 25 (20) | 41 (34) | 3 (3) | 4 (4) | 19 (17) | 16 (13) |
| **Bedroom** | | | | | | |
| 8' × 8' (2.4 × 2.4 m) | 7 (6) | 20 (17) | 2 (2) | 2 (2) | 10 (9) | 8 (7) |
| 8' × 10' (2.4 × 3.0 m) | 9 (7) | 24 (20) | 2 (2) | 2 (2) | 11 (10) | 8 (7) |
| 8' × 12' (2.4 × 3.6 m) | 11 (9) | 26 (22) | 2 (2) | 2 (2) | 12 (11) | 7 (7) |
| 10' × 10' (3.0 × 3.0 m) | 11 (9) | 26 (22) | 2 (2) | 2 (2) | 12 (11) | 8 (7) |
| 10' × 12' (3.0 × 3.6 m) | 13 (11) | 30 (25) | 2 (2) | 2 (2) | 13 (12) | 8 (7) |
| 12' × 12' (3.6 × 3.6 m) | 16 (13) | 32 (27) | 2 (2) | 2 (2) | 14 (13) | 8 (7) |
| 12' × 14' (3.6 × 4.2 m) | 19 (15) | 36 (30) | 2 (2) | 2 (2) | 17 (15) | 8 (7) |
| 12' × 16' (3.6 × 4.8 m) | 21 (17) | 38 (32) | 2 (2) | 2 (2) | 18 (16) | 8 (7) |
| 14' × 14' (4.2 × 4.2 m) | 22 (18) | 38 (32) | 2 (2) | 2 (2) | 18 (16) | 8 (7) |
| 14' × 16' (4.2 × 4.8 m) | 25 (20) | 42 (35) | 2 (2) | 2 (2) | 19 (17) | 8 (7) |
| **Kitchen** | | | | | | |
| 6' × 10' (1.8 × 3.0 m) | 7 (6) | 8 (7) | 3 (3) | 4 (4) | 3 (3) | 14 (13) |
| 6' × 12' (1.8 × 3.6 m) | 8 (7) | 12 (10) | 3 (3) | 4 (4) | 4 (4) | 14 (13) |
| 8' × 10' (2.4 × 3.0 m) | 9 (7) | 12 (10) | 3 (3) | 4 (4) | 4 (4) | 14 (13) |
| 8' × 12' (2.4 × 3.6 m) | 11 (9) | 13 (11) | 3 (3) | 4 (4) | 6 (5) | 14 (13) |

| | Ceiling sq yd (sq m) | Walls sq yd (sq m) | Window sq yd (sq m) | Door sq yd (sq m) | Skirting yd (m) | Frame yd (m) |
|---|---|---|---|---|---|---|
| 10' × 10' | 11 | 13 | 3 | 4 | 6 | 14 |
| (3.0 × 3.0 m) | (9) | (11) | (3) | (4) | (5) | (13) |
| 10' × 12' | 13 | 13 | 3 | 4 | 7 | 14 |
| (3.0 × 3.6 m) | (11) | (11) | (3) | (4) | (6) | (13) |
| 10' × 14' | 16 | 13 | 3 | 4 | 7 | 14 |
| (3.0 × 4.2 m) | (13) | (11) | (3) | (4) | (6) | (13) |
| 12' × 12' | 16 | 16 | 3 | 4 | 7 | 14 |
| (3.6 × 3.6 m) | (13) | (13) | (3) | (4) | (6) | (13) |
| 12' × 14' | 19 | 18 | 3 | 4 | 8 | 14 |
| (3.6 × 4.2 m) | (15) | (15) | (3) | (4) | (7) | (13) |
| **WC** | | | | | | |
| 3'6" × 5' | 2 | 10 | 1 | 2 | 4 | 7 |
| (1.0 × 1.5 m) | (2) | (8) | (1) | (2) | (4) | (6) |
| 4' × 5' | 2 | 11 | 1 | 2 | 4 | 7 |
| (1.2 × 1.5 m) | (2) | (9) | (1) | (2) | (4) | (6) |
| 4' × 6' | 3 | 12 | 1 | 2 | 6 | 7 |
| (1.2 × 1.8 m) | (2) | (10) | (1) | (2) | (5) | (6) |
| 4'4" × 5' | 2 | 11 | 1 | 2 | 6 | 7 |
| (1.3 × 1.5 m) | (2) | (9) | (1) | (2) | (5) | (6) |
| 4'4" × 6' | 3 | 12 | 1 | 2 | 6 | 7 |
| (1.3 × 1.8 m) | (2) | (10) | (1) | (2) | (5) | (6) |
| **Bathroom** | | | | | | |
| 6' × 8' | 5 | 28 | 1 | 7 | 10 | 15 |
| (1.8 × 2.4 m) | (4) | (23) | (1) | (6) | (9) | (14) |
| 6' × 10' | 7 | 30 | 1 | 7 | 12 | 15 |
| (1.8 × 3.0 m) | (5) | (25) | (1) | (6) | (11) | (14) |
| 7' × 8' | 6 | 28 | 1 | 7 | 11 | 15 |
| (2.1 × 2.4 m) | (5) | (23) | (1) | (6) | (10) | (14) |
| 8' × 8' | 7 | 30 | 1 | 7 | 11 | 15 |
| (2.4 × 2.4 m( | (6( | (25) | (1) | (6) | (10) | (14) |
| 8' × 10' | 9 | 34 | 1 | 7 | 12 | 15 |
| (2.4 × 3.0 m) | (7) | (28) | (1) | (6) | (11) | (14) |
| 8' × 12' | 11 | 36 | 1 | 7 | 14 | 15 |
| (2.4 × 3.6 m) | (9) | (30) | (1) | (6) | (13) | (14) |

The rates and hours listed in Table 1 (see page 127) should be applied to the relevant entry in Table 2 (see page 136) to produce the facts necessary to compare the cost of doing the work yourself to employing a painter.

## Example 1

Let us assume that you wish to re-decorate your dining room size 14 × 12 ft (4.2 × 3.6 m). The work consists of:

**(a)** scraping off the existing woodchip wallpaper and hanging new paper (basic price £4.50 per roll);

**(b)** one undercoat and one gloss coat to all woodwork;

**(c)** two coats emulsion paint to the ceiling.

You should then apply the hours and prices in Table 1 (see page 127) to the dimensions in Table 2 (see page 136) as follows:

| | | | | £ |
|---|---|---|---|---|
| Scrape off one layer of woodchip paper from walls | 35 sq yd (29 sq m) | 15:00 (14:50) | – | 1 | 49.00 (49.30) |
| Apply standard patterned wallpaper (BP £4.50 per roll) to walls | 35 sq yd (29 sq m) | 11:40 (12:05) | 31.50 (30.74) | 6 | 80.50 (81.20) |
| One white undercoat and one white coat gloss on | | | | | |
| window | 3 sq yd (3 sq m) | 2:00 (2:10) | 1.92 (2.28) | 5 | 12.60 (15.00) |
| door | 4 sq yd (4 sq m) | 2:40 (3:00) | 2.56 (3.04) | 5 | 16.80 (20.00) |
| skirting not exceeding 6" (150 mm) girth | 17 yd (15 m) | 1:08 (1:42) | 2.04 (2.10) | 5 | 18.70 (18.00) |
| frames 6"–12" (150–300 mm) girth | 16 yd (13 m) | 2:40 (3:12) | 3.52 (3.12) | 5 | 32.80 (28.60) |

| | | 📏 | 🕐 | ✂ | ✋ | £ |
|---|---|---|---|---|---|---|
| Two coats matt brilliant white emulsion paint to ceiling | | 19 sq yd (15 sq m) | 4:56 (4:20) | 13.30 (12.00) | 5 | 70.30 (66.00) |
| | | | 40:04 (42:19) | £54.84 (£53.28) | | £279.90 (£278.10) |

This shows that it should take you about 40 hours to redecorate your living room and the cost of the materials is approximately £55. Alternatively the cost of employing a contractor would be about £280. Note that the difference between the imperial and metric sizes and the effect of rounding off small quantities causes variations in prices and hours.

## Example 2

In this example we will assume that you wish to redecorate your bathroom size 8 × 10 ft (2.4 × 3 m). The work consists of:

**(a)** one undercoat and one gloss coat to all woodwork;

**(b)** two coats emulsion paint to ceiling and approximately half the wall area;

**(c)** scrape off one layer of paper to approximately half the wall area;

**(d)** hang vinyl surface paper (basic price £5.50 per roll) to approximately half the wall area.

The hours and costs for the individual items are set out in Table 1 (see page 127) and the quantities are in Table 2 (see page 136). Notice that the area of 34 square yards (28 square metres) for the walls has been divided into two equal parts of 17 square yards (14 square metres) for part wallpapering and part painting.

> **Don't forget, these prices may need adjustment depending on where you live.**
> Regional adjustments are provided in the Introduction.

| | 📏 | 🕐 | 💷 | ✋ | £ |
|---|---|---|---|---|---|
| Scrape off one layer of vinyl paper from walls | 17 sq yd (14 sq m) | 8:30 (8:16) | – | 1 | 29.75 (29.40) |
| Vinyl surfaced wallpaper (BP £5.50 per roll) to walls | 17 sq yd (14 sq m) | 5:40 (5:50) | 18.70 (18.20) | 6 | 39.10 (39.20) |
| One undercoat and one coat gloss on | | | | | |
| window | 1 sq yd (1 sq m) | 0:40 (0:44) | 0.64 (0.76) | 5 | 4.20 (5.00) |
| door | 6 sq yd (6 sq m) | 4:00 (4:24) | 3.84 (4.56) | 5 | 25.20 (30.00) |
| skirting not exceeding 6" (150 mm) girth | 12 yd (11 m) | 0:48 (1:06) | 1.44 (1.54) | 5 | 12.10 (13.20) |
| frames 6"–12" (150–300 mm) girth | 15 yd (14 m) | 2:30 (2:48) | 3.30 (3.36) | 5 | 12.00 (30.80) |
| Two coats matt coloured emulsion paint on | | | | | |
| walls | 17 sq yd (14 sq m) | 5:40 (5:36) | 12.92 (12.60) | 5 | 64.60 (64.60) |
| ceiling | 9 sq yd (7 sq m) | 3:36 (3:16) | 6.84 (6.30) | 5 | 34.20 (31.50) |
| | | 29:02 (30:44) | £47.68 (£48.42) | | £240.25 (£243.50) |

These figures demonstrate that it should take you about 30 hours to complete the work with a material cost of about £50. A contractor would probably charge about £250 for carrying out the same work.

## EXTERNAL PAINTING

Painting outside can be a real pleasure when the sun is shining but a nightmare if it is cold and windy, particularly if rain is threatening! The information here is based upon the work being done at ground level, 20% to 30% should be added for working from a ladder.

| | | | | | |
|---|---|---|---|---|---|
| **Wash down previously painted surfaces and rub down, width** | | | | | |
| over 12" (300 mm) | 1 sq yd | 0:20 | – | 2 | 2.40 |
| | (1 sq m) | (0:22) | – | | (2.90) |
| 6"–12" (150–300 mm) | 1 yd | 0:08 | – | 2 | 1.00 |
| | (1 m) | (0:09) | – | | (1.10) |
| not exceeding 6" (150 mm) | 1 yd | 0:03 | – | 2 | 0.55 |
| | (1 m) | (0:04) | | | (0.60) |
| **Burn off existing paint from general surfaces, width** | | | | | |
| over 12" (300 mm) | 1 sq yd | 1:15 | – | 3 | 8.35 |
| | (1 sq m) | (1:20) | – | | (10.00) |
| 6"–12" (150–300 mm) | 1 yd | 0:30 | – | 3 | 2.45 |
| | (1 m) | (0:35) | – | | (2.70) |
| not exceeding 6" (150 mm) | 1 yd | 0:20 | – | 3 | 1.28 |
| | (1 m) | (0:22) | | | (1.40) |
| **One coat oil based white undercoat on general surfaces, width** | | | | | |
| over 12" (300 mm) | 1 sq yd | 0:25 | 0.32 | 5 | 2.20 |
| | (1 sq m) | (0:28) | (0.38) | | (2.60) |
| 6"–12" (150–300 mm) | 1 yd | 0:07 | 0.11 | 5 | 1.10 |
| | (1 m) | (0:09) | (0.12) | | (1.20) |
| not exceeding 6" (150 mm) | 1 yd | 0:03 | 0.07 | 5 | 0.80 |
| | (1 m) | (0:04) | (0.08) | | (0.90) |
| **One coat oil based gloss on general surfaces, width** | | | | | |
| over 12" (300 mm) | 1 sq yd | 0:25 | 0.32 | 5 | 2.50 |
| | (1 sq m) | (0:28) | (0.38) | | (2.60) |
| 6"–12" (150–300 mm) | 1 yd | 0:07 | 0.11 | 5 | 1.10 |
| | (1 m) | (0:09) | (0.12) | | (1.20) |
| not exceeding 6" (150 mm) | 1 yd | 0:03 | 0.07 | 5 | 0.80 |
| | (1 m) | (0:04) | (0.08) | | (0.90) |

| | 📏 | 🕐 | ✂ | ✋ | £ |
|---|---|---|---|---|---|
| **Two coats 'Solignum' green preservative on wood** | | | | | |
| wrought (smooth) timber | 1 sq yd (1 sq m) | 0:20 (0:25) | 0.33 (0.40) | 4 | 3.10 (3.70) |
| sawn (rough) timber | 1 sq yd (1 sq m) | 0:22 (0:28) | 0.42 (0.50) | 4 | 3.25 (3.90) |
| **Two coats green preservative on wood** | | | | | |
| wrought (smooth) timber | 1 sq yd (1 sq m) | 0:22 (0:28) | 0.95 (1.00) | 4 | 3.85 (4.60) |
| sawn (rough) timber | 1 sq yd (1 sq m) | 0:25 (0:30) | 0.95 (1.15) | 4 | 4.20 (5.00) |
| **Two coats golden brown preservative on wood** | | | | | |
| wrought (smooth) timber | 1 sq yd (1 sq m) | 0:22 (0:28) | 0.65 (0.70) | 4 | 3.50 (4.20) |
| sawn (rough) timber | 1 sq yd (1 sq m) | 0:25 (0:30) | 0.68 (0.80) | 4 | 3.75 (4.50) |
| **Two coats creosote on wood** | | | | | |
| wrought (smooth) timber | 1 sq yd (1 sq m) | 0:30 (0:35) | 0.25 (0.30) | | 3.20 (3.80) |
| sawn (rough) timber | 1 sq yd (1 sq m) | 0:35 (0:40) | 0.30 (0.35) | 4 | 3.35 (4.00) |
| **One coat 'Blue Circle' stabilising solution and one coat 'Snowcem' finish on** | | | | | |
| brickwork | 1 sq yd (1 sq m) | 0:40 (0:45) | 0.90 (1.10) | 5 | 3.20 (3.80) |
| concrete | 1 sq yd (1 sq m) | 0:40 (0:45) | 1.00 (1.20) | 5 | 3.35 (4.00) |
| cement rendering | 1 sq yd (1 sq m) | 0:35 (0:40) | 1.00 (1.20) | 5 | 3.25 (3.90) |
| rough cast | 1 sq yd (1 sq m) | 0:45 (0:50) | 1.50 (1.80) | 5 | 4.35 (5.20) |

| One coat 'Blue Circle' stabilising solution and one coat 'Sandtex Matt' finish on | | | | | |
|---|---|---|---|---|---|
| brickwork | 1 sq yd | 0:40 | 1.10 | 5 | 4.00 |
| | (1 sq m) | (0:45) | (1.30) | | (4.75) |
| concrete | 1 sq yd | 0:40 | 1.10 | 5 | 4.00 |
| | (1 sq m) | (0:45) | (1.30) | | (4.75) |
| cement rendering | 1 sq yd | 0:35 | 1.10 | 5 | 3.70 |
| | (1 sq m) | (0:40) | (1.30) | | (4.40) |
| rough cast | 1 sq yd | 0:45 | 1.40 | 5 | 4.80 |
| | (1 sq m) | (0:50) | (1.70) | | (5.70) |

**Don't forget, these prices may need adjustment
depending on where you live.**
Regional adjustments are provided in the Introduction.

# INSULATION

The thought of burning bank notes is anathema to everybody but if you don't insulate your home properly that is the equivalent of what you are doing. Significant savings on fuel bills can be achieved by installing insulation, in addition to improving your lifestyle by reducing draughts and coldness. Grants are available in certain circumstances and you can find out more by contacting the Energy Action Grants Agency in Newcastle-upon-Tyne, tel. 0800 181667.

| | 📏 | 🕐 | ⚒ | ✋ | £ |
|---|---|---|---|---|---|
| **Glass fibre quilt laid over joists** | | | | | |
| 60 mm thick | 1 sq yd | 0.11 | 2.00 | 2 | 2.95 |
| | (1 sq m) | (0.13) | (2.40) | | (3.50) |
| 80 mm thick | 1 sq yd | 0.12 | 2.70 | 2 | 4.00 |
| | (1 sq m) | (0.14) | (3.20) | | (4.80) |
| 100 mm thick | 1 sq yd | 0.13 | 3.20 | 2 | 4.50 |
| | (1 sq m) | (0.15) | (3.80) | | (5.30) |
| 150 mm thick | 1 sq yd | 0.14 | 4.85 | 2 | 6.20 |
| | (1 sq m) | (0.16) | (5.80) | | (7.40) |
| 200 mm thick | 1 sq yd | 0.15 | 6.50 | 2 | 7.95 |
| | (1 sq m) | (0.17) | (7.80) | | (9.50) |
| **Glass fibre quilt 600 mm wide laid between joists** | | | | | |
| 100 mm thick | 1 sq yd | 0.15 | 1.85 | 2 | 3.30 |
| | (1 sq m) | (0.16) | (2.00) | | (3.60) |
| 150 mm thick | 1 sq yd | 0.18 | 1.95 | 2 | 3.75 |
| | (1 sq m) | (0.20) | (2.10) | | (4.10) |
| **Glass fibre quilt pinned vertically to softwood** | | | | | |
| 60 mm thick | 1 sq yd | 0.16 | 2.00 | 2 | 3.60 |
| | (1 sq m) | (0.19) | (2.40) | | (4.30) |
| 80 mm thick | 1 sq yd | 0.16 | 2.70 | 2 | 4.35 |
| | (1 sq m) | (0.20) | (3.20) | | (5.20) |
| 100 mm thick | 1 sq yd | 0.17 | 3.20 | 2 | 4.95 |
| | (1 sq m) | (0.21) | (3.80) | | (5.90) |
| 150 mm thick | 1 sq yd | 0.18 | 4.85 | 2 | 6.70 |
| | (1 sq m) | (0.22) | (5.80) | | (8.00) |
| 200 mm thick | 1 sq yd | 0.19 | 6.50 | 2 | 8.40 |
| | (1 sq m) | '0.23) | (7.80) | | (10.00) |

|  | / | ⏱ | ⚖ | ✋ | £ |
|---|---|---|---|---|---|
| **Exfoliated vermiculite 100 mm thick laid between joists at centres** | | | | | |
| 400 mm | 1 yd | 0.03 | 3.12 | 2 | 3.65 |
|  | (1 m) | (0.03) | (3.41) |  | (4.00) |
| 450 mm | 1 yd | 0.04 | 3.52 | 2 | 4.10 |
|  | (1 m) | (0.04) | (3.85) |  | (4.50) |
| 500 mm | 1 yd | 0.04 | 3.90 | 2 | 4.65 |
|  | (1 m) | (0.05) | (4.27) |  | (5.10) |
| **Exfoliated vermiculite 150 mm thick laid between joists at centres** | | | | | |
| 400 mm | 1 yd | 0.04 | 4.70 | 2 | 5.50 |
|  | (1 m) | (0.05) | (5.14) |  | (6.00) |
| 450 mm | 1 yd | 0.05 | 5.30 | 2 | 6.40 |
|  | (1 m) | (0.06) | (5.80) |  | (7.00) |
| 500 mm | 1 yd | 0.06 | 5.89 | 2 | 6.85 |
|  | (1 m) | (0.07) | (6.44) |  | (7.50) |
| **Expanded polystyrene sheeting fixed to walls with adhesive** | | | | | |
| 25 mm thick | 1 sq yd | 0.25 | 1.70 | 4 | 5.85 |
|  | (1 sq m) | (0.30) | (2.00) |  | (7.00) |
| 50 mm thick | 1 sq yd | 0.30 | 3.25 | 4 | 7.50 |
|  | (1 sq m) | (0.35) | (3.90) |  | (9.00) |
| 75 mm thick | 1 sq yd | 0.33 | 4.90 | 4 | 10.00 |
|  | (1 sq m) | (0.40) | (5.85) |  | (12.00) |
| 100 mm thick | 1 sq yd | 0.38 | 6.50 | 4 | 12.50 |
|  | (1 sq m) | (0.45) | (7.80) |  | (15.00) |
| **Cistern jacket in glass fibre with polythene cover with two fixing bands** | | | | | |
| 630 × 450 × 420 mm | 1 no | 1:20 | 9.00 | 3 | 20.00 |
| 700 × 500 × 535 mm | 1 no | 1:30 | 13.00 | 3 | 25.00 |
| 995 × 605 × 595 mm | 1 no | 1:40 | 14.00 | 3 | 28.00 |

# INSULATION

| | | | | | |
|---|---|---|---|---|---|
| Hot water cylinder jacket in glass fibre with PVC cover with two fixing bands for cylinder 450 mm diameter, height | | | | | |
| 300 mm | 1 no | 0:30 | 8.00 | 3 | 15.00 |
| 450 mm | 1 no | 0:35 | 9.00 | 3 | 16.00 |
| 600 mm | 1 no | 0:40 | 10.00 | 3 | 20.00 |
| Pre-formed pipe lagging in fire retardant foam 13 mm thick to pipe | | | | | |
| 15 mm | 1 yd | 0:09 | 0.90 | 3 | 1.80 |
| | (1 m) | (0:10) | (1.00) | | (2.00) |
| 22 mm | 1 yd | 0:11 | 1.10 | 3 | 2.05 |
| | (1 m) | (0:12) | (1.20) | | (2.25) |
| 28 mm | 1 yd | 0:14 | 1.20 | 3 | 2.30 |
| | (1 m) | (0:15) | (1.30) | | (2.50) |

Don't forget, these prices may need adjustment depending on where you live.
Regional adjustments are provided in the Introduction.

# HOME SECURITY

Making your home safe from fire and burglary is vital but the installation of the equipment is probably better left to the expert.
The following prices are approximate and should be regarded as indicative.

## FIRE ALARMS

| Self-contained smoke detector complete with battery and built in warbler | £35 each |
|---|---|

## INTRUDER ALARM SYSTEM

The following prices relate to the installation of the equipment only excluding the cable. The estimated cost of laying 4 core cable is approximately 60p per metre which should be added to the prices below.

| | |
|---|---|
| 12 volt internal alarm siren | £30 each |
| Weatherproof self-activating bell and red housing | £100 each |
| Recessed or surface magnetic door proximity switch | £15 each |
| Stair pressure mat | £9 each |
| Floor pressure mat | £20 each |
| Panic button | £16 each |
| Vibration window contact | £30 each |
| Infra red detector 12 metre range | £75 each |
| Door connector loops | £10 each |
| Self contained ultrasonic space alarm | £200 each |

# PATHS AND EDGINGS

The figures quoted in this section are based upon unit rates, i.e. prices and hours per square yard or square metre and it is assumed that the area to be laid is between 5 and 40 square yards. The unit cost for smaller areas would be more expensive but would be cheaper (per square yard or square metre) for areas over 40 square yards. It is assumed that you will do the excavation by hand and the surplus excavated material will be wheeled to a skip (situated within 30 yards of the working area) which will be filled.

You will notice that in some of the following tables only the total price has been entered in the contractor's price column because a contractor would probably calculate his costs on an overall or job basis rather than on an evaluation of individual items.

## PRECAST CONCRETE FLAGGED PATHS

| Preparatory work | / | ⏱ | £ | 👐 | £ |
|---|---|---|---|---|---|
| Excavate 6" (150 mm) deep by hand to remove soil and load into skip | 1 sq yd (1 sq m) | 0:40 (0:45) | – | 2 | – |
| Remove from site by skip | 0.2 cu yd (0.15 cu m) | – | 1.64 (1.62) | – | – |
| 4" (100 mm) thick bed of sand | 1 sq yd (1 sq m) | 0:20 (0:22) | 1.42 (1.70) | 2 | – |
| per square yard | | 1:00 | £3.06 | | £5.45 |
| per square metre | | (1:07) | (£3.32) | | (£6.52) |

The above costs should be added to the following figures for different finishes to arrive at a composite square yard or square metre rate.

> **Don't forget, these prices may need adjustment depending on where you live.**
> Regional adjustments are provided in the Introduction.

| | 📏 | 🕐 | 🔧 | ✋ | £ |
|---|---|---|---|---|---|
| **2″ (50 mm) thick precast concrete natural colour flags size** | | | | | |
| 1′6″ × 1′6″ | 1 sq yd | 0:40 | 9.10 | 5 | 13.70 |
| (450 × 450 mm) | (1 sq m) | (0:45) | (10.90) | | (16.40) |
| 2′0″ × 1′6″ | 1 sq yd | 0:35 | 7.80 | 5 | 11.70 |
| (600 × 450 mm) | (1 sq m) | (0:40) | (9.30) | | (14.00) |
| 2′0″ × 2′0″ | 1 sq yd | 0:30 | 6.45 | 5 | 10.00 |
| (600 × 600 mm) | (1 sq m) | (0:35) | (7.70) | | (12.00) |
| 2′0″ × 3′0″ | 1 sq yd | 0:25 | 5.50 | 5 | 8.80 |
| (600 × 900 mm) | (1 sq m) | (0:30) | (6.60) | | (10.50) |
| **2″ (50 mm) thick precast concrete coloured flags size** | | | | | |
| 1′6″ × 1′6″ | 1 sq yd | 0:40 | 11.40 | 5 | 16.30 |
| (450 × 450 mm) | (1 sq m) | (0:45) | (13.60) | | (19.50) |
| 2′0″ × 1′6″ | 1 sq yd | 0:35 | 9.60 | 5 | 14.20 |
| (600 × 450 mm) | (1 sq m) | (0:40) | (11.50) | | (17.00) |
| 2′0″ × 2′0″ | 1 sq yd | 0:30 | 8.00 | 5 | 11.90 |
| (600 × 600 mm) | (1 sq m) | (0:35) | (9.60) | | (14.20) |
| 2′0″ × 3′0″ | 1 sq yd | 0:25 | 6.85 | 5 | 10.20 |
| (600 × 900 mm) | (1 sq m) | (0:30) | (8.20) | | (12.20) |
| **Concrete block paving size 8″ × 4″ × 2½″ (200 × 100 × 65 mm) thick** | | | | | |
| natural | 1 sq yd | 1:00 | 5.70 | 5 | 14.90 |
| | (1 sq m) | (1:05) | (6.80) | | (17.80) |
| coloured | 1 sq yd | 1:00 | 6.70 | 5 | 15.90 |
| | (1 sq m) | (1:05) | (8.05) | | (19.00) |
| multicoloured | 1 sq yd | 1:00 | 7.00 | 5 | 16.30 |
| | (1 sq m) | (1:05) | (8.35) | | (19.50) |
| **Concrete block paving size 8″ × 4″ × 3″ (200 × 100 × 80 mm) thick** | | | | | |
| natural | 1 sq yd | 1:10 | 6.30 | 5 | 16.30 |
| | (1 sq m) | (1:15) | (7.30) | | (19.50) |
| coloured | 1 sq yd | 1:10 | 7.60 | 5 | 17.60 |
| | (1 sq m) | (1:15) | (9.05) | | (21.00) |
| multicoloured | 1 sq yd | 1:10 | 7.80 | 5 | 18.00 |
| | (1 sq m) | (1:15) | (9.30) | | (21.50) |

| | / | ⏱ | ₤ | ✋ | £ |
|---|---|---|---|---|---|
| Brick paviours size 8½″ × 4″ × 2½″ (215 × 103 × 65 mm) thick | | | | | |
| bricks laid flat | 1 sq yd (1 sq m) | 1:00 (1:10) | 18.20 (21.75) | 5 | 26.75 (32.00) |
| bricks laid on edge | 1 sq yd (1 sq m) | 1:15 (1:30) | 28.50 (34.00) | 5 | 37.60 (45.00) |

## IN SITU CONCRETE PATHS (1:2:4 MIX)

| | / | ⏱ | ₤ | ✋ | £ |
|---|---|---|---|---|---|
| Excavate 8″ (200 mm) deep by hand to remove soil and load into skip | 1 sq yd (1 sq m) | 0:50 (0:55) | – | 2 | – |
| Remove from site by skip | 0.27 cu yd (0.2 cu m) | – | 2.22 (2.16) | – | – |
| 4″ (100 mm) thick bed of hardcore blinded with sand | 1 sq yd (1 sq m) | 0:25 (0:30) | 0.90 (1.10) | 2 | – |
| 4″ (100 mm) thick bed of concrete trowelled smooth | 1 sq yd (1 sq m) | 0:35 (0:40) | 5.70 (6.80) | 4 | – |
| Formwork and supports to edge of path 4″ (100 mm) high | 2 yd (2 m) | 1:30 (1:40) | 1.40 (1.50) | 4 | – |
| per square yard per square metre | | 2:30 (2:50) | £10.22 (£11.56) | | £22.80 (£27.30) |

In this example it has been assumed that the concrete will be delivered ready mixed and the hours represent the time it will take you to barrow the concrete a distance not exceeding 30 yards including placing and trowelling.

# TARMACADAM PATHS

Laying tarmacadam paths is usually not carried out by DIY enthusiasts mainly because of the plant involved. The following prices are
those you would expect to pay a bona fide contractor. These prices
refer to black bitumen macadam laid on prepared surfaces. For red
bitumen macadam add approximately 50%.

| | |
|---|---|
| Bitumen macadam 70 mm thick in two coats consisting of 50 mm base course and 20 mm wearing course | 12.00 sq m |

# GRAVEL PATHS

The following prices assume the gravel in to be laid on a prepared
surface.

| | 📏 | 🕐 | £ | ✋ | £ |
|---|---|---|---|---|---|
| Gravel bed consisting of 19 mm stone in bed | | | | | |
| 40 mm thick | 1 sq yd | 0.03 | 0.65 | 2 | 1.10 |
| | (1 sq m) | (0.03) | (0.80) | | (1.30) |
| 60 mm thick | 1 sq yd | 0.03 | 1.00 | 2 | 1.50 |
| | (1 sq m) | (0.04) | (1.20) | | (1.80) |
| Gravel bed consisting of 38 mm stone in bed | | | | | |
| 50 mm thick | 1 sq yd | 0.04 | 0.65 | 2 | 1.10 |
| | (1 sq m) | (0.05) | (0.80) | | (1.30) |
| 70 mm thick | 1 sq yd | 0.05 | 1.00 | 2 | 1.50 |
| | (1 sq m) | (0.06) | (1.20) | | (1.80) |

# EDGINGS

Quite often a surface area is bounded by a pin kerb or brick edging
which both delineates a boundary and forms a pleasing feature.
Costings are presented below and it is assumed that the concrete
required for the beds and backings will be ready mixed delivered
within 30 yards of the place of work and that the small amount of
surplus excavated material will be disposed of in the garden area.

| | 📏 | 🕐 | ✂ | ✋ | £ |
|---|---|---|---|---|---|
| **Precast concrete** | | | | | |
| Excavate shallow trench size 12″×6″ (300×150 mm) deep | 1 yd (1 m) | 0:10 (0:12) | – | 2 | – |
| Concrete (1:3:6 mix in bed and backing to kerb) | 1 yd (1 m) | 0:20 (0:22) | 1.37 (1.50) | 2 | – |
| 6″×2″ (150×50 mm) Precast concrete pin kerb | 1 yd (1 m) | 0:35 (0:40) | 1.65 (1.80) | 5 | – |
| per linear yard per linear metre | | 1:05 (1:14) | £3.02 (£3.30) | | £11.50 (£12.60) |
| For different size edging use the following figures | | | | | |
| 8″×2″ (205×50 mm) | 1 yd (1 m) | 0:45 (0:50) | 2.00 (2.20) | 5 | – |
| 10″×2″ (205×50 mm) | 1 yd (1 m) | 0:55 (1:00) | 2.35 (2.55) | 5 | – |
| **Brick edgings** | | | | | |
| Excavate shallow trench size 9″×4″ (225×100 mm) deep | 1 yd (1 m) | 0:09 (0:10) | – | 2 | – |
| Concrete (1:3:6) mix in bed to brick kerb | 1 yd (1 m) | 0:20 (0:22) | 1.37 (1.50) | 2 | – |
| Brick-on-edge facing brick (£400 per thousand) bedded, jointed and pointed in cement mortar | 1 yd (1 m) | 0:36 (0:40) | 1.90 (2.10) | 5 | – |
| per linear yard per linear metre | | 1:05 (1:12) | £3.27 (£3.60) | | £8.70 (£9.50) |

If a more expensive brick is used add 20p per metre to the contractors price for every £50 per thousand over £400.

# FENCING

You have a wide choice of fencing that can be used to mark house boundaries and the erection should be well within the range of skills of the average DIY enthusiast. All the fencing quoted assumes that post holes (where applicable) have been dug by hand and that concrete is ready mixed and deposited within 30 yards of the place of working.

| | | | | | |
|---|---|---|---|---|---|
| **Existing work** | | | | | |
| Remove fencing and posts | | | | | |
| Chainlink fencing, height | | | | | |
| 4' (1200 mm) | 1 yd | 0:20 | – | 2 | 2.20 |
| | (1 m) | (0:22) | | | (2.40) |
| 6' (1800 mm) | 1 yd | 0:30 | – | 2 | 2.75 |
| | (1 m) | (0:35) | | | (3.00) |
| Close boarded timber fencing, height | | | | | |
| 4' (1200 mm) | 1 yd | 0:35 | – | 2 | 3.65 |
| | (1 m) | (0:40) | | | (4.00) |
| 6' (1800 mm) | 1 yd | 0:45 | – | 2 | 5.50 |
| | (1 m) | (0:50) | | | (6.00) |
| Chestnut pale wired fencing, height | | | | | |
| 3' (900 mm) | 1 yd | 0:15 | – | 2 | 1.80 |
| | (1 m) | (0:18) | | | (2.00) |
| 4' (1200 mm) | 1 yd | 0:20 | – | 2 | 2.20 |
| | (1 m) | (0:22) | | | (2.40) |
| **New work** | | | | | |
| Post and galvanised wire fencing | | | | | |
| 2 line | 1 yd | 0:05 | 0.28 | 4 | 1.10 |
| | (1 m) | (0:06) | (0.33) | | (1.20) |
| 3 line | 1 yd | 0:11 | 0.41 | 4 | 1.65 |
| | (1 m) | (0:12) | (0.45) | | (1.80) |
| 4 line | 1 yd | 0:16 | 0.55 | 4 | 2.30 |
| | (1 m) | (0:18) | (0.60) | | (2.50) |

# FENCING

| | / | 🕐 | £ | ✋ | £ |
|---|---|---|---|---|---|
| **Post and plastic coated wire fencing** | | | | | |
| 2 line | 1 yd | 0:05 | 0.18 | 4 | 1.00 |
| | (1 m) | (0:06) | (0.20) | | (1.10) |
| 3 line | 1 yd | 0:11 | 0.27 | 4 | 1.55 |
| | (1 m) | (0:12) | (0.30) | | (1.70) |
| 4 line | 1 yd | 0:16 | 0.37 | 4 | 2.10 |
| | (1 m) | (0:18) | (0.40) | | (2.30) |
| **Extra for pressure treated softwood posts with pointed end driven into ground, height** | | | | | |
| 5' (1.5 m) | 1 no | 0:20 | 3.30 | 4 | 6.00 |
| 6' (1.8 m) | 1 no | 0:25 | 3.80 | 4 | 6.30 |
| 7' (2.1 m) | 1 no | 0:30 | 4.25 | 4 | 7.60 |
| 8' (2.4 m) | 1 no | 0:35 | 4.50 | 4 | 8.00 |
| **Interwoven or waney lap panel fencing, height** | | | | | |
| 4' (1.2 m) | 1 yd | 0:23 | 7.75 | 5 | 11.00 |
| | 1 m) | (0:25) | (8.50) | | (12.00) |
| 5' (1.5 m) | 1 yd | 0:28 | 8.25 | 5 | 11.90 |
| | (1 m) | (0:30) | (9.00) | | (13.00) |
| 6' (1.8 m) | 1 yd | 0:32 | 8.70 | 5 | 12.80 |
| | (1 m) | (0:35) | (9.50) | | (14.00) |
| **Vertical close boarded timber fence fixed to two horizontal rails, height** | | | | | |
| 4' (1.2 m) | 1 yd | 0:35 | 10.50 | 5 | 14.60 |
| | (1 m) | (0:40) | (11.50) | | (16.00) |
| 5' (1.5 m) | 1 yd | 0:40 | 11.50 | 5 | 16.45 |
| | (1 m) | (0:45) | (12.50) | | (18.00) |
| 6' (1.8 m) | 1 yd | 0:45 | 12.35 | 5 | 18.30 |
| | (1 m) | (0:50) | (13.50) | | (20.00) |
| **Extra for pressure treated softwood posts set in concrete base, height** | | | | | |
| 5' (1.5 m) | 1 no | 0:50 | 6.80 | 5 | 15.50 |
| 6' (1.8 m) | 1 no | 0:50 | 7.30 | 5 | 16.00 |
| 7' (2.1 m) | 1 no | 1:00 | 7.75 | 5 | 18.00 |
| 8' (2.4 m) | 1 no | 1:00 | 8.00 | 5 | 18.00 |

| | 📏 | 🕐 | ⚖ | ✋ | £ |
|---|---|---|---|---|---|
| **Galvanised chainlink fencing, height** | | | | | |
| 3' (900 mm) | 1 yd | 0:14 | 4.10 | 5 | 6.40 |
| | (1 m) | (0:15) | (4.50) | | (7.00) |
| 4' (1.2 m) | 1 yd | 0:18 | 5.50 | 5 | 8.20 |
| | (1 m) | (0:20) | (6.00) | | (9.00) |
| 5' (1.5 m) | 1 yd | 0:23 | 5.95 | 5 | 10.00 |
| | (1 m) | (0:25) | (6.50) | | (11.00) |
| 6' (1.8 m) | 1 yd | 0:27 | 7.30 | 5 | 13.70 |
| | (1 m) | (0:30) | (8.00) | | (15.00) |
| **Plastic coated chainlink fencing, height** | | | | | |
| 3' (900 mm) | 1 yd | 0:14 | 3.66 | 5 | 5.95 |
| | (1 m) | (0:15) | (4.00) | | (6.50) |
| 4' (1.2 m) | 1 yd | 0:18 | 5.00 | 5 | 7.75 |
| | (1 m) | (0:20) | (5.50) | | (8.50) |
| 5' (1.5 m) | 1 yd | 0:23 | 5.95 | 5 | 9.60 |
| | (1 m) | (0:25) | (6.50) | | (10.50) |
| 6' (1.8 m) | 1 yd | 0:27 | 6.85 | 5 | 13.25 |
| | (1 m) | (0:30) | (7.50) | | (14.50) |
| **Extra for black coated angle iron posts set in concrete base, height** | | | | | |
| 5' (1.5 m) | 1 no | 0:20 | 8.00 | 5 | 12.00 |
| 6' (1.8 m) | 1 no | 0:25 | 9.50 | 5 | 14.00 |
| 7' (2.1 m) | 1 no | 0:30 | 11.00 | 5 | 16.00 |

**Don't forget, these prices may need adjustment depending on where you live.**
Regional adjustments are provided in the Introduction.

# DRAINAGE

Not many people have a clear idea of how their drainage system works. It is a good idea to lift the manhole covers, make a sketch of the bottom of the manhole and identify where the waste from each sink, WC, bath etc. enters the manhole. You can do this by running each tap individually and watch the flow.

The chances are that if you are going to suffer from a blocked drain it will happen on a cold dark night and having a sketch of the drainage layout can help enormously.

You can hire a set of drain rods for about £8 per day or £10 for a weekend but if you lay some new drains the following figures should help.

| | 📏 | 🕐 | £ | ✋ | £ |
|---|---|---|---|---|---|
| Excavate trench by hand, place excavated material to one side and refill trench later, depth | | | | | |
| 2'6" (750 mm) | 1 yd | 1:22 | – | 3 | 13.80 |
| | (1 m) | (1:30) | | | (15.00) |
| 3'0" (900 mm) | 1 yd | 1:50 | – | 3 | 18.30 |
| | (1 m) | (2:00) | | | (20.00) |
| 3'6" (1050 mm) | 1 yd | 2:20 | – | 3 | 22.80 |
| | (1 m) | (2:30) | | | (25.00) |
| 4'0" (1200 mm) | 1 yd | 2:45 | – | 3 | 27.50 |
| | (1 m) | (3:00) | | | (30.00) |
| Sand bed laid in trench under pipe, thickness | | | | | |
| 4" (100 mm) | 1 yd | 0:09 | 0.90 | 3 | 1.80 |
| | (1 m) | (0:10) | (1.00) | | (2.00) |
| 6" (150 mm) | 1 yd | 0:11 | 1.40 | 3 | 2.60 |
| | (1 m) | (0:12) | (1.50) | | (2.80) |
| Cement bed and surround to 4" (100 mm) pipe | 1 yd | 0:55 | 11.00 | 3 | 18.30 |
| | (1 m) | (1:00) | (12.00) | | (20.00) |
| Vitrified clay drain pipe 4" (100 mm) diameter, with spigot and socket joints and sealing rings, laid to falls | 1 yd | 0:27 | 2.30 | 5 | 6.90 |
| | (1 m) | (0:30) | (2.50) | | (7.50) |

| Extra for | ✎ | 🕐 | 💷 | 🖐 | £ |
|---|---|---|---|---|---|
| bend | 1 no | 0:20 | 3.00 | 5 | 6.50 |
| junction | 1 no | 0:20 | 6.30 | 5 | 10.00 |

## INSPECTION CHAMBERS

It is now possible to buy plastic pre-formed inspection chambers (small manholes). These chambers are available with many different main and side channel layouts in the bottom of the chamber, and they are designed to cover all domestic drainage requirements. The cost of materials excluding the excavation, concrete and cover should be between £50 and £120 depending upon size and depth.

---

**Don't forget, these prices may need adjustment depending on where you live.**
Regional adjustments are provided in the Introduction.

---

# PATIOS

Laying a patio can add a very attractive feature to your house. You can use a wide variety of materials and a selection of them have been included in the costings set out below. It is assumed that all the excavated material will be barrowed to a skip placed within 30 yards of the patio.

| | 📏 | 🕐 | 💷 | ✋ | £ |
|---|---|---|---|---|---|
| **Preparatory work** | | | | | |
| Excavate 6″ (150 mm) by hand to remove soil and load into skip | 1 sq yd (1 sq m) | 0:40 (0:45) | – | 2 | – |
| Remove from site by skip | 0.2 cu yd (0.15 cu m) | – | 1.24 (1.62) | – | – |
| 4″ (100 mm) thick bed of sand | 1 sq yd (1 sq m) | 0:20 (0:22) | 1.42 (1.70) | 2 | – |
| per square yard per square metre | | 1:00 (1:07) | 3.06 (£3.32) | | 5.45 (£6.52) |
| **Patio size 12′ × 9′ (3.66 × 2.75 m)** | | | | | |
| 2″ (50 mm) thick precast concrete natural colour flags, size | | | | | |
| 1′6″ × 1′6″ (450 × 450 mm) | 12 sq yd (10 sq m) | 20:00 (18:40) | 146.20 (142.00) | 5 | 230.00 (229.00) |
| 2′0″ × 1′6″ (600 × 450 mm) | 12 sq yd (10 sq m) | 19:00 (17:50) | 130.00 (126.00) | 5 | 194.00 (205.00) |
| 2′0″ × 2′0″ (600 × 600 mm) | 12 sq yd (10 sq m) | 18:00 (17:00) | 114.00 (110.00) | 5 | 185.00 (183.00) |
| 2′0″ × 3′0″ (600 × 900 mm) | 12 sq yd (10 sq m) | 17:00 (16:10) | 103.00 (99.00) | 5 | 171.00 (170.00) |

| | | | | | |
|---|---|---|---|---|---|
| 2" (50 mm) thick precast concrete coloured flags, size | | | | | |
| 1'6" × 1'6" | 12 sq yd | 20:00 | 173.20 | 5 | 261.00 |
| (450 × 450 mm) | (10 sq m) | (18:40) | (169.00) | | (260.00) |
| 2'0" × 1'6" | 12 sq yd | 19:00 | 152.00 | 5 | 236.00 |
| (600 × 450 mm) | (10 sq m) | (17:50) | (148.00) | | (235.00) |
| 2'0" × 2'0" | 12 sq yd | 18:00 | 129.00 | 5 | 208.00 |
| (600 × 600 mm) | (10 sq m) | (17:00) | (129.00) | | (207.00) |
| 2'0" × 3'0" | 12 sq yd | 17:00 | 119.00 | 5 | 188.00 |
| (600 × 900 mm) | (10 sq m) | (16:10) | (115.00) | | (187.00) |
| Concrete block paving size 8" × 4" × 2½" (200 × 100 × 65 mm) thick | | | | | |
| natural | 12 sq yd | 24:00 | 105.00 | 5 | 244.00 |
| | (10 sq m) | (22:00) | (101.00) | | (243.00) |
| coloured | 12 sq yd | 24:00 | 117.00 | 5 | 256.00 |
| | (10 sq m) | (22:00) | (114.00) | | (255.00) |
| multicoloured | 12 sq yd | 24:00 | 121.00 | 5 | 261.00 |
| | (10 sq m) | (22:00) | (116.70) | | (260.20) |
| Concrete block paving size 8" × 4" × 3" (200 × 100 × 80 mm) thick | | | | | |
| natural | 12 sq yd | 26:00 | 112.00 | 5 | 261.00 |
| | (10 sq m) | (23:40) | (108.00) | | (260.00) |
| coloured | 12 sq yd | 26:00 | 128.00 | 5 | 276.00 |
| | (10 sq m) | (23:40) | (124.00) | | (275.00) |
| multicoloured | 12 sq yd | 26:00 | 130.00 | 5 | 281.00 |
| | (10 sq m) | (23:40) | (126.70) | | (280.00) |

Don't forget, these prices may need adjustment
depending on where you live.
Regional adjustments are provided in the Introduction.

📏  🕐  ⚖  ✍  £

**Patio size 18′ × 9′
(5.5 × 2.75 m)**

2″ (50 mm) thick
precast concrete
natural colour flags,
size

| | | | | | |
|---|---|---|---|---|---|
| 1′6″ × 1′6″ | 18 sq yd | 30:00 | 219.00 | 5 | 345.00 |
| (450 × 450 mm) | (15 sq m) | (28:00) | (213.00) | | (343.00) |
| 2′0″ × 1′6″ | 18 sq yd | 27:30 | 195.00 | 5 | 291.00 |
| (600 × 450 mm) | (15 sq m) | (26:15) | (189.00) | | (307.00) |
| 2′0″ × 2′0″ | 18 sq yd | 27:00 | 171.00 | 5 | 277.00 |
| (600 × 600 mm) | (15 sq m) | (25:30) | (165.00) | | (255.00) |
| 2′0″ × 3′0″ | 18 sq yd | 25:30 | 155.00 | 5 | 257.00 |
| (600 × 900 mm) | (15 sq m) | (24:15) | (148.00) | | (255.00) |

2″ (50 mm) thick
precast concrete
coloured flags, size

| | | | | | |
|---|---|---|---|---|---|
| 1′6″ × 1′6″ | 18 sq yd | 30:00 | 260.00 | 5 | 391.00 |
| (450 × 450 mm) | (15 sq m) | (28:00) | (254.00) | | (390.00) |
| 2′0″ × 1′6″ | 18 sq yd | 28:50 | 228.00 | 5 | 354.00 |
| (600 × 450 mm) | (15 sq m) | (26:15) | (222.00) | | (353.00) |
| 2′0″ × 2′0″ | 18 sq yd | 27:00 | 193.00 | 5 | 312.00 |
| (600 × 600 mm) | (15 sq m) | (25:30) | (194.00) | | (311.00) |
| 2′0″ × 3′0″ | 18 sq yd | 25:30 | 178.00 | 5 | 276.00 |
| (600 × 900 mm) | (15 sq m) | (24:15) | (173.00) | | (280.00) |

Concrete block
paving size
8″ × 4″ × 2½″
(200 × 100 × 65 mm)
thick

| | | | | | |
|---|---|---|---|---|---|
| natural | 18 sq yd | 36:00 | 158.00 | 5 | 366.00 |
| | (15 sq m) | (33:00) | (152.00) | | (365.00) |
| coloured | 18 sq yd | 36:00 | 176.00 | 5 | 384.00 |
| | (15 sq m) | (33:00) | (171.00) | | (382.00) |
| multicoloured | 18 sq yd | 36:00 | 182.00 | 5 | 392.00 |
| | (15 sq m) | (33:00) | (174.70) | | (390.00) |

| | 📏 | 🕐 | 🧵 | ✋ | £ |
|---|---|---|---|---|---|
| **Concrete block paving size 8" × 4" × 3" (200 × 100 × 80 mm) thick** | | | | | |
| natural | 18 sq yd | 39:00 | 168.00 | 5 | 392.00 |
| | (15 sq m) | (35:00) | (162.00) | | (390.00) |
| coloured | 18 sq yd | 39:00 | 192.00 | 5 | 414.00 |
| | (15 sq m) | (35:40) | (186.00) | | (412.00) |
| multicoloured | 18 sq yd | 39:00 | 195.00 | 5 | 421.00 |
| | (15 sq m) | (35:00) | (189.00) | | (420.00) |
| **Patio size 24' × 9' (7.32 × 2.75 m)** | | | | | |
| **2" (50 mm) thick precast concrete natural colour flags, size** | | | | | |
| 1'6" × 1'6" | 24 sq yd | 40:00 | 292.00 | 5 | 460.00 |
| (450 × 450 mm) | (20 sq m) | (37:20) | (284.00) | | (458.00) |
| 2'0" × 1'6" | 24 sq yd | 38:00 | 260.00 | 5 | 388.00 |
| (600 × 450 mm) | (20 sq m) | (35:40) | (252.00) | | (410.00) |
| 2'0" × 2'0" | 24 sq yd | 36:00 | 228.00 | 5 | 370.00 |
| (600 × 600 mm) | (20 sq m) | (34:00) | (220.00) | | (365.00) |
| 2'0" × 3'0" | 24 sq yd | 34:00 | 205.00 | 5 | 342.00 |
| (600 × 900 mm) | (20 sq m) | (32:20) | (198.00) | | (340.00) |
| **2" (50 mm) thick precast concrete coloured flags, size** | | | | | |
| 1'6" × 1'6" | 24 sq yd | 40:00 | 347.00 | 5 | 522.00 |
| (450 × 450 mm) | (20 sq m) | (37:20) | (338.00) | | (520.00) |
| 2'0" × 1'6" | 24 sq yd | 38:00 | 304.00 | 5 | 472.00 |
| (600 × 450 mm) | (20 sq m) | (35:40) | (296.00) | | (470.00) |
| 2'0" × 2'0" | 24 sq yd | 36:00 | 265.00 | 5 | 416.00 |
| (600 × 600 mm) | (20 sq m) | (34:00) | (258.00) | | (414.00) |
| 2'0" × 3'0" | 24 sq yd | 34:00 | 238.00 | 5 | 376.00 |
| (600 × 900 mm) | (20 sq m) | (32:20) | (230.00) | | (374.00) |

|  | 📏 | 🕐 | 💰 | ✋ | £ |
|---|---|---|---|---|---|
| Concrete block paving size 8″ × 4″ × 2½″ (200 × 100 × 65 mm) thick | | | | | |
| natural | 24 sq yd | 48:00 | 210.00 | 5 | 488.00 |
| | (20 sq m) | (44:00) | (202.00) | | (486.00) |
| coloured | 24 sq yd | 48:00 | 234.00 | 5 | 512.00 |
| | (20 sq m) | (44:00) | (227.00) | | (511.00) |
| multicoloured | 24 sq yd | 48:00 | 241.00 | 5 | 519.00 |
| | (20 sq m) | (44:00) | (233.00) | | (517.00) |
| Concrete block paving size 8″ × 4″ × 3″ (200 × 100 × 80 mm) thick | | | | | |
| natural | 24 sq yd | 52:00 | 224.00 | 5 | 522.00 |
| | (20 sq m) | (47:00) | (216.00) | | (520.00) |
| coloured | 24 sq yd | 52:00 | 256.00 | 5 | 552.00 |
| | (20 sq m) | (47:00) | (248.00) | | (550.00) |
| multicoloured | 24 sq yd | 52:00 | 260.00 | 5 | 562.00 |
| | (20 sq m) | (47:20) | (252.00) | | (560.00) |
| **Patio size 24′ × 15′ (7.32 × 4.58 m)** | | | | | |
| 2″ (50 mm) thick precast concrete natural colour flags, size | | | | | |
| 1′6″ × 1′6″ | 40 sq yd | 51:00 | 486.00 | 5 | 766.00 |
| (450 × 450 mm) | (33 sq m) | (48:00) | (476.00) | | (770.00) |
| 2′0″ × 1′6″ | 40 sq yd | 47:00 | 433.00 | 5 | 646.00 |
| (600 × 450 mm) | (33 sq m) | (45:00) | (423.00) | | (639.00) |
| 2′0″ × 2′0″ | 40 sq yd | 44:00 | 380.00 | 5 | 617.00 |
| (600 × 600 mm) | (33 sq m) | (42:00) | (370.00) | | (610.00) |
| 2′0″ × 3′0″ | 40 sq yd | 41:00 | 342.00 | 5 | 570.00 |
| (600 × 900 mm) | (33 sq m) | (39:00) | (333.00) | | (564.00) |

Don't forget, these prices may need adjustment
depending on where you live.
Regional adjustments are provided in the Introduction.

| | | | | | |
|---|---|---|---|---|---|
| 2" (50 mm) thick precast concrete coloured flags, size | | | | | |
| 1'6" × 1'6" | 40 sq yd | 50:00 | 578.00 | 5 | 870.00 |
| (450 × 450 mm) | (33 sq m) | (47:00) | (568.00) | | (861.00) |
| 2'0" × 1'6" | 40 sq yd | 47:00 | 506.00 | 5 | 787.00 |
| (600 × 450 mm) | (33 sq m) | (45:00) | (498.00) | | (780.00) |
| 2'0" × 2'0" | 40 sq yd | 44:00 | 442.00 | 5 | 693.00 |
| (600 × 600 mm) | (33 sq m) | (42:00) | (433.00) | | (686.00) |
| 2'0" × 3'0" | 40 sq yd | 41:00 | 396.00 | 5 | 626.00 |
| (600 × 900 mm) | (33 sq m) | (39:00) | (386.00) | | (619.00) |
| Concrete block paving size 8" × 4" × 2½" (200 × 100 × 65 mm) thick | | | | | |
| natural | 40 sq yd | 80:00 | 350.00 | 5 | 812.00 |
| | (33 sq m) | (73:20) | (339.00) | | (804.00) |
| coloured | 40 sq yd | 80:00 | 390.00 | 5 | 853.00 |
| | (33 sq m) | (73:20) | (382.00) | | (850.00) |
| multicoloured | 40 sq yd | 80:00 | 402.00 | 5 | 870.00 |
| | (33 sq m) | (73:20) | (391.00) | | (867.00) |
| Concrete block paving size 8" × 4" × 3" (200 × 100 × 80 mm) thick | | | | | |
| natural | 40 sq yd | 86:40 | 375.00 | 5 | 870.00 |
| | (33 sq m) | (78:50) | (360.00) | | (866.00) |
| coloured | 40 sq yd | 86:40 | 427.00 | 5 | 932.00 |
| | (33 sq m) | (78:50) | (415.00) | | (923.00) |
| multicoloured | 40 sq yd | 86:40 | 435.00 | 5 | 945.00 |
| | (33 sq m) | (78:50) | (425.00) | | (935.00) |

**Don't forget, these prices may need adjustment depending on where you live.**
Regional adjustments are provided in the Introduction.

**Patio size 30′ × 15′
(9.15 × 4.57 m)**

2″ (50 mm) thick
precast concrete
natural colour flags,
size

| | | | | | |
|---|---|---|---|---|---|
| 1′6″ × 1′6″ | 50 sq yd | 63:20 | 608.00 | 5 | 958.00 |
| (450 × 450 mm) | (42 sq m) | (59:44) | (596.00) | | (962.00) |
| 2′0″ × 1′6″ | 50 sq yd | 59:10 | 542.00 | 5 | 808.00 |
| (600 × 450 mm) | (42 sq m) | (56:14) | (529.00) | | (861.00) |
| 2′0″ × 2′0″ | 50 sq yd | 55:00 | 475.00 | 5 | 771.00 |
| (600 × 600 mm) | (42 sq m) | (52:44) | (462.00) | | (766.00) |
| 2′0″ × 3′0″ | 50 sq yd | 50:50 | 427.00 | 5 | 712.00 |
| (600 × 900 mm) | (42 sq m) | (49:14) | (416.00) | | (714.00) |

2″ (50 mm) thick
precast concrete
coloured flags, size

| | | | | | |
|---|---|---|---|---|---|
| 1′6″ × 1′6″ | 50 sq yd | 63:20 | 723.00 | 5 | 1088.00 |
| (450 × 450 mm) | (42 sq m) | (59:44) | (710.00) | | (1092.00) |
| 2′0″ × 1′6″ | 50 sq yd | 59:10 | 633.00 | 5 | 984.00 |
| (600 × 450 mm) | (42 sq m) | (56:14) | (622.00) | | (987.00) |
| 2′0″ × 2′0″ | 50 sq yd | 55:00 | 552.00 | 5 | 866.00 |
| (600 × 600 mm) | (42 sq m) | (52:44) | (541.00) | | (869.00) |
| 2′0″ × 3′0″ | 50 sq yd | 50:50 | 495.00 | 5 | 783.00 |
| (600 × 900 mm) | (42 sq m) | (49:14) | (483.00) | | (785.00) |

Concrete block
paving size
8″ × 4″ × 2½″
(200 × 100 × 65 mm)
thick

| | | | | | |
|---|---|---|---|---|---|
| natural | 50 sq yd | 100:00 | 437.00 | 5 | 1016.00 |
| | (42 sq m) | (91:40) | (424.00) | | (1020.00) |
| coloured | 50 sq yd | 100:00 | 487.00 | 5 | 1166.00 |
| | (42 sq m) | (91:40) | (478.00) | | (1174.00) |
| multicoloured | 50 sq yd | 100:00 | 502.00 | 5 | 1171.00 |
| | (42 sq m) | (91:40) | (489.00) | | (1176.00) |

Concrete block
paving size
8″ × 4″ × 3″
(200 × 100 × 80 mm)
thick

| | | | | | |
|---|---|---|---|---|---|
| natural | 50 sq yd | 108:20 | 467.00 | 5 | 1087.00 |
| | (42 sq m) | (98:35) | (450.00) | | (1033.00) |
| coloured | 50 sq yd | 108:20 | 533.00 | 5 | 1150.00 |
| | (42 sq m) | (98:35) | (516.00) | | (1145.00) |
| multicoloured | 50 sq yd | 108:20 | 542.00 | 5 | 1171.00 |
| | (42 sq m) | (98:35) | (529.00) | | (1176.00) |

Don't forget, these prices may need adjustment
depending on where you live.
Regional adjustments are provided in the Introduction.

# WALLING

Brick or stone walling constructed in gardens usually acts as a demarcation line between different surfaces and/or levels. Information given in this section generally applies to walls up to 3 feet (approximately 1 metre) high. It is assumed that you will excavate by hand and that the surplus excavated material will be spread and levelled over the garden area and also that concrete is ready mixed and will be deposited within 30 yards of the place of work. The mortar is assumed to be mixed by hand at the point of use.

The comments at the front of the Paths and edgings section (see page 149) on the single entry in the contractor's price column also apply here.

| *Preparatory work* | | | | | |
|---|---|---|---|---|---|
| Excavate trench size 18″ × 9″ (450 × 225 mm) | 1 yd (1 m) | 0:20 (0:25) | – | 2 | – |
| Concrete (1:3:6 cement, sand, aggregate) in wall foundation | 1 yd (1 m) | 0:15 (0:20) | 5.50 (6.00) | 3 | – |
| per linear yard per linear metre | | 0:35 (0:45) | £3.35 (£4.00) | | £10.00 (£11.00) |

These costs should be added to the following figures for different kinds of walling to arrive at a composite rate per linear yard or metre for walling 1 yard or metre high as shown.

| **Walls in common bricks (£120 per 1000) in cement mortar** | | | | | |
|---|---|---|---|---|---|
| Half brick wall 4½″ (112 mm) thick, height | | | | | |
| 3′ (900 mm) | 1 yd (1 m) | 2:00 (2:10) | 9.50 (10.40) | 6 | 28.00 (30.50) |
| 4′ (1.2 m) | 1 yd (1 m) | 2:40 (3:00) | 12.65 (13.80) | 6 | 37.25 (40.60) |

| | / | 🕐 | 🪢 | ✋ | £ |
|---|---|---|---|---|---|
| One brick wall 9″ (225 mm) thick, height | | | | | |
| 3′ (900 mm) | 1 yd | 2:40 | 19.00 | 6 | 56.00 |
| | (1 m) | (3:00) | (20.70) | | (61.00) |
| 4′ (1.2 m) | 1 yd | 3:30 | 25.30 | 6 | 74.50 |
| | (1 m) | (3:50) | (27.60) | | (81.20) |
| 5′ (1.5 m) | 1 yd | 4:25 | 31.60 | 6 | 93.00 |
| | (1 m) | (4:50) | (34.50) | | (101.40) |
| 6′ (1.8 m) | 1 yd | 5:20 | 38.00 | 6 | 112.00 |
| | (1 m) | (5:50) | (41.40) | | (122.00) |

**Walls in common bricks (£130 per 1000) in cement mortar**

| | / | 🕐 | 🪢 | ✋ | £ |
|---|---|---|---|---|---|
| Half brick wall 4½″ (112 mm) thick, height | | | | | |
| 3′ (900 mm) | 1 yd | 2:00 | 10.30 | 6 | 29.50 |
| | (1 m) | (2:10) | (11.20) | | (32.20) |
| 4′ (1.2 m) | 1 yd | 2:40 | 13.40 | 6 | 39.00 |
| | (1 m) | (3:00) | (14.60) | | (42.50) |
| One brick wall 9″ (225 mm) thick, height | | | | | |
| 3′ (900 mm) | 1 yd | 2:40 | 20.60 | 6 | 57.50 |
| | (1 m) | (3:00) | (22.45) | | (62.70) |
| 4′ (1.2 m) | 1 yd | 3:30 | 27.40 | 6 | 77.00 |
| | (1 m) | (3:50) | (29.90) | | (83.90) |
| 5′ (1.5 m) | 1 yd | 4:25 | 34.25 | 6 | 96.00 |
| | (1 m) | (4:50) | (37.35) | | (106.60) |

**Walls in common bricks (£140 per 1000) in cement mortar**

| | / | 🕐 | 🪢 | ✋ | £ |
|---|---|---|---|---|---|
| Half brick wall 4½″ (112 mm) thick, height | | | | | |
| 3′ (900 mm) | 1 yd | 2:00 | 11.20 | 6 | 31.50 |
| | (1 m) | (2:10) | (12.20) | | (34.30) |
| 4′ (1.2 m) | 1 yd | 2:40 | 14.90 | 6 | 41.50 |
| | (1 m) | (3:00) | (16.25) | | (45.25) |
| 6′ (1.8 m) | 1 yd | 5:20 | 41.00 | 6 | 115.00 |
| | (1 m) | (5:50) | (44.70) | | (125.40) |

| | | ⏲ | £ | ✋ | £ |
|---|---|---|---|---|---|

**One brick wall 9″ (225 mm) thick**

| | | | | | |
|---|---|---|---|---|---|
| 3′ (900 mm) | 1 yd | 2:40 | 22.20 | 6 | 59.20 |
| | (1 m) | (3:00) | (24.20) | | (64.50) |
| 4′ (1.2 m) | 1 yd | 3:30 | 29.50 | 6 | 79.20 |
| | (1 m) | (3:50) | (32.20) | | (86.30) |
| 5′ (1.5 m) | 1 yd | 4:25 | 36.90 | 6 | 99.00 |
| | (1 m) | (4:50) | (40.20) | | (107.90) |
| 6′ (1.8 m) | 1 yd | 5:20 | 44.30 | 6 | 118.50 |
| | (1 m) | (5:50) | (48.30) | | (129.15) |

**Walls in facing bricks (£240 per 1000) in cement mortar**

Half brick wall 4½″ (112 mm) thick, height

| | | | | | |
|---|---|---|---|---|---|
| 3′ (900 mm) | 1 yd | 2:20 | 16.00 | 6 | 42.00 |
| | (1 m) | (2:30) | (17.44) | | (45.80) |
| 4′ (1.2 m) | 1 yd | 3:10 | 21.30 | 6 | 56.00 |
| | (1 m) | (3:30) | (23.30) | | (61.00) |

**One brick wall 9″ (225 mm) thick, height**

| | | | | | |
|---|---|---|---|---|---|
| 3′ (900 mm) | 1 yd | 3:00 | 32.00 | 6 | 74.00 |
| | (1 m) | (3:20) | (34.90) | | (80.70) |
| 4′ (1.2 m) | 1 yd | 4:00 | 42.60 | 6 | 98.50 |
| | (1 m) | (4:20) | (41.40) | | (107.40) |
| 5′ (1.5 m) | 1 yd | 5:00 | 53.20 | 6 | 123.00 |
| | (1 m) | (5:30) | (58.00) | | (134.20) |
| 6′ (1.8 m) | 1 yd | 6:00 | 63.80 | 6 | 148.00 |
| | (1 m) | (6:30) | (69.55) | | (161.30) |

**Walls in facing bricks (£300 per 1000) in cement mortar**

Half brick wall 4½″ (112 mm) thick, height

| | | | | | |
|---|---|---|---|---|---|
| 3′ (900 mm) | 1 yd | 2:20 | 20.00 | 6 | 46.00 |
| | (1 m) | (2:30) | (21.80) | | (50.15) |
| 4′ (1.2 m) | 1 yd | 3:10 | 26.60 | 6 | 61.20 |
| | (1 m) | (3:30) | (29.00) | | (66.70) |

| | / | ⏲ | ⚖ | ✊ | £ |
|---|---|---|---|---|---|
| One brick wall 9" (225 mm) thick, height | | | | | |
| 3' (900 mm) | 1 yd | 3:00 | 40.00 | 6 | 82.00 |
| | (1 m) | (3:20) | (43.69) | | (89.00) |
| 4' (1.2 m) | 1 yd | 4:00 | 53.20 | 6 | 109.00 |
| | (1 m) | (4:20) | (58.00) | | (118.80) |
| 5' (1.5 m) | 1 yd | 5:00 | 66.50 | 6 | 136.30 |
| | (1 m) | (5:30) | (72.50) | | (148.50) |
| 6' (1.8 m) | 1 yd | 6:00 | 79.80 | 6 | 163.60 |
| | (1 m) | (6:30) | (87.00) | | (178.30) |
| **Walls in facing bricks (£350 per 1000) in cement mortar** | | | | | |
| Half brick wall 4½" (112 mm) thick, height | | | | | |
| 3' (900 mm) | 1 yd | 2:20 | 23.50 | 6 | 50.00 |
| | (1 m) | (2:30) | (25.60) | | (54.50) |
| 4' (1.2 m) | 1 yd | 3:10 | 31.20 | 6 | 66.50 |
| | (1 m) | (3:30) | (34.40) | | (72.50) |
| One brick wall 9" (225 mm) thick, height | | | | | |
| 3' (900 mm) | 1 yd | 3:00 | 47.00 | 6 | 90.00 |
| | (1 m) | (3:20) | (51.25) | | (98.00) |
| 4' (1.2 m) | 1 yd | 4:00 | 65.50 | 6 | 120.50 |
| | (1 m) | (4:20) | (68.10) | | (131.00) |
| **Random rubble walling (£70 per tonne) laid dry** | | | | | |
| 1' (300 mm) thick, height | | | | | |
| 3' (900 mm) | 1 yd | 2:20 | 40.00 | 8 | 85.00 |
| | (1 m) | (3:20) | (43.60) | | (92.60) |
| 4' (1.2 m) | 1 yd | 4:00 | 53.20 | 8 | 113.00 |
| | (1 m) | (4:20) | (58.00) | | (123.20) |
| 5' (1.5 m) | 1 yd | 5:00 | 66.50 | 8 | 141.00 |
| | (1 m) | (5:30) | (72.50) | | (153.70) |

Don't forget, these prices may need adjustment
depending on where you live.
Regional adjustments are provided in the Introduction.

| | / | ⏰ | & | ✋ | £ |
|---|---|---|---|---|---|
| **1'6" (450 mm) thick, height** | | | | | |
| 3' (900 mm) | 1 yd | 3:30 | 60.00 | 8 | 105.00 |
| | (1 m) | (3:50) | (65.40) | | (114.50) |
| 4' (1.2 m) | 1 yd | 4:40 | 80.00 | 8 | 140.00 |
| | (1 m) | (5:10) | (87.20) | | (152.60) |
| 5' (1.5 m) | 1 yd | 5:50 | 100.00 | 8 | 175.00 |
| | (1 m) | (6:20) | (109.00) | | (190.00) |

## Random rubble walling (£70 per tonne) in cement mortar

| | / | ⏰ | & | ✋ | £ |
|---|---|---|---|---|---|
| **1' (300 mm) thick, height** | | | | | |
| 3' (900 mm) | 1 yd | 2:00 | 42.00 | 8 | 80.00 |
| | (1 m) | (2:10) | (45.70) | | (87.20) |
| 4' (1.2 m) | 1 yd | 2:40 | 55.90 | 8 | 106.00 |
| | (1 m) | (2:50) | (60.90) | | (115.50) |
| 5' (1.5 m) | 1 yd | 3:20 | 69.80 | 8 | 133.00 |
| | (1 m) | (3:00) | (76.00) | | (145.00) |
| **1'6" (450 mm) thick, height** | | | | | |
| 3' (900 mm) | 1 yd | 2:20 | 63.00 | 8 | 100.00 |
| | (1 m) | (2:30) | (68.70) | | (109.00) |
| 4' (1.2 m) | 1 yd | 3:10 | 83.80 | 8 | 133.00 |
| | (1 m) | (3:30) | (91.30) | | (145.00) |
| 5' (1.5 m) | 1 yd | 3:50 | 104.70 | 8 | 160.00 |
| | (1 m) | (4:10) | (114.10) | | (174.50) |

## Irregular coursed rubble walling (£70 per tonne) in cement mortar

| | / | ⏰ | & | ✋ | £ |
|---|---|---|---|---|---|
| **1' (300 mm) thick, height** | | | | | |
| 3' (900 mm) | 1 yd | 2:30 | 50.00 | 8 | 92.00 |
| | (1 m) | (2:45) | (54.50) | | (100.30) |
| 4' (1.2 m) | 1 yd | 3:20 | 66.50 | 8 | 122.30 |
| | (1 m) | (3:40) | (72.50) | | (133.30) |
| 5' (1.5 m) | 1 yd | 4:10 | 83.10 | 8 | 153.00 |
| | (1 m) | (4:30) | (90.60) | | (166.80) |

| | / | ⏱ | 💷 | ✋ | £ |
|---|---|---|---|---|---|
| **1'6" (450 mm) thick, height** | | | | | |
| 3' (900 mm) | 1 yd | 3:00 | 70.00 | 8 | 110.00 |
| | (1 m) | (3:20) | (76.30) | | (120.00) |
| 4' (1.2 m) | 1 yd | 4:00 | 93.00 | 8 | 146.30 |
| | (1 m) | (4:20) | (101.40) | | (160.00) |
| 5' (1.5 m) | 1 yd | 5:00 | 116.00 | 8 | 182.90 |
| | (1 m) | (5:30) | (126.50) | | (200.00) |
| **Coursed rubble walling (£70 per tonne) in cement mortar** | | | | | |
| **1' (300 mm) thick, height** | | | | | |
| 3' (900 mm) | 1 yd | 1:50 | 55.00 | 8 | 98.00 |
| | (1 m) | (2:00) | (60.00) | | (106.80) |
| 4' (1.2 m) | 1 yd | 2:20 | 73.00 | 8 | 130.00 |
| | (1 m) | (2:30) | (79.50) | | (141.70) |
| 5' (1.5 m) | 1 yd | 3:00 | 91.50 | 8 | 163.00 |
| | (1 m) | (3:20) | (100.00) | | (178.00) |
| **1'6" (450 mm) thick, height** | | | | | |
| 3' (900 mm) | 1 yd | 2:20 | 75.00 | 8 | 130.00 |
| | (1 m) | (2:30) | (82.00) | | (141.70) |
| 4' (1.2 m) | 1 yd | 3:10 | 100.00 | 8 | 173.00 |
| | (1 m) | (3:30) | (109.00) | | (188.50) |
| 5' (1.5 m) | 1 yd | 3:50 | 125.00 | 8 | 216.90 |
| | (1 m) | (4:10) | (136.25) | | (235.50) |

Don't forget, these prices may need adjustment
depending on where you live.
Regional adjustments are provided in the Introduction.

# ORNAMENTAL POOLS

There are two types of ornamental pools – preformed plastic and those you construct. The plastic type are so diverse in size and shape that it is not possible to include them – visit your local garden centre for the cost and add it to the excavation figures listed below.

You can easily construct an ornamental pool these days thanks to new techniques and materials that are available. Concrete and brickwork are no longer the only choices so the whole job can now be completed much quicker.

When designing your pool, remember to make part of the pool deeper than the rest, at least 450 mm (1 ft 6 in), so that the fish can survive when the pool is frozen over.

It is assumed that the excavation will be done by hand and the surplus excavated material will be placed in another part of the garden. If it is necessary to hire a skip you should use the costs as set out in 'Disposal of rubbish'.

| | | / | ① | & | ♍ | £ |
|---|---|---|---|---|---|---|
| Excavate and place surplus material within 15 yards distance | 1 cu yd (1 cu m) | 3:00 (3:45) | – | | 2 | 18.00 (22.50) |
| Butyl sheeting | 1 sq yd (1 sq m) | 0:02 (0:03) | 4.70 (5.70) | | 3 | 7.00 (8.00) |
| Coloured PVC sheeting standard single | 1 sq yd (1 sq m) | 0:02 (0:03) | 3.00 (2.60) | | 3 | 5.50 (6.20) |
| double sheet | 1 sq yd (1 sq m) | 0:03 (0:04) | 4.70 (5.60) | | 3 | 7.00 (8.20) |
| single sheet, heavy duty | 1 sq yd (1 sq m) | 0:03 (0:04) | 3.40 (4.10) | | 3 | 5.40 (6.50) |

Ornamental pools can be greatly enhanced by the strategic placing of jets, fountains and lighting. Here are some costings covering these items but excluding the length of cable from the pool to the power source. (GPH refers to gallons per hour.)

**Pumps**

| | | | | | |
|---|---|---|---|---|---|
| Bell jet 700 mm diameter and submersible pump 1200 GPH | 1 no | 0:15 | 265.00 | 4 | 300.00 |
| Bell jet 300 mm diameter and submersible pump 250 GPH | 1 no | 0:15 | 85.00 | 4 | 100.00 |
| Straight plume single jet and submersible pump 120 GPH | 1 no | 0:15 | 55.00 | 4 | 70.00 |

**Underwater floodlights**

| | | | | | |
|---|---|---|---|---|---|
| Plain white. 135 mm diameter × 75 mm deep, 50 W | 1 no | 0:20 | 225.00 | 4 | 250.00 |
| Plain white, 135 mm diameter × 65 mm deep, 25 W | 1 no | 0:20 | 110.00 | 4 | 130.00 |
| Coloured, filters | | | | | |
| blue or green | 1 no | 0:20 | 50.00 | 4 | 70.00 |
| yellow or red | 1 no | 0:20 | 70.00 | 4 | 90.00 |

# TOTAL PROJECT COSTS

This chapter lists the approximate costs of complete items of work, e.g. conservatories, swimming pools. The cost of the materials is stated together with the cost of the erection where it is carried out by a contractor. The comments made at the end of the Introduction about the relationship between the cost of this type of improvement and the increased value of the property should be studied carefully. Briefly, it is only worth having swimming pools, sun lounges and conservatories built if you are going to enjoy the facility yourself, because it is unlikely that you will be able to recover the whole of the capital cost on the sale of the house.

---

**Don't forget, these prices may need adjustment
depending on where you live.**
Regional adjustments are provided in the Introduction.

---

# EXTENSIONS

Building an extension to your home can be the easiest way of creating more living space without the harassment of moving. It is difficult to produce accurate square foot prices for the cost of construction because of wide variations in the quality of materials available. However, for a brick built, flat roof extension constructed in traditional materials a guide figure of £50 to £55 per square foot could be used. This is based upon the most popular size extension of 12 ft × 8 ft and the figures quoted would increase per square foot if the area was smaller and decrease if the area was larger.

If the extension is two storey you should add the areas of both floors together to make the calculation.

## CONSERVATORIES AND SUN LOUNGES

There is a profusion of firms supplying and installing conservatories these days and they all seem to have special offers and sales for most of the time! If you are considering building a conservatory you should use a supplier or erector who is a member of The Conservatory Association, 2nd Floor, Godwin House George Street, Huntington, Cambs. PE18 6BU (Telephone 0480 458278). They produce a free booklet called 'Choosing a Conservatory' which you can obtain by calling the above telephone number. You will also be sent brochures from their members in your area. Stand by for a deluge!

The prices below represent an average of several firms' offers and should be regarded an indicative only. The prices include VAT but exclude the cost of the concrete base.

If the base is laid by a builder it should cost you about £42 sq yd (approximately £50 sq m). If you laid the base yourself the materials should cost about £12.50 sq yd (£15 sq m) and take about 2½ hours per sq yd (3 hours per sq m).

It is assumed in these figures that there are no complications with the existing drains or services and no other obstructions on the site of the conservatory that would have cost or time implications.

# CONSERVATORIES AND SUN LOUNGES

|  | Supply only £ | Supply and erect £ |
|---|---|---|
| Lean-to-conservatory in aluminium, glazed full height on prepared base, size | | |
| 10′ × 8′ (3 × 2.4 m) | 2,800 | 3,100 |
| 12′ × 8′ (3.6 × 2.4 m) | 3,000 | 3,350 |
| 14′ × 8′ (4.2 × 2.4 m) | 3,200 | 3,700 |
| Hipped roof conservatory in aluminium, glazed full height on prepared base, size | | |
| 10′ × 8′ (3 × 2.4 m) | 3,100 | 3,400 |
| 12′ × 8′ (3.6 × 2.4 m) | 3,300 | 3,650 |
| 14′ × 8′ (4.2 × 2.4 m) | 3,500 | 4,000 |
| 'Victorian' type conservatory in stained hardwood, glazed full height on prepared base | | |
| 11′ × 10′ (3.3 × 3 m) | 3.300 | 3,600 |
| 11′ × 12′ (3.3 × 3.6 m) | 4,000 | 4,400 |
| 11′ × 14′ (3.3 × 4.2 m) | 4,800 | 5,500 |

Don't forget, these prices may need adjustment
depending on where you live.
Regional adjustments are provided in the Introduction.

# GREENHOUSES

There are two main types of greenhouses – cedar or aluminium, and each can be sub-divided into free-standing or lean-to against an existing building. The following prices which include VAT represent the cost of a basic greenhouse including glass and a list of accessories is given at the end of this section.

If you need a concrete base for the greenhouse and if it is laid by a builder it should cost about £15 sq yd (£18 sq m). If you lay the base yourself it should cost about £6.50 sq yd (£8 sq m) for the materials and take about 1 hour 40 minutes per sq yd (2 hours per sq m).

| | Supplied only £ | Supplied and erected £ |
|---|---|---|
| **Cedar, free standing including base, size** | | |
| 6′ × 6′ (1.8 × 1.8 m) | 600 | 680 |
| 6′ × 8′ (1.8 × 2.4 m) | 680 | 760 |
| 6′ × 10′ (1.8 × 3 m) | 750 | 850 |
| 6′ × 12′ (1.8 × 3.6 m) | 880 | 980 |
| 8′ × 8′ (2.4 × 2.4 m) | 780 | 880 |
| 8′ × 10′ (2.4 × 3 m) | 950 | 1,050 |
| 8′ × 12′ (2.4 × 3.6 m) | 1,100 | 1,220 |
| 8′ × 14′ (2.4 × 4.2 m) | 1,150 | 1,270 |
| 8′ × 16′ (2.4 × 4.8 m) | 1,320 | 1,470 |
| 10′ × 10′ (3 × 3 m) | 1,050 | 1,170 |
| 10′ × 12′ (3 × 3.6 m) | 1,220 | 1,350 |
| 10′ × 14′ (3 × 4.2 m) | 1,350 | 1,500 |
| 10′ × 16′ (3 × 4.8 m) | 1,500 | 1,650 |
| 10′ × 18′ (3 × 5.4 m) | 1,650 | 1,800 |
| 10′ × 20′ (3 × 6 m) | 1,750 | 1,900 |
| **Cedar, lean-to including base size** | | |
| 5′ × 8′ (1.5 × 2.4 m) | 620 | 700 |
| 5′ × 10′ (1.5 × 3 m) | 700 | 800 |
| 5′ × 12′ (1.5 × 3.6 m) | 780 | 880 |
| 6′ × 6′ (1.8 × 1.8 m) | 600 | 680 |
| 6′ × 8′ (1.8 × 2.4 m) | 680 | 760 |
| 6′ × 10′ (1.8 × 3 m) | 720 | 820 |
| 6′ × 12′ (1.8 × 3.6 m) | 680 | 880 |

| | Supplied only £ | Supplied and erected £ |
|---|---|---|
| Aluminium, free-standing, size | | |
| 6'×4' (1.8×1.2 m) | 250 | 300 |
| 6'×6' (1.8×1.8 m) | 280 | 320 |
| 6'×8' (1.8×2.4 m) | 300 | 360 |
| 6'×10' (1.8×3 m) | 340 | 400 |
| 6'×12' (1.8×3.6 m) | 430 | 520 |
| 8'×6' (2.4×1.8 m) | 380 | 440 |
| 8'×8' (2.4×2.4 m) | 450 | 530 |
| 8'×10' (2.4×3 m) | 500 | 580 |
| 8'×12' (2.4×3.6 m) | 550 | 630 |
| | | |
| Aluminium, lean-to size | | |
| 6'×6' (1.8×1.8 m) | 370 | 530 |
| 6'×8' (1.8×2.4 m) | 430 | 600 |
| 6'×10' (1.8×3 m) | 500 | 655 |
| 8'×10' (2.4×3 m) | 580 | 780 |
| 8'×12' (2.4×3.6 m) | 640 | 850 |

| **Accessories** | Cedar £ | Aluminium £ |
|---|---|---|
| Staging (per ft) | 7 | 8 |
| Shelving (per ft) | 5 | 5 |
| Automatic vent opener (each) | 25 | 22 |
| Roof vent (each) | 25 | 22 |
| Extra door (each) | 100 | 60 |

**Don't forget, these prices may need adjustment depending on where you live.**
Regional adjustments are provided in the Introduction.

# SWIMMING POOLS

There are two types of swimming pools. Firstly, the type with a preformed lining which arrives in sections and is welded together on site and placed in the prepared excavation. Secondly, the type which is constructed on site in concrete and blockwork. There are many firms in this very competitive business and you will almost certainly obtain a good discount if you shop around.

Some firms will supply the pools in kit form for you to construct and this is well within the capability of a DIY enthusiast although you probably need to sub-contract the excavation and may need the help of a plumber to instal the filtration equipment.

The following prices exclude the cost of the excavation (a contractor should charge you about £10–£12 per cubic metre for excavation and disposal, providing the ground is clay and the access is not difficult), and the connection of electricity from the mains, pool heating or covers. These prices are for the supply and installation of the pool and include VAT.

Remember you can have irregular shaped pools for between 5% and 10% extra of the equivalent size rectangular pool.

| Size of pool | £ |
|---|---|
| 20′ × 10′ (6 × 3 m) | 11,000–13,000 |
| 23′ × 12′ (7 × 3.5 m) | 12,500–14,000 |
| 26′ × 13′ (8 × 4 m) | 14,000–16,000 |
| 30′ × 15′ (9 × 4.5 m) | 15,500–17,500 |
| 33′ × 16′ (10 × 5 m) | 17,500–19,500 |
| 40′ × 20′ (12 × 6 m) | 21,000–24,000 |

**Don't forget, these prices may need adjustment depending on where you live.**
Regional adjustments are provided in the Introduction.

# HIRING PLANT

The success of carrying out do-it-yourself jobs depends upon having the right tools and equipment. Most householders own standard tools such as hammers, screwdrivers and chisels but there is a wide range of other tools which may only be needed every couple of years or so. You would be foolish to buy equipment and tools for these occasional needs and the answer lies in hiring them.

The following comprehensive list of plant, tools and equipment for domestic use is based upon information kindly supplied by Hire Service Shops (HSS), 23 Willow Lane, Mitcham, Surrey, CR4 4TS who have over 160 shops all over the country. It should be noted that although the prices are correct at the time of going to press, there may have been an increase since then. The price *excludes* VAT and any delivery charges.

## FIXING, GRINDING AND SANDING

|  | First 24 hrs £ | Addit. 24 hrs £ | Per week £ |
|---|---|---|---|
| Cartridge hammer | 13.00 | 6.50 | 26.00 |
| Staple tacker, light duty | 4.00 | 2.00 | 8.00 |
| Hammer stapler | 9.50 | 4.75 | 19.00 |
| Impact wrench, electric | 11.00 | 5.50 | 22.00 |
| Screwdriver, electric | 8.50 | 4.25 | 17.00 |

## ACCESS AND SUPPORT

| | First 24 hrs £ | Addit. 24 hrs £ | Per week £ |
|---|---|---|---|
| Span tower base size 4'3" × 5'0" (1.3 × 1.5 m), height | | | |
| 8'3" (2.5 m) | 25.00 | 12.50 | 50.00 |
| 15'0" (4.5 m) | 36.00 | 18.00 | 72.00 |
| 21'6" (6.5 m) | 47.00 | 23.50 | 96.00 |
| 28'0" (8.5 m) | 58.00 | 29.00 | 116.00 |
| 34'6" (10.5 m) | 69.00 | 34.50 | 138.00 |
| Add extra 3'0" (1 m) | 5.50 | 2.75 | 11.00 |
| Span tower base size 4'3" × 8'3" (1.3 × 2.5 m), height | | | |
| 8'3" (2.5 m) | 25.00 | 12.50 | 50.00 |
| 15'0" (4.5 m) | 36.00 | 18.00 | 72.00 |
| 21'6" (6.5 m) | 47.00 | 23.50 | 96.00 |
| 28'0" (8.5 m) | 58.00 | 29.00 | 116.00 |
| 34'6" (10.5 m) | 69.00 | 34.50 | 138.00 |
| Add extra 3'0" (1 m) | 5.50 | 2.75 | 11.00 |
| Narrow span towers base size 2'8" × 5'0" (0.8 × 1.5 m) | | | |
| 8'3" (2.5 m) | 25.00 | 12.50 | 50.00 |
| 15'0" (4.5 m) | 36.00 | 18.00 | 72.00 |
| 21'6" (6.5 m) | 47.00 | 23.50 | 94.00 |
| 28'0" (8.5 m) | 58.00 | 29.00 | 116.00 |
| 34'6" (10.5 m) | 69.00 | 34.50 | 138.00 |
| Add extra 3'0" (1 m) | 5.50 | 2.75 | 11.00 |
| Narrow span tower base size 2'8" × 8'3" (0.8 × 2.5 m) | | | |
| 8'3" (2.5 m) | 25.00 | 12.50 | 50.00 |
| 15'0" (4.5 m) | 36.00 | 18.00 | 72.00 |
| 21'6" (6.5 m) | 47.00 | 23.50 | 94.00 |
| 28'0" (8.5 m) | 58.00 | 29.00 | 116.00 |
| 34'6" (10.5 m) | 69.00 | 34.50 | 138.00 |
| Add extra 3'0" (1 m) | 5.50 | 2.75 | 11.00 |
| Alloy chimney scaffold unit half chimney surround unit | 39.50 | 19.75 | 79.00 |
| Lightweight staging length | | | |
| 8'0" (2.4 m) | 6.50 | 3.25 | 13.00 |
| 10'0" (3.0 m) | 7.50 | 3.75 | 15.00 |
| 12'0" (3.6 m) | 8.50 | 4.25 | 17.00 |
| 13'9" (4.2 m) | 9.50 | 4.75 | 19.00 |

| | First 24 hrs £ | Addit. 24 hrs £ | Per week £ |
|---|---|---|---|
| 15'9" (4.8 m) | 11.00 | 5.50 | 22.00 |
| 19'9" (6.0 m) | 13.00 | 6.50 | 26.00 |
| 23'6" (7.2 m) | 17.00 | 8.50 | 34.00 |
| **Decorators trestles, height** | | | |
| 4'6" (1.4 m) | 6.00 | 3.00 | 12.00 |
| 8'0" (2.4 m) | 7.00 | 3.50 | 14.00 |
| 10'0" (3.0 m) | 8.00 | 4.00 | 16.00 |
| 12'0" (3.6 m) | 9.00 | 4.50 | 18.00 |
| **Alloy ladders** | | | |
| double 3.5 m extending to 6.2 m | 7.50 | 3.75 | 15.00 |
| double 5.0 m extending to 9.0 m | 10.50 | 5.25 | 21.00 |
| treble 2.5 m extending to 6.0 m | 7.50 | 3.75 | 15.40 |
| treble 3.5 m extending to 9.1 m | 10.50 | 5.25 | 21.00 |
| **Roof ladders** | | | |
| Alloy and wooden 4.9 m, 5.9 m and 6.9 m | 11.50 | 5.75 | 23.00 |
| Ladder stay (each) | 3.50 | 1.25 | 7.00 |
| **Builder's steps** | | | |
| 8 tread, height 1.5 m | 6.50 | 3.25 | 13.00 |
| 10 tread, height 2.1 m | 7.50 | 3.75 | 15.00 |
| 12 tread, height 2.7 m | 8.50 | 4.25 | 17.00 |
| **Steel trestles, nos 1 to 4** | | | |
| 0.5 m extending to 2.4 m | – | – | 2.60 |
| **Jackall props** | 6.00 | 3.00 | 12.00 |
| **Steel props (for hire between 1 and 9 weeks, per week)** | | | |
| No 0 | – | – | 3.00 |
| No 1 | – | – | 3.00 |
| No 3 | – | – | 3.00 |
| No 4 | – | – | 3.00 |
| **Steel props (for hire between 10 and 49 weeks, per week)** | | | |
| No 0 | – | – | 2.40 |
| No 1 | – | – | 2.40 |
| No 3 | – | – | 2.40 |
| No 4 | – | – | 2.40 |
| **Strongboy wall prop** | 3.00 | 1.50 | 6.00 |
| **Scaffold boards, length 2.4 m to 3.9 m** | – | – | 1.55 |

## LIGHTING, WELDING AND POWER

|  | First 24 hrs £ | Addit. 24 hrs £ | Per week £ |
|---|---|---|---|
| **Generators** | | | |
| Petrol, 110/240 volt | | | |
| 3.0 KVA | 28.00 | 14.00 | 56.00 |
| Diesel, 110/240 volt | | | |
| 4.0 kVA | 35.00 | 17.50 | 65.70 |
| 8.0 kVA | 53.00 | 26.50 | 106.00 |
| 15.0 kVA | 71.00 | 35.50 | 142.00 |
| **Transformers** | | | |
| 2.2 kVA | 4.20 | 2.10 | 8.40 |
| 3.0 kVA | 6.40 | 3.20 | 12.80 |
| 5.0 kVA | 8.00 | 4.00 | 16.00 |
| 7.5 kVA | 11.80 | 5.90 | 23.60 |
| 10–15 kVA | 20.00 | 10.00 | 40.00 |
| Extension leads length 50' (15 m) | | | |
| 240 V | 3.40 | 1.70 | 6.80 |
| 110 V | 3.40 | 1.70 | 6.80 |
| Fourway junction box | 5.80 | 2.90 | 11.60 |
| Power breakers | | | |
| RCD 240 V | 1.80 | 0.90 | 3.60 |
| Heavy duty | 2.50 | 1.25 | 5.00 |
| **Floodlights** | | | |
| Gas | | | |
| tripod mounted 240 W | 7.00 | 3.50 | 14.00 |
| tripod mounted, propane | 9.00 | 4.50 | 18.00 |
| Festoon lights industrial | 9.00 | 4.50 | 18.00 |
| Twin 500 W flood 5 m tower mast | 13.00 | 6.50 | 24.00 |
| **Welding** | | | |
| Site welder, petrol 20–170 amp | 37.00 | 18.50 | 74.00 |
| Welder/generator, d.c. diesel | | | |
| 180 amp | 44.00 | 22.00 | 88.00 |
| 300 amp, silenced | 71.50 | 35.75 | 143.00 |
| Arc welder, 240 volt 140/180 amp | 14.00 | 7.00 | 28.00 |
| Oxyacetylene welding kit | 21.00 | 10.50 | 42.00 |
| MIG welder, 240 volt | 14.00 | 7.00 | 28.00 |
| Spot welder, 240 volt (30 amp) | 14.00 | 7.00 | 28.00 |

# CONCRETING AND COMPACTION

|  | First 24 hrs £ | Addit. 24 hrs £ | Per week £ |
|---|---|---|---|
| Concrete mixers |  |  |  |
| 6/4 cu ft diesel | 17.00 | 8.50 | 34.00 |
| 4/3 cu ft (½ bag), petrol | 7.50 | 3.75 | 15.00 |
| 4/3 cu ft (½ bag), electric | 7.50 | 3.75 | 15.00 |
| Concrete power finishing trowel, petrol | 26.00 | 13.00 | 52.00 |
| Poker vibrator |  |  |  |
| electric | 22.00 | 11.00 | 44.00 |
| petrol | 25.50 | 12.50 | 50.00 |
| Floor grinder, |  |  |  |
| diesel | 42.00 | 21.00 | 84.00 |
| electric | 42.00 | 21.00 | 84.00 |
| Floor saw, diesel |  |  |  |
| 350 mm | 29.00 | 14.50 | 58.00 |
| 450 mm | 39.00 | 19.75 | 79.00 |
| Surface scaler/roof dechipper | 65.00 | 15.00 | 95.00 |
| Needle gun, scaler, air driven | 10.00 | 5.00 | 20.00 |
| Indent roller | 5.00 | 2.50 | 10.00 |
| Scaler/scabbler |  |  |  |
| long reach | 10.00 | 5.00 | 20.00 |
| single head | 10.00 | 5.00 | 20.00 |
| triple head | 14.50 | 7.25 | 29.00 |
| **Compactors** |  |  |  |
| Compactor, 2 stroke, petrol | 24.00 | 12.00 | 48.00 |
| Vibrating plate |  |  |  |
| petrol, 450 × 450 mm | 25.00 | 12.50 | 50.00 |
| petrol, 305 × 405 mm | 19.00 | 9.50 | 50.00 |
| Vibrating roller, diesel/petrol |  |  |  |
| medium duty | 41.00 | 20.50 | 82.00 |
| light duty | 36.00 | 18.00 | 72.00 |

## PLUMBING/PUMPING/DRAIN CLEARING

| | First 24 hrs £ | Addit. 24 hrs £ | Per week £ |
|---|---|---|---|
| **Water pumps** | | | |
| Submersible | | | |
| 25 mm, electric | 9.00 | 4.50 | 18.00 |
| 32 mm, electric | 12.00 | 6.00 | 24.00 |
| 50 mm, petrol | 21.00 | 10.50 | 42.00 |
| Centrifugal, petrol | | | |
| 50 mm | 25.00 | 12.50 | 50.00 |
| 75 mm | 27.00 | 13.50 | 54.00 |
| **Drain testing/clearing tools** | | | |
| Drain test kit 'U' gauge | 5.00 | 2.50 | 10.00 |
| Air bag drain stopper | 4.20 | 2.10 | 8.40 |
| Drain plugs 100–150 mm | 2.20 | 1.10 | 4.40 |
| Drain rods and fittings 9 m (per set) | 6.50 | 3.25 | 13.00 |
| Sink cleaner, hand operated | 6.50 | 3.25 | 13.00 |
| Drain cleaner, hand operated | 9.00 | 4.50 | 18.00 |
| Powered drain cleaner, electric | 27.00 | 13.50 | 54.00 |
| **Plumber's tools** | | | |
| Blowlamp | 4.60 | 2.30 | 9.20 |
| Pipe freezing kit, $CO_2$ | 16.50 | 8.25 | 33.00 |
| Steel pipe bender, hydraulic | 25.00 | 12.50 | 50.00 |
| Copper pipe bender | | | |
| hand | 5.50 | 2.75 | 11.00 |
| large | 13.00 | 6.50 | 26.00 |
| Clay pipe cutter | 10.00 | 5.00 | 20.00 |
| Pipe wrenches | | | |
| stillson 450 mm | 3.20 | 1.60 | 6.40 |
| stillson 600 mm | 4.40 | 2.20 | 8.80 |
| stillson 900 mm | 5.60 | 2.80 | 11.20 |
| chain | 6.50 | 3.25 | 13.00 |
| Die stock | | | |
| electric | 29.50 | 14.75 | 59.00 |
| ratchet | 11.00 | 5.50 | 22.00 |
| Pipe threading machine, electric | | | |
| ½"–4" | 57.00 | 28.50 | 114.00 |
| ½"–3" | 49.00 | 24.50 | 98.00 |
| Pipe pressure tester | 11.00 | 5.50 | 22.00 |

# BUILDING AND DECORATING

|  | First 24 hrs £ | Addit. 24 hrs £ | Per week £ |
|---|---|---|---|
| Damp proof injection unit | 22.00 | 11.00 | 44.00 |
| Wallpaper steam strippers, gas/electric | 7.50 | 3.75 | 15.00 |
| Wallpaper perforator | 1.50 | 0.75 | 3.00 |
| Bitumen boiler | 17.00 | 8.50 | 34.00 |
| Metal detector | 9.00 | 4.50 | 18.00 |
| Cable avoiding tool | 25.00 | 12.50 | 50.00 |
| CAT signal generator | 15.00 | 7.50 | 30.00 |

# BUILDING/DECORATING TOOLS

|  | First 24 hrs £ | Addit. 24 hrs £ | Per week £ |
|---|---|---|---|
| Blowlamp with extension hose | 4.60 | 2.30 | 9.20 |
| Bolt croppers | 5.00 | 2.30 | 10.00 |
| Crowbar | 2.50 | 1.25 | 5.00 |
| Floorboard cramps | 3.00 | 1.50 | 6.00 |
| G clamps | 2.00 | 1.00 | 4.00 |
| Paving mallet | 2.50 | 1.25 | 5.00 |
| Pickaxe/matlock | 2.50 | 1.25 | 5.00 |
| Punner | 2.50 | 1.25 | 5.00 |
| Sash clamps | 2.00 | 1.00 | 4.00 |
| Shovel/spade | 2.50 | 1.25 | 5.00 |
| Sledgehammer 3 kg and 6.5 kg | 2.50 | 1.25 | 5.00 |
| Spirit level | 2.50 | 1.25 | 5.00 |
| Tarpaulins | 5.00 | 2.50 | 10.00 |
| Tyrolean roughcast machine | 5.00 | 2.50 | 10.00 |
| Wheelbarrow | 2.60 | 1.30 | 5.20 |
| Workmate | 5.00 | 2.50 | 10.00 |

## HEATING/COOLING/DRYING

|  | First 24 hrs £ | Addit. 24 hrs £ | Per week £ |
|---|---|---|---|
| **Industrial heaters, gas** | | | |
| Plaque heater 9500 Btu | 7.50 | 3.75 | 15.00 |
| Forced air, 30–125,000 Btu | 21.00 | 10.50 | 42.00 |
| Forced air, 108–250,000 Btu | 29.00 | 14.50 | 58.00 |
| **Industrial heaters, paraffin** | | | |
| Forced air, 60,000 Btu | 19.00 | 9.50 | 38.00 |
| Forced air, 100,000 Btu | 21.00 | 10.50 | 42.00 |
| Forced air, 160,000 Btu | 29.00 | 14.50 | 58.00 |
| **Home/office heaters** | | | |
| Cabinet, gas 3–16,000 Btu/hr | 7.00 | 3.50 | 14.00 |
| Electric fan heater, 3 kW | 4.00 | 2.00 | 8.00 |
| **Cooling** | | | |
| Space cooler | 37.00 | 18.50 | 74.00 |
| Air conditioning unit | 41.00 | 20.50 | 82.00 |
| **Drying** | | | |
| Building dryer, dehumidifier, industrial | 27.50 | 13.75 | 55.00 |
| Portable building dryer, 140m$^3$ | 17.00 | 8.50 | 34.00 |
| Portable fume extractor | 31.00 | 15.50 | 62.00 |

## PAINT SPRAYING AND BLASTING

|  | First 24 hrs £ | Addit. 24 hrs £ | Per week £ |
|---|---|---|---|
| **Spray units** | | | |
| Heavy duty airless | 65.00 | 32.50 | 130.00 |
| Medium duty airless | 50.00 | 25.00 | 100.00 |
| Easy spray portable | 18.00 | 9.00 | 36.00 |
| Compressors and gravity feed gun system | 38.00 | 19.00 | 76.00 |
| Small cellulose spray | 18.50 | 9.25 | 37.00 |

## ROAD HAZARD EQUIPMENT

|  | First 24 hrs £ | Addit. 24 hrs £ | Per week £ |
|---|---|---|---|
| Traffic warning cones | – | – | 2.75 |
| Road warning lamps, battery | – | – | 4.00 |
| Flashing lamp and stand, battery | – | – | 4.00 |
| Road signs | – | – | 7.50 |
| Road barrier, and cone cap | – | – | 2.75 |

## BREAKING AND DRILLING

|  | First 24 hrs £ | Addit. 24 hrs £ | Per week £ |
|---|---|---|---|
| **Breakers** | | | |
| heavy duty, diesel | 47.00 | 23.50 | 94.00 |
| medium duty petrol | 37.50 | 18.75 | 75.00 |
| heavy duty, electric | 27.50 | 13.75 | 55.00 |
| **Electric hammers** | | | |
| heavy duty, 2200 W | 27.50 | 13.75 | 55.00 |
| medium duty | 11.00 | 5.50 | 22.00 |
| **Rotary hammers** | | | |
| medium duty | 11.00 | 5.50 | 22.00 |
| light duty | 10.00 | 5.00 | 20.00 |
| **Hammer drills** | | | |
| heavy duty | 14.00 | 7.10 | 28.00 |
| medium duty | 12.50 | 6.25 | 25.00 |
| **Electric drills** | | | |
| Two speed | 5.50 | 2.75 | 11.00 |
| Right angle drill | 12.00 | 6.00 | 24.00 |
| Cordless drill | 9.00 | 4.50 | 18.00 |
| Four speed drill | 12.00 | 6.00 | 24.00 |
| Cordless drill | 12.00 | 6.00 | 24.00 |
| **Magnetic base drills** | | | |
| Magnetic drill stand (drill extra) | 22.00 | 11.00 | 44.00 |

189

# SAWING AND CUTTING

| | First 24 hrs £ | Addit. 24 hrs £ | Per week £ |
|---|---|---|---|
| **Metal/masonry saw benches** | | | |
| Masonry saw bench, petrol | 40.00 | 20.00 | 80.00 |
| Masonry saw bench, electric | 36.50 | 18.25 | 73.00 |
| Bench top cut off saw | 22.00 | 11.00 | 44.00 |
| Tile saw | 26.00 | 13.00 | 52.00 |
| **Timber saw benches** | | | |
| Combination bench 200 mm | 25.00 | 12.50 | 50.00 |
| **Floor saw** | | | |
| Track/floor saw 450 mm | 29.00 | 14.50 | 58.00 |
| Chain saws, inc. chain | 28.00 | 14.00 | 56.00 |
| **Cutting/grinding/sanding** | | | |
| Angle grinders | | | |
| 100 mm | 5.50 | 2.75 | 11.00 |
| 125 mm | 5.50 | 2.75 | 11.00 |
| 230 mm | 7.50 | 3.75 | 15.00 |
| 300 mm | 13.50 | 6.75 | 27.00 |
| **Metal cutters** | | | |
| Metal shears | 14.50 | 7.25 | 29.00 |
| Metal nibblers | 14.50 | 7.25 | 29.00 |
| **Sanders** | | | |
| Belt sander | 11.00 | 5.50 | 22.00 |
| Disc sander 180 mm | 11.00 | 5.50 | 22.00 |
| Orbital sander industrial | 11.00 | 5.50 | 22.00 |
| Domestic 200 mm | 20.00 | 10.00 | 40.00 |
| Edging sander | 15.00 | 7.50 | 30.00 |
| Router, laminate trimmers | 13.00 | 6.50 | 26.00 |
| Power plane | 13.00 | 6.50 | 26.00 |

# LIFTING/MATERIALS HANDLING

| | First 24 hrs £ | Addit. 24 hrs £ | Per week £ |
|---|---|---|---|
| Mini excavator/digger (wheeled) | 52.00 | 52.00 | 156.00 |
| Rubbish chute, per 1 m section | 3.10 | 1.55 | 4.00 |
| **Winching** | | | |
| Tirfor | | | |
| 1600 kg | – | – | 26.00 |
| 3200 kg | – | – | 32.00 |
| Gin wheel, 250 kg | 3.00 | 1.50 | 6.00 |
| Chainfall | | | |
| 6 m | – | – | 18.00 |
| 12 m | – | – | 18.00 |
| **Hoisting** | | | |
| Scaffold hoist, electric, 150 kg | 37.50 | 18.75 | 75.00 |
| Chain hoist | | | |
| 10 cwt (500 kg) | – | – | 55.00 |
| 20 cwt (1000 kg) | – | – | 70.00 |
| 30/40 cwt (1500/2000 kg) | – | – | 100.00 |

## GARDENING EQUIPMENT

|  | First 24 hrs £ | Addit. 24 hrs £ | Per week £ |
|---|---|---|---|
| Hedge trimmers |  |  |  |
| petrol engine | 13.00 | 13.00 | 39.00 |
| electric | 6.50 | 6.50 | 19.50 |
| Cultivators |  |  |  |
| 5.0 hp digger | 18.00 | 18.00 | 54.00 |
| Medium duty rotovator | 34.00 | 34.00 | 102.00 |
| Heavy duty rotovator | 48.00 | 48.00 | 144.00 |
| Mowers |  |  |  |
| 19" rotary, petrol | 8.50 | 8.50 | 25.50 |
| 28" rotary, petrol | 37.00 | 37.00 | 110.00 |
| Flame gun, gas operated | 7.00 | 7.00 | 21.00 |
| Ride-on mower | 48.00 | 48.00 | 144.00 |
| **Lawn care** |  |  |  |
| Powered scarifier/thatcher | 16.50 | 16.50 | 49.00 |
| Manual aerator | 3.00 | 3.00 | 9.00 |
| Powered aerator | 24.00 | 24.00 | 72.00 |
| Lawn rake, electric | 6.50 | 6.50 | 19.50 |
| Lawn edger | 5.75 | 5.75 | 17.25 |
| Tree stump, chipper | 25.00 | 25.00 | 75.00 |
| Log splitter, hydraulic | 22.00 | 22.00 | 66.00 |
| **Post hole borers** |  |  |  |
| Powered earth drill, 7"/9" | 17.00 | 17.00 | 51.00 |
| Manual post hole borer, 6"/9" | 3.50 | 3.50 | 10.50 |

# GENERAL DATA

## THE METRIC SYSTEM

**Linear**
| | |
|---|---|
| 1 centimetre (cm) | = 10 millimetres (mm) |
| 1 decimetre (dm) | = 10 centimetres (cm) |
| 1 metre (m) | = 10 decimetres (dm) |
| 1 kilometre (km) | = 1000 metres (m) |

**Area**
| | |
|---|---|
| 100 sq millimetres ($mm^2$) | = 1 sq centimetre ($cm^2$) |
| 100 sq centimetres ($cm^2$) | = 1 sq decimetre ($dm^2$) |
| 100 sq decimetres ($dm^2$) | = 1 sq metre ($m^2$) |

**Capacity**
| | |
|---|---|
| 1 millilitre (ml) | = 1 cubic centimetre ($cm^3$) |
| 1 centilitre (cl) | = 10 millilitres (ml) |
| 1 decilitre (dl) | = 10 centilitres (cl) |
| 1 litre (l) | = 10 decilitres (dl) |

**Weight**
| | |
|---|---|
| 1 centigram (cg) | = 10 milligrams (mg) |
| 1 decigram (dg) | = 10 centigrams (cg) |
| 1 gram (g) | = 10 decigrams (dg) |
| 1 decagram (dag) | = 10 grams (g) |
| 1 hectogram (hg) | = 10 decagrams (dag) |

# METRIC/IMPERIAL AREA CONVERSION TABLE

| Imperial dimension (ft) | Square feet | Square yards | Square metres | Metric dimension (mm) | Metric dimension (mm) |
|---|---|---|---|---|---|
| 3' × 5' | 15 | 1.66 | 1.39 | 914 × 1524 | 0.91 × 1.52 |
| 3' × 6' | 18 | 2.00 | 1.67 | 914 × 1829 | 0.91 × 1.83 |
| 3' × 7' | 21 | 2.33 | 1.95 | 914 × 2134 | 0.91 × 2.13 |
| 3' × 8' | 24 | 2.67 | 2.23 | 914 × 2438 | 0.91 × 2.44 |
| 3' × 9' | 27 | 3.00 | 2.51 | 914 × 2743 | 0.91 × 2.74 |
| 3' × 10' | 30 | 3.34 | 2.79 | 914 × 3048 | 0.91 × 3.05 |
| 4' × 5' | 20 | 2.22 | 1.86 | 1219 × 1524 | 1.22 × 1.52 |
| 4' × 6' | 24 | 2.67 | 2.23 | 1219 × 1829 | 1.22 × 1.83 |
| 4' × 7' | 28 | 3.11 | 2.60 | 1219 × 2134 | 1.22 × 2.13 |
| 4' × 8' | 32 | 3.55 | 2.97 | 1219 × 2438 | 1.22 × 2.44 |
| 4' × 9' | 36 | 3.99 | 3.34 | 1219 × 2743 | 1.22 × 2.74 |
| 4' × 10' | 40 | 4.45 | 3.72 | 1219 × 3048 | 1.22 × 3.05 |
| 5' × 5' | 25 | 2.77 | 2.32 | 1524 × 1524 | 1.52 × 1.52 |
| 5' × 6' | 30 | 3.34 | 2.79 | 1524 × 1829 | 1.52 × 1.83 |
| 5' × 7' | 35 | 3.89 | 3.25 | 1524 × 2134 | 1.52 × 2.13 |
| 5' × 8' | 40 | 4.45 | 3.72 | 1524 × 2438 | 1.52 × 2.44 |
| 5' × 9' | 45 | 5.00 | 4.18 | 1524 × 2743 | 1.52 × 2.74 |
| 5' × 10' | 50 | 5.56 | 4.65 | 1524 × 3048 | 1.52 × 3.05 |
| 6' × 6' | 36 | 3.99 | 3.34 | 1829 × 1829 | 1.83 × 1.83 |
| 6' × 7' | 42 | 4.66 | 3.90 | 1829 × 2134 | 1.83 × 2.13 |
| 6' × 8' | 48 | 5.33 | 4.46 | 1829 × 2438 | 1.83 × 2.44 |
| 6' × 9' | 54 | 6.00 | 5.02 | 1829 × 2743 | 1.83 × 2.74 |
| 6' × 10' | 60 | 6.66 | 5.57 | 1829 × 3048 | 1.83 × 3.05 |
| 6' × 11' | 66 | 7.33 | 6.13 | 1829 × 3353 | 1.83 × 3.35 |
| 6' × 12' | 72 | 8.00 | 6.69 | 1829 × 3658 | 1.83 × 3.66 |
| 7' × 7' | 49 | 5.44 | 4.55 | 2134 × 2134 | 2.13 × 2.13 |
| 7' × 8' | 56 | 6.22 | 5.20 | 2134 × 2438 | 2.13 × 2.44 |
| 7' × 9' | 63 | 7.00 | 5.85 | 2134 × 2743 | 2.13 × 2.74 |
| 7' × 10' | 70 | 7.77 | 6.50 | 2134 × 3048 | 2.13 × 3.05 |
| 7' × 11' | 77 | 8.55 | 7.15 | 2134 × 3353 | 2.13 × 3.35 |
| 7' × 12' | 84 | 9.33 | 7.80 | 2134 × 3658 | 2.13 × 3.66 |
| 8' × 8' | 64 | 7.12 | 5.95 | 2438 × 2438 | 2.44 × 2.44 |
| 8' × 9' | 72 | 8.00 | 6.69 | 2438 × 2743 | 2.44 × 2.74 |
| 8' × 10' | 80 | 8.89 | 7.43 | 2438 × 3048 | 2.44 × 3.05 |
| 8' × 11' | 88 | 9.78 | 8.18 | 2438 × 3353 | 2.44 × 3.35 |
| 8' × 12' | 96 | 10.67 | 8.92 | 2438 × 3658 | 2.44 × 3.66 |
| 9' × 9' | 81 | 9.01 | 7.53 | 2743 × 2743 | 2.74 × 2.74 |
| 9' × 10' | 90 | 10.00 | 8.36 | 2743 × 3048 | 2.74 × 3.05 |
| 9' × 11' | 99 | 11.00 | 9.20 | 2743 × 3353 | 2.74 × 3.35 |
| 9' × 12' | 108 | 12.00 | 10.03 | 2743 × 3658 | 2.74 × 3.66 |

# THE METRIC SYSTEM

| Imperial dimension (ft) | Square feet | Square yards | Square metres | Metric dimension (mm) | Metric dimension (mm) |
|---|---|---|---|---|---|
| 10′ × 10′ | 100 | 11.11 | 9.29 | 3048 × 3048 | 3.05 × 3.05 |
| 10′ × 11′ | 110 | 12.22 | 10.22 | 3048 × 3353 | 3.05 × 3.35 |
| 10′ × 12′ | 120 | 13.34 | 11.15 | 3048 × 3658 | 3.05 × 3.66 |
| 10′ × 13′ | 130 | 14.45 | 12.08 | 3048 × 3962 | 3.05 × 3.96 |
| 10′ × 14′ | 140 | 15.56 | 13.01 | 3048 × 4267 | 3.05 × 4.27 |
| 10′ × 15′ | 150 | 16.67 | 13.94 | 3048 × 4572 | 3.05 × 4.57 |
| 10′ × 16′ | 160 | 17.77 | 14.86 | 3048 × 4877 | 3.05 × 4.88 |
| 11′ × 11′ | 121 | 13.44 | 11.24 | 3353 × 3353 | 3.35 × 3.35 |
| 11′ × 12′ | 132 | 14.66 | 12.26 | 3353 × 3658 | 3.35 × 3.66 |
| 11′ × 13′ | 143 | 15.89 | 13.29 | 3353 × 3962 | 3.35 × 3.96 |
| 11′ × 14′ | 154 | 17.11 | 14.31 | 3353 × 4267 | 3.35 × 4.27 |
| 11′ × 15′ | 165 | 18.33 | 15.33 | 3353 × 4572 | 3.35 × 4.57 |
| 11′ × 16′ | 176 | 19.55 | 16.35 | 3353 × 4877 | 3.35 × 4.88 |
| 12′ × 12′ | 144 | 16.00 | 13.38 | 3658 × 3658 | 3.66 × 3.66 |
| 12′ × 13′ | 156 | 17.33 | 14.49 | 3658 × 3962 | 3.66 × 3.96 |
| 12′ × 14′ | 168 | 18.67 | 15.61 | 3658 × 4267 | 3.66 × 4.27 |
| 12′ × 15′ | 180 | 20.00 | 16.72 | 3658 × 4572 | 3.66 × 4.57 |
| 12′ × 16′ | 192 | 21.34 | 17.84 | 3658 × 4877 | 3.66 × 4.88 |
| 12′ × 17′ | 204 | 22.66 | 18.95 | 3658 × 5182 | 3.66 × 5.18 |
| 12′ × 18′ | 216 | 24.00 | 20.07 | 3658 × 5486 | 3.66 × 5.49 |
| 13′ × 13′ | 169 | 18.78 | 15.70 | 3962 × 3962 | 3.96 × 3.96 |
| 13′ × 14′ | 182 | 20.22 | 16.91 | 3962 × 4267 | 3.96 × 4.27 |
| 13′ × 15′ | 195 | 21.67 | 18.12 | 3962 × 4572 | 3.96 × 4.57 |
| 13′ × 16′ | 208 | 23.11 | 19.32 | 3962 × 4877 | 3.96 × 4.88 |
| 13′ × 17′ | 221 | 24.55 | 20.53 | 3962 × 5182 | 3.96 × 5.18 |
| 13′ × 18′ | 234 | 26.00 | 21.74 | 3962 × 5486 | 3.96 × 5.49 |
| 14′ × 14′ | 196 | 21.78 | 18.21 | 4267 × 4267 | 4.27 × 4.27 |
| 14′ × 15′ | 210 | 23.33 | 19.51 | 4267 × 4572 | 4.27 × 4.57 |
| 14′ × 16′ | 224 | 24.88 | 20.80 | 4267 × 4877 | 4.27 × 4.88 |
| 14′ × 17′ | 238 | 26.44 | 22.11 | 4267 × 5182 | 4.27 × 5.18 |
| 14′ × 18′ | 252 | 28.00 | 23.41 | 4267 × 5486 | 4.27 × 5.49 |
| 15′ × 15′ | 225 | 25.00 | 20.90 | 4572 × 4572 | 4.57 × 4.57 |
| 15′ × 16′ | 240 | 26.67 | 22.30 | 4572 × 4877 | 4.57 × 4.88 |
| 15′ × 17′ | 255 | 28.33 | 23.69 | 4572 × 5182 | 4.57 × 5.18 |
| 15′ × 18′ | 270 | 30.00 | 25.08 | 4572 × 5486 | 4.57 × 5.49 |
| 16′ × 16′ | 256 | 28.44 | 23.78 | 4877 × 4877 | 4.88 × 4.88 |
| 16′ × 17′ | 272 | 30.22 | 25.27 | 4877 × 5182 | 4.88 × 5.18 |
| 16′ × 18′ | 288 | 32.00 | 26.76 | 4877 × 5486 | 4.88 × 5.49 |
| 17′ × 17′ | 289 | 32.11 | 26.85 | 5182 × 5182 | 5.18 × 5.18 |
| 17′ × 18′ | 306 | 34.00 | 28.43 | 5182 × 5486 | 5.18 × 5.49 |
| 18′ × 18′ | 324 | 36.00 | 30.10 | 5486 × 5486 | 5.49 × 5.49 |

## IMPERIAL/METRIC CONVERSIONS

**Linear**
| | |
|---|---|
| 1 in = 25.4 mm | 1 mm = 0.03937 in |
| 1 ft = 304.8 mm | 1 cm = 0.3937 in |
| 1 yd = 914.4 mm | 1 dm = 3.397 in |
| | 1 m = 39.37 in |

**Area**
| | |
|---|---|
| 1 sq in = 645.16 mm$^2$ | 1 cm$^2$ = 0.155 sq in |
| 1 sq ft = 0.0929 m$^2$ | 1 m$^2$ = 10.7639 sq ft |
| 1 sq yd = 0.8361 m$^2$ | 1 m$^2$ = 1.196 sq yd |

**Capacity**
| | |
|---|---|
| 1 cu in = 16.3871 cm$^3$ | 1 cm$^3$ = 0.061 cu in |
| 1 cu ft = 0.0283 m$^3$ | 1 m$^3$ = 35.3148 cu ft |
| 1 cu yd = 0.7646 m$^3$ | 1 m$^3$ = 1.307954 cu yd |

**Capacity**
| | |
|---|---|
| 1 fl oz = 28.4 ml | 1 ml = 0.0352 fl oz |
| 1 pt = 0.568 l | 1 dl = 3.52 fl oz |
| 1 gallon = 4.546 l | 1 l = 1.7598 pt |

**Weight**
| | |
|---|---|
| 1 oz = 28.35 g | 1 g = 0.035 oz |
| 1 lb = 0.4536 kg | 1 kg = 35.274 oz |
| 1 st = 6.35 kg | 1 t = 2204.6 lb |
| 1 ton = 1.016 t | 1 t = 0.9842 ton |

## TEMPERATURE EQUIVALENTS

In order to convert Fahrenheit to Celsius deduct 32, multiply by 5 and divide by 9. To convert Celsius to Fahrenheit multiply by 9, divide by 5 and add 32.

| Fahrenheit | Celsius | Fahrenheit | Celsius | Fahrenheit | Celsius |
|---|---|---|---|---|---|
| 230 | 110.0 | 150 | 65.6 | 60 | 15.6 |
| 220 | 104.4 | 140 | 60.0 | 50 | 10.0 |
| 210 | 98.9 | 130 | 54.4 | 40 | 4.4 |
| 200 | 93.3 | 120 | 48.9 | 30 | -1.1 |
| 190 | 87.8 | 110 | 43.3 | 20 | -6.7 |
| 180 | 82.2 | 90 | 32.2 | 10 | -12.2 |
| 170 | 76.7 | 80 | 26.7 | 0 | -17.8 |
| 160 | 71.1 | 70 | 21.1 | | |

# BUILDING MATERIALS

**Brickwork**
Number of bricks per square metre in half brick
thick wall in stretcher bond

| | |
|---|---|
| 50 × 102.5 × 215 mm | 74 |
| 65 × 102.5 × 215 mm | 59 |
| 75 × 102.5 × 215 mm | 52 |

**Blockwork**
Number of blocks per square metre

| | |
|---|---|
| 450 × 225 mm | 10 |
| 450 × 300 mm | 7 |
| 600 × 115 mm | 7 |

**Timber**
1 standard = 4.67227 cubic metres
1 cubic metre = 35.3148 cubic feet
10 cubic metres = 2.140 standards

# ROOFING

**Number of fibre cement slates per m$^2$**

| Size (mm) | Lap (mm) | No of slates |
|---|---|---|
| 400 × 200 | 70 | 30.0 |
| 400 × 200 | 76 | 30.9 |
| 400 × 200 | 90 | 32.3 |
| 400 × 240 | 80 | 26.1 |
| 500 × 250 | 90 | 19.5 |
| 500 × 250 | 80 | 19.1 |
| 500 × 250 | 70 | 18.6 |
| 500 × 250 | 76 | 18.9 |
| 500 × 250 | 90 | 19.5 |
| 500 × 250 | 106 | 20.5 |
| 500 × 250 | 100 | 20.0 |
| 600 × 300 | 106 | 13.6 |
| 600 × 300 | 100 | 13.4 |
| 600 × 300 | 90 | 13.1 |
| 600 × 300 | 80 | 12.9 |
| 600 × 300 | 70 | 12.7 |
| 600 × 350 | 100 | 11.5 |

**Number of Blue Welsh slates per m$^2$**

| | No of slates |
|---|---|
| 16″ × 8″ (405 × 205 mm) | 29.59 |
| 16″ × 10″ (405 × 255 mm) | 23.75 |
| 16″ × 12″ (405 × 305 mm) | 19.00 |
| 18″ × 9″ (460 × 230 mm) | 23.00 |
| 18″ × 10″ (460 × 255 mm) | 20.37 |
| 18″ × 12″(460 × 305 mm) | 17.00 |
| 20″ × 10″ (510 × 255 mm) | 18.02 |
| 20″ × 12″ (510 × 305 mm) | 15.00 |
| 22″ × 11″ (560 × 280 mm) | 14.81 |
| 22″ × 12″ (560 × 305 mm) | 14.00 |
| 24″ × 12″ (610 × 305 mm) | 12.27 |

Westmorland Green slates 1 ton (Imperial) standard quality covers approximately 18–20 m$^2$. 1 ton (Imperial) Peggies covers approximately 15–16 m$^2$.

| Leadwork | Code | kg/m$^2$ |
|---|---|---|
| Green | 3 | 14.97 |
| Blue | 4 | 20.41 |
| Red | 5 | 25.40 |
| Black | 6 | 30.05 |
| White | 7 | 36.72 |
| Orange | 8 | 40.26 |

# FINISHINGS

FINISHINGS

**Number of tiles per square metre**

| | |
|---|---|
| 150 × 150 mm | 44 |
| 100 × 200 mm | 50 |
| 200 × 200 mm | 25 |
| 250 × 125 mm | 32 |
| 230 × 230 mm | 19 |

| Coverage of plasters | | $m^2$/1000 kg |
|---|---|---|
| Carlite premixed | | |
| browning | 11 mm floating coat | 130–150 |
| Metal lathing | 11 mm pricking up and floating | 60–70 |
| Bonding coat | 8 mm floating coat on concrete | 145–155 |
| | 11 mm floating coat on brickwork and blockwork | 100–110 |
| | 8 mm floating coat on plasterboard | 150–165 |
| Finish | 2 mm finishing coat on floating coat | 410–500 |

| Thistle final coat plasters | | |
|---|---|---|
| Thistle finish | 2 mm finishing coat on sanded undercoat | 350–450 |
| Thistle board finish | 5 mm finishing in two coats | 160–170 |

| Thistle renovating plasters | | |
|---|---|---|
| Thistle undercoat | 11 mm thick | 120 |
| Thistle finish | 2 mm thick | 380–420 |

| Sirapite B plaster | | |
|---|---|---|
| Sirapite B | 3 mm finishing coat | 250–270 |

**Mortar mixes**

| | | |
|---|---|---|
| Cement mortar | 1:3 | 0.48 tonnes cement/$m^3$ |
| | | 1.45 tonnes sand/$m^3$ |
| | 1:4 | 0.36 tonnes cement/$m^3$ |
| | | 1.45 tonnes sand/$m^3$ |
| Cement lime mortar | 1:1:6 | 0.22 tonnes cement/$m^3$ |
| | | 0.11 tonnes lime/$m^3$ |
| | | 1.45 tonnes sand/$m^3$ |
| | 1:2:9 | 0.16 tonnes cement/$m^3$ |
| | | 0.14 tonnes lime/$m^3$ |
| | | 1.45 tonnes sand/$m^3$ |

# AVERAGE WEIGHTS OF MATERIALS

| Material | tonnes per m³ |
|---|---|
| Ashes | 0.68 |
| Aluminium | 2.68 |
| Asphalt | 2.31 |
| Brickwork – engineering | 2.24 |
| Brickwork – common | 1.86 |
| Bricks – engineering | 2.40 |
| Bricks – common | 2.00 |
| Cement – Portland | 1.45 |
| Cement – rapid hardening | 1.34 |
| Clay – dry | 1.05 |
| Clay – wet | 1.75 |
| Coal | 0.90 |
| Concrete | 2.30 |
| Concrete – reinforced | 2.40 |
| Earth – topsoil | 1.60 |
| Glass | 2.60 |
| Granite – solid | 2.70 |
| Gravel | 1.76 |
| Iron | 7.50 |
| Lead | 11.50 |
| Limestone – crushed | 1.75 |
| Plaster | 1.28 |
| Sand | 1.90 |
| Slate | 2.80 |
| Tarmacadam | 1.57 |
| Timber – general construction | 0.70 |
| Water | 1.00 |

# GLOSSARY

The following terms have been included to assist you in your DIY activities. If you come across other words or unfamiliar specialist terms, consult a good DIY manual such as *Collins Complete DIY Manual*.

| | |
|---|---|
| Accelerator | A chemical additive used to speed up the setting of mortar or concrete. |
| Acoustic plaster | Plaster with porous and/or textured surface plaster to absorb sound. |
| Aggregate | The material which is usually the largest element in a concrete mix, e.g. stone or gravel. |
| Agricultural drain | Unglazed, unsocketted and unjointed pipe to drain sub-soil. Sometimes perforated on top surface to allow water to enter. |
| Anaglypta | A heavy embossed wallpaper. |
| Architrave | A piece of timber covering the joint between a door or window frame and the plaster. |
| Airlock | A bubble of air in a pipe preventing the passage of liquid. |
| Angle bead | A galvanised steel right angle fixed at corners of walls to strengthen and protect plaster. |
| Angle grinder | A power operated drill tool with hard disc for cutting metal or masonry. |
| Apron flashing | A flashing usually placed at the cill of dormer windows or the lower side of a chimney stack. |
| Arris | The sharp edge of a brick or other building element. |
| Ashlar | Dressed stone facings laid in courses. |
| Auger | A corkscrew shaped tool used for drilling holes. |

| | |
|---|---|
| Awl | A sharp pointed tool for marking or piercing timber sheeting. |
| Backing coat | The coat in plasterwork under the finishing coat. |
| Back drop | A vertical pipe at a manhole connecting the branch to the invert pipe. It is used to save long lengths of unnecessary excavation. |
| Backfilling | The excavated material that is returned, filled and rammed around foundations. |
| Back lintel | The lintel supporting the back of the wall which cannot be seen from the front. |
| Back putty | The narrow strip of putty between the inside face of the glass and the edge of the rebate. |
| Barge board | A sloping board fixed to the gable end of a roof. |
| Batten | A small section of non-structural timber. |
| Beam filling | Brickwork infilling between joists. |
| Benching | The arrangement of concrete in a manhole at the sides of the main channel and branches. |
| Bending spring | A helical shaped coiled spring inserted in copper pipes to protect the wall of the pipe during bending. |
| Bibcock | A tap supplied by a horizontal water pipe. |
| Blinding | The top surface of hardcore or broken bricks filled with sand to provide a smooth surface to receive concrete. |
| Bloom | A film on gloss painted surfaces caused by defective workmanship or materials. |
| Bodying in | The first stage of French polishing. |
| Bond | The arrangement of bricks or blocks in a pattern to present an attractive appearance and provide structural strength, which is usually achieved by arranging the vertical joints in non-continuous lines. |
| Bonding | The tying in of old and new brickwork (see Toothing). |
| Bradawl | Hand tool used for making holes in wood for screws. |
| Browning coat | A mixture of gypsum plaster, sand and water which acts as a backing coat for plaster work. |
| Butt joint | A joint between two members where they meet face to face with no overlapping. |

# GLOSSARY

| | |
|---|---|
| Built up roofing | Two or three layers of bituminous roofing felt bedded in bitumen. |
| Butterfly wall tie | A wall tie made of galvanised wire formed into a double triangular shape. |
| Came | An 'H' shaped piece of lead to receive the glass in leaded windows. |
| Capillary joint | A joint in copper pipework made by placing a fitting over the end of a copper pipe which is marginally smaller than the fitting. The small space between the two is filled with molten solder to make the joint watertight. |
| Casement door | A fully glazed door. |
| Casement window | The hinged opening part of a window. |
| Casing | The timber lining to a window or door opening. |
| Caulked joint | A joint where the jointing material (usually lead or asbestos rope) is pressed into place by a caulking tool. |
| Cavity flashing | A metal tray fixed across the cavity in a cavity wall. |
| Cavity wall | An external wall constructed of two leaves with a cavity between them. |
| Cement fillet | A triangular section of mortar at the junction of a vertical and horizontal surface to prevent water penetration. |
| Cement grout | A liquefied mix of cement and water. |
| Cheek | The side of a dormer window. |
| Close boarded | Vertical softwood boards fixed to horizontal fencing rails to form solid fence. |
| Closer | A cut brick inserted to maintain the bond at the end of a brick wall. |
| Comb | A toothed metal plate used for spreading adhesive or scratching plaster to receive the next coat. |
| Common brick | A brick of poor appearance normally used where it will not be seen e.g. in foundations or the inner leaf of a cavity wall. |
| Compo | A mortar consisting of cement, lime and sand. |
| Compression joint | A method of jointing copper pipework in which the pipe ends are connected by tightening up brass nuts which force glands into the walls of the pipes. |

# GLOSSARY

| | |
|---|---|
| Conduit | A plastic or metal pipe to receive electric cables. It is used to provide easy renewal or repair of the cables without disturbing the plaster or concrete. |
| Coping | The course of bricks or concrete slab on the top of a wall. |
| Countersinking | A depression made so that the head of a screw can be driven flush with the surface. |
| Curtain wall | The infilling to a frame which has no structural properties. |
| Dado | The lower part of an internal wall with two different finished surfaces. |
| Damp-proof course | A layer of impervious material laid in walls to prevent the rising of moisture. |
| Decking | Horizontal rigid sheeting secured to joists as a floor or roof surface. |
| De-humidifier | Air conditioning unit which cools the air to reduce its humidity. |
| Dormer window | An attic window which projects through a sloping roof. |
| Dowel | A short round piece of hardwood or metal sunk into two separate members to strengthen the connection. |
| Dressed stone | Stone which has been squared and made smooth all round. |
| Dry lining | The system of using plasterboard or similar to form the surface of walls instead of wet plastering. |
| Dry walling | Walls where the stones are laid dry without the use of mortar. |
| Eaves | That part of the roof that projects beyond the face of the external wall. |
| Eaves tile | A short tile nailed at the eaves of a roof as an extra course. |
| Efflorescence | The unsightly deposit of crystallized salts on walls caused by the evaporation of water leaving the salt deposit on the surface. Can be removed by washing or brushing. |
| Elbow | A 90 degrees bend in a pipe. |
| Elevation | A drawing showing the vertical face of a building. |

| | |
|---|---|
| Engineering brick | A very dense clay brick used where strength and durability is required. |
| Exfoliated vermiculite | Vermiculite which has been heated to increase its size. |
| Expansion pipe | An overflow pipe from a hot water cylinder discharging over the cold water tank in case of the water overheating. |
| Extrados | The upper surface of an arch. |
| Eyebrow | A type of dormer window formed by constructing a curved continuous upper surface of roof without any sharp angles. |
| Facing brick | A brick which is generally more attractive in appearance than common bricks and used mainly in external walls. |
| Fascia | A vertical timber board fixed to the end of rafters to receive rainwater gutter. |
| Fenestration | The arrangement of windows on a building elevation. |
| Fibrous plaster | Plaster containing fibrous material to maintain its strength but makes it lighter. |
| Field drain | see Agricultural drain. |
| Firring piece | Splayed pieces of timber nailed to the top of roof joists to create the fall on a flat roof. |
| Flashing | A method of making the joint between a roof and wall watertight by inserting a strip of flexible metal or bitumen. |
| Flaunching | The cement mortar placed around chimney pots to deflect rainwater on to the roof. |
| Flitch beam | A composite beam constructed of two timber beams with a metal strengthening plate between them. They are held together by bolts. |
| Float glass | Glass produced by floating it on molten metal. |
| Free standing | An element which is not supported by an adjacent structure. |
| Frustum | Lower part of cone whose top surface is parallel to the base. |
| Gable end | The triangular shape of a house end where the roof sits vertically above the end wall. |

| | |
|---|---|
| Gabion | A wire basket filled with rock to act as a permanent retaining feature. Usually placed on steep embankments or sides of rivers. |
| Going | The width of the horizontal tread in a staircase. The total going is the sum of tread goings. |
| Granolithic concrete | A hard wearing concrete used for floor finishes. The aggregate used in the mix is selected to produce extra strength. |
| Hardcore | Broken brick or stones laid as a base to receive concrete beds. |
| Haunching | The placement of concrete around drain pipes up to the crown of the pipe. |
| Header | A brick laid so that only the ends are exposed. |
| Heave | A swelling of the clay caused by excess water which can cause movement in buildings. |
| Holderbat | A bracket which encircles a pipe and is fixed to a wall. |
| Hollow wall | see Cavity wall. |
| Honeycomb wall | A brick wall usually built under a floor to support joists. The brickwork has gaps left in to allow air to circulate freely. |
| Immersion heater | A single or double electric element fitted inside an insulated copper cylinder. |
| Inspection chamber | A shallow manhole positioned at junction of main drain and branches. |
| Interceptor trap | A trap set at the end of a drainage system between the main sewer and the drain to prevent the ingress of vermin and gases. |
| Irregular coursing | The arrangement of stone in a rubble wall where the stones are of varying depths. |
| Jamb | The inside vertical face of an opening or the vertical side member of a window or door frame. |
| Jointing | The mortar placed between the vertical and horizontal faces of bricks. |
| Joist | A supporting beam in floors or roofs usually made of timber or steel. |
| Key | The scoring effect on a surface to assist the adhesion of a further coat. |

# GLOSSARY

| | |
|---|---|
| Keying in | The bonding or joining of old and new brickwork. |
| Kicking plate | A metal plate screwed to the lower part of a door to prevent damage. |
| King post | A type of roof truss. |
| Latex screed | A screed applied in thin layers to existing concrete or screed to provide level surface for floor finish. |
| Lining paper | A thin paper pasted to walls or ceiling to conceal irregularities before papering or painting. |
| Lintol | A timber or steel structural member placed over a door or window opening to take the weight of the wall above. |
| Lost headed nail | A nail whose head is only slightly larger than the nail so that it can be driven below the surface of the timber. |
| Luminaire | A light fitting. |
| Mansard roof | A roof where each side has two different angled slopes. |
| Marine plywood | Exterior quality plywood. |
| Masonry nail | A hardened nail that can be driven or fired into concrete or brickwork. |
| Mastic | A non-setting material used for sealing joists. |
| Mirror screw | A screw with a detachable dome head which is fixed after the screw has been secured. |
| Mist coat | A thin coat of emulsion paint usually applied to seal the surface. |
| Mono-pitched roof | A roof with only one sloping face. |
| Mortise | A recess cut in timber to receive tongue or tenon from another member. |
| Mullion | A vertical structural member of a window. |
| Muntin | A vertical member of a framed door. |
| Needle | A horizontal beam used in shoring. |
| Newel | A post in a staircase that supports the handrail. |
| Nogging | A short horizontal timber member between vertical studding in partition. |

# GLOSSARY

| | |
|---|---|
| Nominal size | The original size of timber before planing or dressing and is usually 3 mm larger than the finished size. At this stage the timber is described as sawn. |
| Open eaves | An arrangement where the soffit board is fixed between the projecting rafters so that the rafters are partially exposed. |
| Opening light | The part of a window that opens. |
| Oriel window | A window above ground floor level that projects beyond the face of the wall. |
| Overhand | Brickwork that is laid from the inside of a building to save scaffolding costs. |
| Pantile | Roof tile which is undulating in appearance. |
| Pargetting | The rendering to a chimney flue. |
| Pebble dash | An external finish to walls produced by throwing pebbles on to rendering before it has set. |
| Pin kerb | A small precast concrete kerb usually 6 ft × 2 in (150 × 50 mm) used mainly as path edging. |
| Pointing | The operation of raking out the mortar between the bricks (see Jointing). |
| Purlin | A horizontal roof member which supports the rafters. |
| Raft foundation | A reinforced concrete slab with extra concrete at perimeter to form a ground beam. Used mainly in poor ground conditions. |
| Rag bolt | A bolt with an irregular shaped end, cast into concrete for greater strength. |
| Rebate | A rectangular recess cut into the edge of a timber member such as a window frame to form seating for glass. |
| Reconstructed stone | Precast concrete made by adding stone dust to the cement to produce a stone effect. |
| Rendering | The application of mortar to a wall. |
| Reveal | Vertical face of opening. |
| Router | A tool for cutting grooves in wood. |
| Sash | see Opening light. |
| Sand blasting | A process of cleaning stone or brickwork by hosing with high pressure water and sand. |

| | |
|---|---|
| Screed | A layer of material laid on concrete to provide base to receive finishing material. |
| Scrimmed and filled joint | A technique of concealing plasterboard joints by filling with cloth and applying a thin coat of plaster. |
| Sett | Stone block used for decorative paving. |
| Sharp sand | Used in mixing concrete. |
| Skim coat | The final finish coat on plaster, usually about 3 mm thick. |
| Skip | Steel container for the removal of rubbish. |
| Soakaway | A stone filled pit to receive surface water. |
| Socket | The end of the pipe in 'spigot and socket' pipework which receives the spigot of the adjacent pipe. |
| Soffit | The horizontal surface under an arch or opening. |
| Soffit board | Horizontal board secured to underside of rafters beneath an overhanging eaves. |
| Soft sand | Used in mixing mortar. |
| Spigot | The end of the pipe in 'spigot and socket pipework' which is inserted into the next pipes socket. |
| Spur | A branch from a ring main usually for a new socket outlet. |
| Stucco | Smooth external rendering. |
| Studding | Timber framed partition. |
| Sump | A pit below floor level. |
| Tanking | A vertical and horizontal waterproofed membrane to prevent the ingress of water. |
| Taped and filled joint | A technique of concealing joints between paper tape in lieu of cloth prior to plastering (see Scrimmed and filled joint). |
| Template | A full size pattern used for cutting round to produce required profile of permanent material. |
| Tile hanging | The vertical fixing of roofing tiles. |
| Toothing | The arrangement of leaving alternate courses of brickwork projecting where a new wall is to be tied in to an existing one. |
| Tyrolean finish | The application of external plasterwork to provide an attractive rough textured finish. It can be hand |

applied but is usually done by machine to ensure uniformity.

| | |
|---|---|
| Uncoursed | The arrangement of irregular stones in a wall without a continuous horizontal bed. |
| Underpinning | The technique of replacing a load bearing wall below ground level by providing temporary supports in short lengths whilst the new wall and foundation is constructed. |
| Upstand | A vertical flashing usually at junction of horizontal and vertical surfaces. |
| Vapour barrier | A layer of impermeable material to prevent the penetration of moist air. |
| Verge | The edge of a sloping roof at the gables. |
| Vermiculite | A lightweight insulating material often used in floor and roof screeds. |
| Wall plate | A horizontal timber member set on top of wall to receive rafters or joists. |
| Wall tie | A piece of twisted metal built into each leaf of a cavity wall. |
| Wrought face | The face of timber after it has been planed. |

# INDEX